Encyclopedia of

Money Making Sales Letters

D1416061

Encyclopedia of

Money Making Sales Letters

Nate Rosenblatt

Edited by Margaret Morgan Bynum and
Marjory Rosenblatt

Round Lake Publishing
Ridgefield, Connecticut

Round Lake Publishing Co.
31 Bailey Avenue
Ridgefield, CT 06877

Printed in the United States of America

098765432

Library of Congress Cataloging-in-Publication Data

Rosenblatt, Nate, 1942-
    Encyclopedia of money making sales letters / Nate Rosenblatt;
edited by Margaret Morgan Bynum and Marjory Rosenblatt.
      p.   cm.
    Includes index.
    ISBN 0-929543-08-4 : $19.95
    1. Sales letters. I. Bynum, Margaret Morgan. II. Rosenblatt,
Marjory, 1945- . III. Title. IV. Title: Money making sales
letters.
HF5730.R73 1990   90-8791
658.8'1--dc20   CIP

Special thanks to a great group of people who gave me insights into their professions and persuasive techniques:

Bernard Arons, import/export; Lee Attix, construction; John Bader, training; Martha Biafor, insurance; Amanda Blumenthal, advertising; Victor Brody, seminars; Wayne Bunting, real estate; Jeffrey Cramp, advertising; Robert Didio, collections; Linda Golin, medicine; Lou Golin, drug testing; Don Giorgione, Ph. D., engineering; Stanley Greenblatt, Ph. D., computers and telecommunications; Steve Lember, mutual funds; Chuck McLeester, direct response; Bradley Smith, D.D.S., dentistry; Joseph and Sylvia Soltoff, retail clothing; Betty Tascione, optometry; Peter Zakroff, recording/music.

CONTENTS

Chapter 2   SETTING UP THE SALES CALL

New Customers

Current Customers

Chapter 3   PROPOSALS AND QUOTATIONS

Cover Letters, Responses and Follow-ups

Proposals and Quotations

Chapter 4   FOLLOW-UPS TO SALES CALLS

After Contact

After Sale

Chapter 5 CLOSING THE SALE

Chapter 6 KEEPING THE CUSTOMER BUYING

Chapter 7 CUSTOMER RELATIONS

Chapter 8 SELLING YOURSELF

Job Search

On the Job

Selling Your Product

Chapter 9 SELLING WITH THE FAX

Sending Timely Information

Dealing with Problems

Chapter 10   SELLING BY DIRECT MAIL

Products

Services

Special Formats

Chapter 11   COMMUNICATING WITH THE SALES FORCE

Sales Management

Employee Motivation

Chapter 12   PROMOTIONAL ANNOUNCEMENTS

New Products and Services

Chapter 13 LETTERS FROM PROFESSIONALS

Chapter 14 SELLING INVESTMENTS, REAL ESTATE, INSURANCE, AND BANKING SERVICES

Chapter 15 CREDIT AND COLLECTIONS

Preface

Everyone sells. You may be the owner of a small business about to request a $100,000 line of credit from a bank vice president. Or an engineer trying to convince management that a certain project deserves priority treatment. Maybe you're a consultant trying to convince a multinational corporation of the need for a new telecommunications network. Or an importer seeking to become a source of supply for a national gift chain.

Perhaps you're a parent trying to persuade the school board to fund a new playground, or you're in charge of a committee to get business contributions for your church building fund.

All of us—bank managers, supervisors, salespersons, parents, community leaders, realtors, scientists—use the written word to convince others to agree to, support or buy our ideas, beliefs, products, and services. We all write sales letters. We all seek successful results from those written messages.

This book was developed to ensure those successes. Every model letter was created to help you achieve your selling goal—getting the reader to do as you wish.

Before you start a letter, identify exactly what you're aiming to accomplish. What do you want the reader to do? Buy your product? Support your research? Lend you money? Recommend you for a raise? Whatever it is, be very sure about why you're writing. Everything in your letter should lead to your goal.

Next, select the sample letter that comes closest to suiting your needs. Use the table of contents or one of the two indexes to locate the letter. Then refer to the brief comments at the bottom of the letter to help you focus on its main points.

In adapting the letter for your use, write as if you were speaking to the person face-to-face. By doing this, you'll find that your letter sounds natural, a quality that is often missing in written communications.

Don't make the mistake of using $5 words where 50 cent words will do. Many people think their letters improve with the use of long words and paragraphs. Take the advice of the American poet, William Cullen Bryant:

> Never use a long word where a short one will do. Call a spade by its name, not a well-known instrument of manual labor. Let a home be a home and not a residence; speak of a place, not a locality; and so on of the rest. When a short word will do, you always lose by using a long one. You lose in clearness. You lose in honest expression of meaning, and in the estimation of all men who are capable of judging, you lose reputation for ability...Elegance of language may not be in the power of all of us, but simplicity and straightforwardness are.

Remember: every letter you write says something about you. A badly written letter is the equivalent of showing up for an important meeting in wrinkled clothing and with uncombed hair. Aesthetics count. Make the appearance of your letters inviting. Don't combine your thoughts into long, forbidding-looking paragraphs. Sending a letter doesn't guarantee it will be read. Entice your reader with brief, sharp ideas presented with logic and purpose.

What about content? The secret is to focus on the reader—what the reader knows and believes, and what the reader needs and wants. Your background, knowledge, and desires are important only if you can show how the reader will benefit from them.

Keep the spotlight on the reader as you choose each word and thought. What will the reader find interesting or useful? What ideas will lead the reader to do what you want done? Keeping the focus on what interests the reader, rather than what interests you, takes constant vigil, but it's absolutely essential for success in written communication.

Ideally, a reader should understand a letter with one reading. There's less impact with each rereading and less likelihood of fulfilling the writer's objective. Of course, there are times when details must be checked by rereading. But always aim for the one-reading-mastery of your ideas.

There are four parts to every effective sales letter.

1. Get the reader's attention.

Do this in the first paragraph or headline. Ask a provocative question, challenge the reader, give the reader a sense that he or she is important, make a strong offer or promise.

2. **Identify a need the reader has and show how you can fill that need.**

   Does the reader want to expand his business or improve his profits? Does she want to find a less expensive manufacturer? Does he want to look more youthful? Once the need is identified, state how your product or service can satisfy that need.

3. **Persuade the reader to buy.**

   Use an inducement such as special price, free-trial offer, testimonials from satisfied buyers.

4. **Get the reader to act.**

   Whether you want the person to order, agree to see a product demonstration, let you use his name as a reference, etc., specify the action you want and how the reader is to respond (send a purchase order, call an 800 phone number, sign the enclosed contract, write a referral letter, etc.). And stress the need for immediacy ("Act today," "Don't delay," "Order now"). An action postponed is likely to be left undone.

In addition to the 4 critical elements of every letter, the reader must also know what _you_ promise to do and when. State that you will:

- Call on Tuesday
- Meet Monday at ten
- Send a proposal next week

Think of letters as scripts for interaction between you and your reader. You must always keep the dialogue active between you and your prospect or customer.

As you go through these letters, be aware that they respect the reader by avoiding stale cliches and overworked introductions. You won't find tired phrases such as "enclosed herein ..." or "pursuant to our conversation..." You will discover language that doesn't bore the reader. The opening lines lead naturally and conversationally to your objective for writing—getting the sale.

Above all, be sure your letters are honest and sincere. Never, ever, promise something you can't deliver—or state an untruth. Your customer will never forgive you. And credibility, once lost, is never regained.

Every letter is a sales letter. By keeping that thought in mind—and keeping in mind the reader's interests and motivations—you'll produce the kinds of letters that get results. Good selling!

Prospecting for New Customers 1

Even seasoned salespeople experience chills, butterflies, and a certain wild-eyed anxiety when prospecting for new customers. But the anxiety can be reduced dramatically if you know that the prospect will be receptive. Finding a receptive prospect—one who is likely to have an interest in your product or service—makes cold calling much easier, and your chances for success much greater. There are a number of methods to reach these people effectively, and this chapter deals with them.

Your prospecting letter makes your first impression for you—and you only make one first impression. First impressions establish the relationship for all future interaction.

A first contact by mail must get the reader's attention <u>and</u> set the tone for what follows. Sell yourself as competent, capable of accepting challenges, and able to meet the prospect's needs.

After the door is opened, you must convince the potential buyer that you have the answer he or she is seeking. You may even <u>be</u> the answer. But he'll never know that unless you tell him.

Good sales letters can help you drum up business less expensively, and frequently more effectively, than any other prospecting tool. Here's how to find and develop new customers.

Door Openers. Trade journals, local newspapers, civic and religious groups, and industry newsletters are just a few of the sources that can provide you with a steady supply of potential new buyers and contacts. These sources list people who have just been hired, promoted, or received awards. Or those who have recently moved into a community. These events present excellent reasons for writing. You're telling prospects about yourself and your company when they're most receptive, and at a time when, in many cases, you know their needs.

Lead Generaters. These are the lifeblood of a sales force. It's no surprise that the giant corporations devote tremendous amounts of time and energy to generating leads for their sales people. NCR, according to <u>The Direct Marketing Handbook</u>, uses over 200 lead-generating letters to specific industries.

It also points out the benefits of a solid lead generating program: ADP, for example, spent $700,000 in lead-generating direct mail, and can trace $18,000,000 in annual sales to those mailings.

Well written letters can pull a better response than glossy brochures or fancy promotion pieces, particularly as your prospects go up the managerial ladder. Prospecting letters should concentrate on your offer, as opposed to your product.

You can generate leads through special events. Trade shows provide excellent opportunities because you can identify the kinds of companies that will be attending. Enthusiastically invite people to your booth or hospitality suite for a personalized introduction to a new product or service. And if you're a retailer, get people excited about coming to your store through a discount offer, coupon, or contest.

Appeals to Special Interest Groups. Mail to groups of prospects that have common interests. Customize your appeal to fit that audience. Point out how your product or service fits in with their specific needs. Don't just talk about your travel packages, for example; tell educators you have a s pecial plan that caters to their summer schedule. Think about your audience's needs and you'll have a new group of buyers.

Company Name
Address
City, State Zip

Date

Mr. and Mrs. John Banks
24 Conestoga Highway
Richland Hills, TX 76118

WELCOME TO RICHLAND HILLS!

Dear Mr. and Mrs. Banks:

We'd like to help make you and your family feel right at home in
Richland Hills. We'll contact your old pharmacy for you and have your
prescriptions and medical history put on file here so we'll be ready to
serve you without delay.

Having a local pharmacy prepared to meet your prescription needs
quickly is a real security blanket when you move into a new community.
You'll find that the staff at Richard's Drug Store will help you feel as if
you lived here for years!

One more welcome note. Bring this letter on your first visit and take
10% off any non-prescription item in the store. Come in, say hello, and
let us help you settle into your new life in a great community.

Your Neighbor,

Harold Baines
Pharmacist

- Don't be afraid to be creative. A big "welcome sign" above the salutation adds a friendly touch to this letter.

- Always sell benefits: a sense of security, all your needs taken care of, becoming an immediate part of the community.

- The letter requires an action ("come in") in order for the reader to receive the full benefits.

Company Name
Address
City, State Zip

Date

Mr. Louis Grossman
Vista Marketing Corp.
1211 Avenue West
Carbondale, IL 62902

Dear Mr. Grossman:

A new job is a cause for celebration! We'd like to add to the festivities by reserving a table for you (and someone special to you) at the Hideaway, the distinguished restaurant where Carbondale's community leaders gather for special events. A complimentary bottle of our house wine is waiting for you as our way of saying congratulations.

Just call by the end of the month to reserve your table and complimentary wine. I'm looking forward to serving you personally.

Sincerely,

Angelo Morganti
Maitre d'

- Explain the reason for the "celebration" immediately.

- Create a parallel between your prospect's new status and your service; both are steps up.

- A deadline hastens action.

Company Name
Address
City, State Zip

Date

Ms. Susan Gross
Director of Purchasing
Hydra Technical Products
4118 S. Lincoln Highway
St. Louis, MO. 63143

Dear Ms. Gross:

What an impressive achievement—to jump from buyer to Director of
Purchasing in less than two years, particularly at a company like Hydra,
which prides itself on professionalism. Congratulations.

Because of your rapid rise, you'll appreciate Standard Office Supplies'
similar success story. Three years ago we didn't exist, and now we're
the leading office products distributor in the area.

You understand the commitment it takes to move to the top quickly, so I
think you'll also understand why I'm convinced our companies should be
working together.

I'll call next week for an appointment. I'm looking forward to offering my
congratulations in person.

Yours truly,

Louise Potter
Sales Representative

- Local newspapers and magazines list promotions, new jobs, transfers, etc. They're a great source of leads.

- Appeal to the sense of pride that follows a promotion.

- Always indicate an action (calling next week).

Company Name
Address
City, State Zip

Date

Mr. Arthur Donnelly
Vice President, Finance
Worldwide Trucking Corp.
5218 Cold Duck Lane
Bismarck, ND 58501

Dear Mr. Donnelly:

I can't help but wonder who got the "pats on the back" for the phenomenal turn-around year your organization just completed. Was it the sales and marketing team? The advertising department? Manufacturing? The CEO? Too often, the contributions of strong financial leadership are taken for granted.

The professional money management community knows how much the guidance of a strong financial manager adds to the equation. Congratulations on a remarkable fiscal performance, particularly in light of the new regulations and taxes the government has thrown at your industry.

I'd like the opportunity to demonstrate how our various investment and tax strategies can help you maintain your new position of strength for many years to come. I think you'll find our client list one you'd be proud to join.

How does the week of the 15th sound to you for a meeting? Perhaps we can get to know each other over lunch. I'll call next week.

Sincerely,

Adam Rangel

- Show your appreciation and understanding of the prospect's accomplishment.

- Suggest that your service can help maintain the success.

- Offer a time frame for a meeting to help focus the subsequent phone conversation.

Company Name
Address
City, State Zip

Date

Ms. Julie Dowell
906 N. 2nd Street
Snow Hill, MD 21863

Dear Julie:

When I read about your selection as president of the Snow Hill Civic Association, my first thought was how much your drive, enthusiasm, and good old American "can-do" attitude will mean to the group. I'm so pleased that your community has finally opted for new, fresh ideas.

My second thought was that I can help you attain a number of the association's long-stated goals—particularly getting a traffic light on Route 70 and expanding the play area behind Roberts Elementary School. My public relations firm was instrumental in helping civic associations in nearby Shelltown and Scarboro accomplish similar goals, and I'd like to repeat those successes for you.

I'll call you before your next meeting to renew old acquaintances and give you an idea how we can work together.

Kindest regards,

Pam Messner

- People love to read about their own strengths and accomplishments.

- Highlight your successes as they relate to the prospect's needs.

Company Name
Address
City, State Zip

Dear Value-Conscious Neighbor:

I won't beat around the bush. We're new and, yes, different from other men's and boys' clothing stores. For example:

- Does anyone else within a 100-mile radius (500? 1,000?) offer a FREE sport shirt with the purchase of two others?

- Have you ever heard of a men's store that gives a FREE magazine subscription to <u>Outdoor World</u> with the purchase of new hiking boots?

- Do you know of any other clothing store that gives you a special "premium buyer" discount that delivers bigger and bigger savings with <u>everything</u> you buy?

We're new and different all right, and you're going to <u>love</u> the difference. Stop in and see for yourself...and while you're here sign up for our FREE drawing for a white water raft and a complete new camping outfit!

"New" takes on a special meaning at our first store in this area...so come and say hello. You're going to see some of the most amazing bargains and values ever offered!

Sincerely,

Buck Youngblood
Manager

- The salutation appeals to price conscious shoppers.

- Sell your store's major strengths.

- Offer a reason (the drawing) for the prospect to visit your store.

Company Name
Address
City, State Zip

Date

Mr. And Mrs. Samuel Fishbein
23 Grays Ferry Road
Goldsboro, NC 27530

Dear Mr. and Mrs. Fishbein:

<u>Roger Arons has a deal for you!</u>

Yes, <u>that</u> Roger Arons. Your neighbor and president of the Goldsboro
Civic Association has just joined Goodfellow Tires as retail manager.
And one of the first things he did on the job was think of his neighbors!

Roger wants you to come in any time next week (from 8:00 a.m. to 6:00
p.m.), have a cup of coffee or soft drink with him, and see for yourself
the <u>unadvertised specials</u> he can't wait to show his neighbors from
Goldsboro.

I'm very pleased to have Roger join our team of tire specialists, and
since he says his neighbors are the nicest people in the township, I'm
looking forward to meeting and greeting you myself.

Cordially,

Arthur Goodfellow

- Establish the neighborhood relationship immediately.

- Emphasize that there is a special reason for the prospect to visit.

Company Name
Address
City, State Zip

How many times have you been
stuck in traffic and wished you had
something of value to listen to?

Dear Commuter:

While you're waiting for the crane to lift the overturned tractor trailer
three miles ahead of you, you could be sharpening your negotiating
skills, learning how to make criticism work for you, practicing a foreign
language for your overseas trip, or enhancing your vocabulary.

If you attended seminars given by the authors of the tapes in the
enclosed catalog, you'd pay thousands of dollars, not counting time
away from the job. But now you can learn while you drive to the office...
and make time work for you while you're on the road.

As always, our tapes are satisfaction guaranteed or your money is
refunded. Call 1-800-555-TAPE or send the enclosed order form to
make your driving time pay off for you!

Sincerely,

Mike Bruton
Publisher

- Attract customer interest by asking a question that plays to your product's strength.

- Illustrate how your product can be a profitable solution to an everyday problem.

- Prominently display the phrase "satisfaction guaranteed" in your letter as well as the catalog.

Company Name
Address
City, State Zip

How would you like your best work
to be featured in a $25,000 advertisement
seen by discriminating buyers
throughout the United States?

Dear Interior Designer:

Atlas Exquisite Wall Coverings is sponsoring the Atlas Room-of-the-Year Contest. That means you have an opportunity to demonstrate your talents—and advertise your business—to more than one million decorating-minded homeowners.

All you have to do is complete the entry form that's enclosed with this letter and include a photograph of the work described. Remember: the room must be showcased with Atlas Exquisite paper for you to be eligible for the award.

If our panel of judges selects your entry as the Atlas Room-of-the-Year, you and your work will be featured in our September advertisement in Design and Decor Magazine. That's our way of thanking you for using the best wallpaper in the world!

Sincerely,

Carl Maerstrom
Vice President, Marketing

P.S. Be sure to send in your entry by June 1 to be eligible.

- An effective contest generates sales and/or interest in your product.

- Highlight the reason the prospect should enter the contest.

- To encourage response, stress the ease of entering the contest.

Company Name
Address
City, State Zip

Date

Mr. Miles Slaughter
Meeting Planner
American Manufacturers Association
8432 Willow Brook Road
St. Paul, MN 55155

Dear Mr. Slaughter:

Frequent travelers like you are tough to impress. But wait till you see what Monarch Hotels have to offer. We deliver a free morning paper, complimentary overnight shoeshine, valet services, fax and computer access, private dining and health clubs, luxury suites, and superb concierge services. But you may be thinking that other quality hotel chains offer similar services.

Our services are better, but we need to get you and your guests here to prove it. So here's a special offer to show how much we want your business: If you can guarantee 100 nights a year in reservations, we'll give you a 20% discount on our world-class rooms; 200 nights a year earns you a 30% discount; and if you guarantee 300 or more nights per year, your members and guests will enjoy an incredible 40% discount.

Luxury and economy aren't usually mentioned in the same breath...except by our customers! Just send the enclosed postage-paid reply card and I'll rush you complete information about our discount package. Or call me at 612-555-5989, and we'll arrange to meet over lunch at our gourmet Fountain Restaurant. I'd like you to be my guest.

Sincerely,

Patrick Forte
Vice President

P.S. In case your calculator isn't handy, 300 nights @ 40% discount means a savings of $24,000!

- Recognize the prospect as a seasoned professional, someone who recognizes quality.

- Demonstrate that you want the business and are willing to provide deep incentives to get it.

Company Name
Address
City, State Zip

Date

Mr. Nick Greene
Waldman Specialty Sales
491 E. Ellison Avenue
Stamford, CT 06925

Dear Nick:

This isn't just an invitation to an ordinary new product presentation. You're going to be in on the launch of a product that will revolutionize the training industry...and have lots of other applications as well. First, the details:

WHERE: The Empire Room, Parker Hotel
57th Street and Fifth Avenue, New York

WHEN: Tuesday, May 26, 12:00 noon

WHO: Top executives from the premium, advertising agency, and video production industries

WHAT: Luncheon and presentation to announce a breakthrough product.

You're going to see the first throw-away videotape (the case is cardboard). That means you can now duplicate video for about as much as it costs to duplicate audio...opening huge new markets to video messages!

More at the presentation. I'll call to confirm your attendance. You have to attend, Nick. I guarantee it will be well worth your time.

Regards,

Donald Cranston

- Express your enthusiasm for the event.

- List who, what, where, when; leave nothing to chance.

- Follow up.

Company Name
Address
City, State Zip

Date

Mr. Delbert Russell
Delta Printers & Lithographers
1809 Apple Boulevard
Greenfield, WI 53220

Dear Mr. Russell:

The rumors are true! The revolutionary new Heinrich 4000 half-web you've read so much about will be premiering at the PRINT EXPO show this year...

<u>and you're invited to join me
for a personal inspection
of this amazing new equipment!</u>

I can't wait to show you the <u>fastest</u> half-web in the world (which means you can produce more work during every shift). And wait until you see for yourself the computer-corrected registration to within 1/64th of an inch (which means superb quality and happier customers). Plus, I want to explain our financing plan that makes it possible to put the Heinrich 4000 to work for you <u>immediately!</u>

If you have the chance, call me before the show, and I'll schedule your personal inspection so you'll have no delay whatsoever. But even if you can't schedule the time in advance, don't miss the opportunity to visit Booth 1050. You'll see why we call the 4000 the profit-maker!

Sincerely,

Walter Nemeier
Sales Manager

- Invite the prospect for a <u>specific</u> reason. Avoid the temptation to say, "We have lots of new things to show you."

- Point out the benefits of taking the time to visit.

- Be sure to give the booth number.

Company Name
Address
City, State Zip

Date

Mr. Harrison Guthrie
Savings and Loan Partnership, Inc.
280 Hartford Road
Tyler, TX 75712

Dear Mr. Guthrie:

We missed you at the recent International Banking Conference. You were probably very busy and may not have found time to visit the exhibit floor. We were busy, too. Hundreds of your fellow banking executives reviewed our high yield, high quality cash management products.

We didn't want you to miss out on this important information, so we've enclosed the packet you would have received at our booth. This will give you the opportunity to review the history, philosophy, and successful record of our cash management services with financial institutions throughout the United States.

You also missed the chance to have your questions answered about our services. I'll call in just a few days to take care of that last bit of "show" business.

Cordially,

Louise Carner

• Attendee lists from trade shows include excellent prospects. Be sure to get a complete roster.

Office of the President
Company Name
Address
City, State Zip

Mr. Charles Overmeyer
President and CEO
Overmeyer Brands
300 Coleman Blvd.
Newark, NJ 07114

Dear Mr. Overmeyer:

You can't wait any longer to get involved. Policy decisions which may adversely affect <u>your</u> company's health care benefits are being made by insurance carriers...and your benefits manager is helpless against them.

It's vitally important that you understand the forces at work in today's health care industry. Why is your company paying more—much more! —than ever before, but getting much less? Why has your company inadvertently allowed medical decisions to be made by groups that seem far more interested in their fiscal well-being than your physical well-being?

<u>You</u> need to know what forces are driving the nearly $200 billion health care benefits industry. And I invite you to find out during a CEO-only seminar on Friday, March 25. You'll have the opportunity to meet and swap ideas with senior executives from a number of leading firms, as well as with government officials.

I invite you to join your colleagues. Send the enclosed reply form <u>today.</u>

Very truly yours,

Daniel C. Daras
President and CEO

- CEOs like to talk to CEOs.

- Identify a specific problem that is important enough for a CEO's attention.

- Offer a solution by the CEO's peers.

Company Name
Address
City, State Zip

Do you have what it takes to be an entrepreneur?
Take our free test—and find out!

Many people don't. They don't have the skills, drive, or temperament. They don't have the stomach to take the risks, even though the rewards can far outweigh the dangers.

If you've ever wondered if you have what it takes to get out of the 9 to 5 rut, to stop envying the person you work for, to be the one who drives the fancy car, then take ten to fifteen minutes of your time to complete the enclosed GET (General Entrepreneurial Test) questionnaire.

We'll send you our analysis of your answers to help you decide if you're a candidate for your own business. And it won't cost you a cent! This is a service of my company, Entrepreneur's Press, that was created to help people like you find their place in life. A little over ten years ago, someone helped convince me that I had what it took to have my own business, and I'm determined to help others.

Let me hear from you. Send in the enclosed questionnaire and GET the answers you've been seeking.

Cordially,

Don Francis
Publisher

- Everyone likes to test his/her abilities, so mailings like this produce better-than-average responses.

- This is a classic two-step approach. First, you qualify the prospect with his/her interest in entrepreneurship, then you send him offers geared to that interest.

Company Name
Address
City, State Zip

Date

The Reverend Lester Beach, S.J.
St. Joan of Arc
4250 Kaiser Boulevard
Morrisville, NC 27560

Dear Reverend Father:

How do you introduce prospective new parishioners to your church? How do you keep current communicants apprised of the state of the church? We'd like to help you put your best face forward with the ST. JOAN OF ARC VIDEO.

If you have at least 50 members, we'll work with you on this wonderful new promotional tool for the church. You supply us with your history and give us access to your parishioners, and we'll give you a 60-minute color video that will be the talk of the community.

We'll videotape church members during a service or function, and include each family in the presentation. You'll receive an official church copy, with special introduction, at no cost. We'll make the tape available to parishioners for only $39.95 (and give the church 10% of each sale).

This will become an annual event that will always be eagerly anticipated. And it will help you tell the church's story to the community-at-large. I'll call next week to explain all the details of this exciting, motivational package. And I'll give you names of churches that are using this service.

Very truly yours,

Alfred Barnes

- Use questions that relate to challenges in the prospect's life. Then show how your answers deal with those challenges.

- Be sure to highlight the benefits (free offer and income-raising possibilities).

- Indicate a follow-up.

Company Name
Address
City, State Zip

Date

Ms. Claudia Kauffman
President
Roosevelt High School Class of 1960
33 Brook Drive
Caldwell, ID 83605

Dear Ms. Kauffman:

Whatever happened to the guy who always wore a beret and recited the Pledge of Allegiance backwards? Did everybody's All-American quarterback ever marry the cheerleader who broke her leg doing a split?

We're the reunion specialists! We'll help you locate your entire class...we'll take care of your invitations and track the responses (we'll mail three reminders!)...we'll create the theme and the buttons with the yearbook pictures on them...we'll make your reunion an event to remember and cherish.

There's not a detail we won't cover for you. Questionnaires to update everyone's lives. The music from your graduation year. The teachers who made learning so special. And we'll arrange everything within your budget including the food, beverages, and band.

Let us help you plan your next reunion. Check with Bob Hardison in Cambridge (555-7623) and ask him about the reunion we staged for him last month.

We'll make your reunions unforgettable events.

Cordially,

Larry Noble

- Try an opening that paints a picture of school days. After you've established the mood, begin to sell.

- List your services in detail.

- Use local references to help cement the sale.

Company Name
Address
City, State Zip

<u>If you can clear your calendar
for just two days,
we'll give you everything you need to know
to make you more effective
the other 363 days!</u>

Dear DP Professional:

At our special two-day event (March 6 and 7 in Chicago), you'll learn PRECIS features, timesavers, tips, and troubleshooting techniques that will make your PRECIS system work for you, including how to:

- Understand terminal server port assignments for device identification and relocation.
- Establish system independence by initializing your back-up media.
- Streamline your periodic and day-end processing schedules.
- Optimize your customer support services.

You'll have the opportunity to work side-by-side with your colleagues from all over the country. You'll interact with them and our team of specialists who will walk you through the program that makes <u>you</u> the PRECIS authority in your computer operation.

Enroll now. Attendance is strictly first-come, first-served. We'll accept <u>only 35 registrants</u> to insure that the learning is intense and the training personal. Return the enclosed enrollment form that spells out the registration details, or call 1-800-HOT-TIPS.

Cordially,

Lisa Brodie
VP, Training

- Qualify the prospect in the salutation. This is <u>not</u> a course for non-technical people.

- Establish the intensity of the time and training to appeal to top level people.

- Create a sense of urgency with limited enrollment.

Company Name
Address
City, State Zip

Date

Mr. Courtland Fox
American Educators Association
3 Belvedere Street
Fort Lauderdale, FL 33333

Dear Mr. Fox:

How would you like to help your members <u>save up to 60%</u> on cruises, tours, and travel plans?

The SHORT-TERM TRAVEL CLUB rewards people who can travel on short notice. And since many of your members have that sort of flexibility—particularly in the summer—I think this would suit your members' needs perfectly.

How do we do it? We're the biggest buyer of unsold space on airlines, cruise ships, and hotels. When tour operators get nervous (about 8 weeks before departure time), they call us, and we buy the unsold space at a significant discount... then turn around and offer huge savings to groups like yours.

Your members will sit in the same seats, occupy the same cabins, be housed in the same luxury accommodations as people who pay hundreds, even thousands of dollars more.

I'll be happy to come down to discuss this exciting program. I'd love to have an excuse to trade our northern cold for your Florida sun. I'll call next week.

Cordially,

Lowell Rooker

P.S. The handsome brochure I've enclosed is the one given to its members by the Society of College and University Professors. Our program has been a <u>big hit</u> with them for ten years.

- Explain why this group should be interested in your services.

- Offer a credible explanation of how you can provide such phenomenal savings (or your letter will be tossed!).

- If possible, show a similar group that has accepted.

Company Name
Address
City, State Zip

<u>Your home may be your castle,
but what do you do when the
moat needs fixing?</u>

Dear Home Owner:

Have you needed a plumber lately? (Worse yet, have you been able to get one?) Have you stayed home for days waiting for an unreliable or incompetent contractor to show up? Have you just flat-out had it with no-shows, high bills, and shoddy workmanship?

By joining the Maintenance Co-op, you'll eliminate the hassles, avoid surly repairmen and pay about 20% less for home repairs than non-members. <u>And that's a guarantee</u>!

Maintenance Co-op was started by two local people—Sidney and Carole Mills—who had reached a state of utter frustration over the simplest home repair. With a solution born of despair, they created MC along with a group of neighbors and really started something <u>big</u>. Maintenaince Co-op now serves over 5,000 families.

If you'd like your plumbing, electrical repairs, carpentry, window replacement, caulking, and other home repairs done quickly, efficiently, and reasonably, mail the reply card for more information.

You're under no obligation whatsoever to take this service...but if you want to regain control of your castle, mail the postpaid card today for FREE information.

Sincerely,

Nelson Morsky
Vice President

- Set the stage with your headline/salutation.

- Create a sense of identification with people in similar circumstances.

- Assure the prospect that there is no obligation.

Company Name
Address
City, State Zip

Question: If you were in <u>my</u> shoes what would you do?

Answer: Run in the Pine Hill 5K teen race and win bonus prizes!

This year's 5K Teen Race has a special twist. If you finish the race and are wearing running shoes from The Racing Place, you will win a valuable gift certificate from our store!

1st place:	$100 gift certificate
2nd place:	$ 75 gift certificate
3rd place:	$ 50 gift certificate
4th place:	$ 25 gift certificate
Finishers:	$ 5 gift certificate

Don't forget: to be eligible for our great gift certificates, you have to be wearing running shoes with our special RP mark on them. Just come to the van at the finish line to claim your gift certificate. Everyone's a winner at the Racing Place!

Yours for better racing,

Bob Weinerman
The Racing Place

- Reinforce the headline by making the supporting information stand out (the prizes).

- Take advantage of events that can tie in with your product line.

- "Everyone wins" contests are excellent for promoting good will among your prospects.

Company Name
Address
City, State Zip

Date

Mr. Harold Leshner, C.P.A.
Mankowitz, Brown and Harris
60 Park Place
Eugene, OR 97403

Dear Mr. Leshner:

You're part of an outstanding accounting firm. I run one of the top computer consulting firms. You know and understand your clients' businesses. I know and understand how to integrate electronic data processing into their business functions. Together, we can help your clients select microcomputer software (accounting as well as spreadsheet, data base, and others) and generate additional income for you.

Think how much more valuable your services would be if you could help your clients:

- Fit a computer into their businesses with virtually no disruption in their operation.

- Use a computer to decrease costs, increase productivity.

- Train their staffs to get maximum productivity.

Stop giving away business. Let us be your subcontractor (you maintain complete client control) and help you get tens of thousands of dollars in fees that have traditionally gone to other firms.

I'll call you next week to tell you what you have to gain.

Yours truly,

Dr. Frank Springs

• Explain the proposed relationship.

• State what the prospect has to gain.

• Affix a dollar value to the gain.

Company Name
Address
City, State Zip

Date

Mr. Malcolm Wetherington, Sales Manager
Pitman Controls
696 Commerce Way
Tupelo, MS 38801

Dear Mr. Wetherington:

The sales manager at MBI looked me in the eye, didn't crack a smile, and said: "I've got salespeople all over the world. Our business is fast-paced, and we need information quickly. If you're as good as you think you are, here's what I want from you: a system where my salespeople can

(1) dial in from anywhere and at anytime for up-to-the-minute reports on product movement, purchase orders, and scheduling

(2) send and receive messages from anywhere, and at anytime

(3) have access to a central data bank that has all their product information.

Oh, and one other thing. I don't have any money in the budget for programming. If you can do all this on a zero based budget, you've got the job."

Today, six-and-a-half-months later, the MBI sales manager has a broad grin on his face because I helped him achieve <u>all</u> of his goals. With no programming charges. And, by his own estimate, he has <u>dramatically</u> enhanced productivity.

I'll call you in a few days to spell out the specifics. Then you'll understand how we turned the computer into the sales manager's best friend.

Cordially,

Aaron Levin
VP, Sales

- A narrative style is a very effective attention-getter.

- Avoid too many details in the introductory letter.

- Use a problem/solution approach. (He gave me a difficult problem; I solved it and made him look good.)

Company Name
Address
City, State Zip

Date

Mr. Arthur Fowler
New England Telephone, Inc.
13 Abington Place
N. Woodstock, NH 03293

Dear Mr. Fowler:

If I said I could train your managers to speak more effectively, what would your response be?

— I'd like you to, but we don't have the money.
— I'd like you to, but we don't have the time.
— I'd like you to, but I can't take our employees away
    from the job.

If you're like many trainers, you may have selected all three perfectly valid answers. But suppose my responses to you were as follows...would you be interested?

1. You don't have to lay out a penny.
2. You don't have to expend a minute in time or energy.
3. You don't have to take away employees' work time.

Companies such as General Electronics, McTavish Restaurants, Public Service of Florida, and American Communication Enterprises have taken us up on this offer.

If you'll take about 30 seconds to complete and mail the enclosed reply card, I'll send you complete information on how they did it...and what the improvement has meant to these companies.

Cordially,

Troy Atwood

- These are three common excuses for doing nothing. This letter will be read because it confronts them.

- Be sure you can deliver on your offer. (In this case, it's accomplished through an employee-paid self-study program.)

Company Name
Address
City, State Zip

Date

Ms. Joan Glass
American Businesswoman Magazine
13 East Hawthorne Street
Evanston, IL 60201

Dear Ms. Glass:

When American Publishing Group purchased <u>School & University Magazine</u>, the industry joke was that SUM ranked 17th in a 5-magazine field. And that wasn't much of an exaggeration. As you're probably aware, SUM is now the #1 publication, with more ad pages than the next two magazines combined.

I was brought in to find the elusive marketing niche for SUM, and it didn't take very long to fuel the turnaround. I decided to approach the school and university market as a single market, while the other magazines insisted the market was divided into two segments, high school and college.

With some survey work and a lot of promotion, we were able to show advertisers they could reach the entire market with one publication instead of having to pay for two. (Schools buy bleachers; colleges buy bleachers.)

I'm telling you all this because I've been studying your market, and I believe I have several innovative ideas that will catapult you into the number one position among women's magazines. I'll need no more than 45 minutes to explain.

I'll call next week to set up a meeting.

Sincerely,

Alex Mayer
President

- Get right into the success story. Don't start by branding yourself as a consultant. Weave a story that shows you're a problem-solver and profit-maker.

- Set a time limit for the meeting; this increases your chances for having the meeting.

Company Name
Address
City, State Zip

Date

Marie McCoy, D.V.M.
790 Amity Avenue
Medford, OR 97501

Dear Dr. McCoy:

Do you know the real questions pet owners have? Concerns such as: "How do I get a 160 pound Great Dane with a broken leg to the vet?" Or "What do I do about a three-pound toy poodle that's sick to her stomach since I don't want to ruin my $25,000 car?"

Do you know how much people hate wasting time in crowded vet offices? Or how upset they get when they put their pets through the anxiety of being dragged there? Do you know what vets pay in rent and staff dollars? Or how difficult it is to start a practice without going deeply into debt?

Become a MOBILE VET. We now have MOBILE VETS in seventeen states, and we're growing. We supply you with a fully equipped van—the latest in veterinary technology. And we supply complete training in using all the equipment. Plus, we supply you with advertising material and national marketing support.

The cost of getting started is far less than for a traditional office, and you have the advantage of dealing with more relaxed animals (and owners) in their homes. Instead of spending years working for someone else, you can start your own MOBILE VET practice immediately.

Please read the enclosed brochure, then return the reply card for complete information about obtaining your own MOBILE VET franchise.

Sincerely,

Dale Farmer
Senior Vice President

- By asking the right questions, you can help people arrive at answers that will sell your product or service.

- Focus on the basics (it costs less, can get you started immediately, and serves a need).

Setting Up the Sales Call 2

The sales call provides an opportunity for you to sell a prospect or customer face-to-face, which, after all, is the most effective method of selling. To be virtually guaranteed a meeting, your letter has to sell your services in such a convincing manner that a sales call will naturally follow.

Convincing a busy person to see you—especially if you don't know the prospect—can be a real challenge. As with all sales letters, the most important aspect of setting up a sales call is to get the reader's attention. Once that has been accomplished, focus on the reader's needs and how you can satisfy those needs. Then convince the reader that your product or service is the best one to do the job. Finally, ask for the sale—in this case, an agreement to meet.

New Customers. Your primary goal is to get an appointment with someone who may know little or nothing about you or your company. So you need to "size up" the prospect to determine what might be important to him or her, and what would induce that person to take time to see you.

Where does the company fit within the industry? Is it a market leader? Or is it trying to catch up? What particular needs does the person to whom you're writing have? Has her product line grown stale? Is he looking for new markets or new distribution channels? In other words, do some homework before you dash off a letter. If you don't, you're missing the opportunity to make the kinds of quality calls that will generate sales.

Don't limit what you can offer until you know what the prospect might want. If you guess wrong, you may never have another chance to offer other possibilities.

Include samples, discounts, coupons, and other enticements to break down walls. Past successes with comparable firms show you aren't new to the business—just to the prospect.

Current Customers. Taking people for granted has ruined many relationships, and is one of the leading causes for losing customers. You have to work to keep the relationship fresh and valuable to the customer.

Everyone likes to see something new. Do you have a new product? A new service or new employee? Or perhaps new equipment? You can create a sense of urgency ("I want you to see this before anyone else does...").

You have a unique opportunity to create additional sales with existing customers. No matter what you offer, emphasize the pleasure of doing business with them, how bright the future is for both of you, and how a continued relationship increases their profits.

Reactivating old accounts—especially those who were dissatisfied in the past—can be very satisfying, though the technique is not easy to master. Accentuating positives is a must, and accepting honest blame when you've been wrong wins points. The emphasis always must be on the future and what benefits it can hold.

Company Name
Address
City, State Zip

Date

Mr. Ned Strang
Correspondence Schools of America
Second Street at Astoria Place
Newark, NJ 07185

Dear Mr. Strang:

May I be frank with you?

CSA has missed opportunity after opportunity to create a major new profit center, probably because management—your old management—insisted that things be done exactly as they had always been done.

When I told them how much profit could be produced by renting their mailing lists, they shook their heads "no." I showed them estimates of the huge income that list rental would generate...but for some reason they preferred to do nothing.

I've enclosed a projection of the rental income your lists could generate for the next five years—and I've been conservative. I think you'll agree that the numbers are extraordinary! And remember, this income is yours without any expenditure or any risk. Your two competitors have been renting their lists for years, and have a tremendous amount of incremental income to show for it.

I can help you introduce new profits to your new company. All we have to do is alter some old thinking. I'll call in a few days to set an appointment.

Sincerely,

Kent Grantham
Vice President, Marketing

Enclosure

- A new person may be eager to pursue revenue producing ideas that require no cash risk.

- Support your position with facts and figures the new prospect can use.

Company Name
Address
City, State Zip

Date

Mr. Lewis Triolla
Advanced Engineering
Point Pleasant Road
Newport, RI 02841

Dear Mr. Triolla:

I want your meeting business, and I'll do just about anything to get it. If you get the idea that I'm aggressive, you're correct. But that aggressiveness works for you.

We just hosted a 200-person conference for a group that had green and white as its colors. We painted the meeting room in their company colors, then repainted it after they left. Last week we had a meeting of the Orthodox Jewish Council of New England, and we set up a temporary kitchen, under the supervision of a rabbi, to meet their dietary needs.

I've only been the manager at the Newport Surf Inn and Lodge for six months, but in that time we've had a dramatic upsurge in business. I think one of the reasons is that I'll do almost anything to please you and your guests. And, of course, the Inn still has the same fine dining and wide range of facilities to please the most discriminating guest.

Can I convince you to come in and inspect our grand old "new" hotel? A combination of new personnel, new attitudes, and massive renovations have made the Newport Surf Inn and Lodge your number one meeting selection.

I'll call you to arrange your visit. And don't worry about transportation. I'll send our limo.

Cordially,

John (Skip) Carlisle
Manager

- There's a certain advantage to being new. Don't hide it.

- List achievements that make you unique.

- Make it difficult for the prospect to say "no" to a visit.

Company Name
Address
City, State Zip

Date

Ms. Elizabeth Mullins
Manager, Computer Services
Credit BankCard Corporation
1776 Walt Whitman Boulevard
Burlington, VT 05401

Dear Ms. Mullins:

As a consultant in the EDP field, I'll bet that you're not getting the most from your computer equipment.

I've enclosed a standard PC diskette (cost about forty cents) to prove my point. I created an application that most people think can be implemented only by costly CD ROM.

I generated the disk on a $1,200 IBM-compatible. (As you know, to create a CD ROM master can cost thousands of dollars.) Just pop the diskette in your computer and type A:CONTROL to get an understanding of the kinds of savings I can provide your company without any upgrade to your equipment.

If you're willing to risk a half-hour of your time, I can show you a number of exciting ways you can enhance the management and utilization of your technology while containing (or reducing) the costs.

I'll call you next week.

Very truly yours,

Arthur Levitz

Enclosure

- A challenge is a sure-fire way to grab a prospect's attention.

- An "involvement" device (interactive disk) is an effective method for demonstrating your creativity, and grabbing the reader's attention.

- Suggest that there will be a benefit as a result of meeting.

Company Name
Address
City, State Zip

Date

Mr. Richard Pei
President
Far East Trading Company, Ltd.
20, Chung Hsiao W. Road, Sec. 12
Taipei, Taiwan, R.O.C.

Dear Mr. Pei:

Mr. Beryl Harmon of Star*Bound Gifts suggested that we had something in common. You need a U.S. distributor, and I'd like to carry your line of quality bath fashion goods.

My company has been responsible for a number of successful product launches in the States. If you're aware of the success of Trim-Slim Jogging Outfits , you may know that it broke every sales record for a new line of sports clothing. We also did the recent Australian merchandising program that has performed so well.

We think your fabric massage straps, gloves, and belts will fit nicely with the current American enthusiasm for better health and looks. And your emphasis on products that stimulate blood circulation will tie in perfectly with beauty promotions as well as health.

I'm going to work on some preliminary sales projections for you. Until then, please review the enclosed literature on my company. I'll be in touch within two weeks.

I can help you move merchandise, Mr. Pei.

Sincerely,

Leonard Wynn

Enclosure

- Name dropping can pay off. Mention whatever companies or individuals will be of interest to your prospect.

- List successes.

- Tell the prospect what steps need to be taken.

Company Name
Address
City, State Zip

Date

Ms. Patricia Liberts
American Society for Trucking
100 W. Magnolia Trail
Orlando, FL 32801

Dear Ms. Liberts:

Bill Curry indicated that you were looking for someone to "syndicate" promotional mailings to your membership. I've called repeatedly for a clarification (syndication means different things to different people), but since you've been unavailable, I'll make some assumptions.

Assumption number one is that you're seeking an organization to (a) find products of interest to your members (personal as well as career) and (b) take care of all the details and costs for promotion, warehousing, shipping, invoicing, etc.

Assumption number two is that you'd be interested in talking to me since my company has been successfully handling the promotional/fulfillment operation for seven highly respected non-profit associations similar to yours.

I'd be delighted to present a full proposal of what we can do for you, if I can first have a moment of your time. Bill said this was a pressing need, so I assume (there's that word again) that I'll hear from you this week. I think you'll find what I have to offer is of great value.

Sincerely,

Leonard La Rosa

- Let the prospect know someone else sponsored your call and is aware of her actions.

- Be as general as possible when guessing at what the prospect might want. If you're wrong, you may never get the opportunity to bid.

- Make it clear that the prospect stands to benefit by being responsive.

Company Name
Address
City, State Zip

Date

Mr. Daniel Baker
Guthrie-Chalmers Engineers, Inc.
Chalmers Building
Riverside, NJ 08080

Dear Dan:

I'm glad I had the opportunity to get to know you better. Thanks for making the time available, especially with no prior notice.

As Jim mentioned when he brought me into your office, we've started to move ahead on a number of special projects that should give your division a major sales boost this year. Jim also suggested that you and I work together on the development of a number of proposals, including the national seminar on electronic data banks for technical professionals.

Please feel free to use me as a resource, Dan. I'm fortunate that I've been able to serve as a consultant to Jim for more than fifteen years, and I hope that I'll have an opportunity to bring you similar successes.

I'll call you soon. I'd enjoy continuing the discussion over lunch.

Cordially,

Nat Paulson

- Don't presume the same relationship you had with his predecessor. You have to re-sell yourself.

- Reinforce the concept that the prospect's predecessor relied on you in the past, and that you brought him much success.

Company Name
Address
City, State Zip

Dear Audio/Visual Duplicator:

Take a hard look at the audio and video housings we've included with this letter. How do they compare with the ones you use?

You may not see any difference between ours and yours if you're using top quality housings. But what about price? If you're paying more than 12 cents for audio housings or 45 cents for video housings, you now have a way to lower your cost of product.

As the head of production for Cherry Blossom Cassette Manufacturing Company in Tokyo, I'm responsible for producing over one million housings each week.

We ship weekly to the States, and we always maintain a minimum inventory of one full month's production in raw materials. When I call you next week, I'll supply a list of very satisfied users who can vouch for our on-time delivery, superior quality, and unbeatable prices.

If you'd like to place an order or obtain more information, use the enclosed order form. I'm looking forward to helping you lower your cassette housing costs.

Very truly yours,

Albert Lom
Vice President, Sales

Enclosure

- Title-only mailings often have a sameness about them. If you can include a product sample or premium, it will dramatically add to readership of your message.

- Stress your key selling point more than once (in this case, price).

- If you're selling "blind," let the prospect know that references are available.

Company Name
Address
City, State Zip

Date

Byron Stuart
Chemco International
32 Bethesda
Philadelphia, PA 19123

Dear Mr. Stuart:

I'd like to extend an invitation to you and your staff to attend a tour of our facilities.

I think once you see our factory, you'll understand not only how we achieve our low pricing (through the latest automation techniques), but also how we maintain extremely high quality (by using the most contemporary QC hardware and software available).

I'll call you next week to set up the tour.

Sincerely,

Jane Fabiani
Vice President, Marketing

- A plant tour is a great opportunity to sell your company and your products.

Company Name
Address
City, State Zip

Date

Mr. David Niles
American Book Combine
888 Third Avenue
New York, NY 10022

Dear Mr. Niles:

Most American publishers ignore the Asian market because they have no idea how thirsty Asian business people are for American books.

Did you know, for example, that Fine-Tuning the Art of Negotiating, published by Watson Publishing Company, sold 50,000 copies in one year—and is now in its third printing in Japan? Or that "Manufacturing for the Future," from Matrix Press, sold 35,000 copies in just six months?

We set up distribution for both these books in the Far East. And we can do the same for you. Will you give me a few minutes to explain how you can build new sales by taking advantage of the opportunities in the English-speaking Asian market? I'll call to schedule an appointment.

Sincerely,

Carol Lopinson

- Opening a new market for a company is exciting news, and will get attention.

- Point to a competitor, if possible, who has experienced success with your service.

Company Name
Address
City, State Zip

Date

Mr. Elliot Spring
Asian Showrooms Ltd.
35 Parker Place
New York, NY 10020

Dear Mr. Spring:

I've just been advised by my Chinese agent that shipment of the "Emperor Tea Cup" collection has been delayed.

As much as I'd like to see you again, our scheduled meeting on June 7 (10:00 a.m.) doesn't make much sense without the merchandise. I had the opportunity to examine the cups during my last visit to China, and the catalog just doesn't do them justice.

The moment I'm notified of shipment, I'll call to reschedule. I believe these cups will become a major seller for your chain.

Thanks for your understanding. I should be back to you within two weeks.

Sincerely,

Julius Rappoport

- Explain why a postponement is to the <u>prospect's</u> benefit—not yours.

- Set the stage for a new appointment.

Company Name
Address
City, State Zip

Date

Ms. Elaine Altman
Viking Electronics
2195 Capitol Street
Billings, MT 59101

Dear Elaine:

You're the primary reason I worked so hard to find my "perfect" replacement. It's really important to me that you continue to receive the kind of service and attention I feel you deserve.

I think you and Norm Baseman will pick up where we left off. He has more of a technical background than I do, and you'll find that he's the sort of person who will give you straight answers to tough questions. He's good.

I'd like the opportunity to say goodbye to you and also to introduce you to Norm. Are you free for lunch any day next week? We'll work around your schedule.

Talk to you in a few days.

Cordially,

Stan Douglass

- Personalize the replacement process.

- Tell the client that the commitment remains every bit as strong as when you provided the service.

Company Name
Address
City, State Zip

Date

Mr. Bernard Adamczak
Culinary Gifts, Inc.
5090 Elverson Place
Tysons Corner, VA 22180

Dear Bernie:

We've just acquired a Hong Kong company that has been a respected manufacturer for nearly twenty years. Their specialty is top quality meat, oven, and refrigerator freezer thermometers. I think the top-of-the-line thermometers are a natural for your kitchenware catalog, and the bottom-of-the-line should be a great addition to your premium business. We can private label for you in <u>any</u> quantity.

I'd like to show you samples while you still can include them in your upcoming catalog. Please check your calendar for next Wednesday or Thursday. This is an exciting opportunity.

Talk to you soon.

Cordially,

Kim Shimamura

- Make suggestions as to how the customer can use the new products. (Never assume he/she will make the connection.)

- Ask for an appointment to demonstrate the new product, and offer a sense of urgency.

Company Name
Address
City, State Zip

Date

Ms. Jane Miller
Federal Marketing, Inc.
#1 Willingboro Way
Anchorage, AK 99510

Dear Jane:

It's been a long time since we developed any new promotions for you, so I thought I'd update you on a few things we're doing that should be of interest.

I've enclosed two new direct response kits that are not only innovative but have proven to be powerful sales generators. One is a name change kit for a national fuel company; the other is an employee motivation piece for a national convenience store chain.

On the television front, we've had great success recently for Colonial Mortgage. We produced two new TV commercials. Our spots beat the control with a cost per lead that was less than half of the control spot's cost per lead. But rather than talk about it, I've enclosed a reel that I think you'll enjoy viewing. (It'll only take 6 minutes.)

I'll call you in a few days to answer any questions and to see if we can put our team to work on developing new customers for you.

Cordially,

Gordon Bright

- Make an inactive client understand that you are creating winning promotions for others.

- Stress new business—and successes—that you've developed since your last contact.

Company Name
Address
City, State Zip

Date

Mr. Joseph Deacon
Alverthorp & Mohl Advertising
888 Commonwealth Way
Harrisburg, PA 17111

Dear Joe:

You may not recognize the company name on the letterhead, but I think it will become familiar quickly—I've started my own recording company.

As you know, I've spent nearly eighteen years as a producer and sound engineer. (We've worked together for almost ten of them.) I'm putting that background to use in my new company, producing radio spots and live and remote recordings and handling all facets of post-production editing and remix.

I know what you demand in a production, Joe, and I hope you'll continue to let me give it to you. I have a complete new music library, access to the best talent, and I can even manage any duplicating and fulfillment needs you may have. We're located in the new Highland Industrial Park, about a 6-minute drive from your office.

I've always been noted for giving my clients a little "extra." Now that I have my own studio, you'll get even more.

I'll talk to you soon.

Regards,

Sid Jones

- Unless you had an employment agreement prohibiting contact, there are no prospects as good as the people with whom you've been working.

- List all your new capabilities, and offer some reason for keeping the business, in addition to friendship (better rates, better equipment, etc.).

Company Name
Address
City, State Zip

Date

Mr. Ernest Laver
Forms Research Company
221 Albidale Street
Guilford, CT 06437

Dear Ernie:

The more I thought about your possible acquisition of Tribute Publishing Company, the more I believed it would be an excellent deal for everyone.

As you review the enclosed financials, keep in mind that I estimate them to be about $400,000 too fat in overhead. By deleting that excess, you have a very profitable addition to your burgeoning empire (and I've seen you wield a very sharp knife in the past).

I'm going to be in Chicago at the end of the month. I'll sit down with Tribute management and set up an appointment for you to visit. Don't call them. I'd rather it appear that I'm forcing you to consider this deal.

I'll call you after the meeting.

Regards,

Owen Wooster

Enclosure

- Explain why you think the deal is worth pursuing (company too fat; prospect knows how to slash costs).

- Offer a strategy for setting it up.

Proposals and Quotations 3

During a writing class conducted for a major New York City financial organization, a participant expressed his frustration with his job. "I'm paid to analyze all phases of our operations and develop proposals for improving them. But I've been here for a year," he said, "and nothing has ever come of any of my proposals. I'm this close (he held his thumb and forefinger a fraction of an inch apart) to quitting. I'm not contributing."

Surprisingly, it turned out that this individual was an excellent writer. His sentences were crisp, his grammar was precise. He was bright, and carefully articulated his requests. So what was wrong? Why weren't his proposals acted upon?

The answer was that the analyst never asked for anything to happen. He just assumed things would happen because of his outstanding research. It never occurred to him that (1) he had to sell his ideas and (2) his management needed to be motivated to read key sections of his reports and proposals.

The analyst's self-esteem recovered dramatically when he learned how to summarize and highlight recommended actions. He discovered that a simple cover letter, supporting memo, or executive summary could pinpoint important areas and excite management about the positive values of change.

The moral of the story? Remember that proposals and quotations must also be selling vehicles. The good ones are more than just numbers; they're motivators.

Cover Letters, Responses, and Follow-Ups. Proposals and quotations are often colorless. Inflexible organizational and governmental requirements may dictate a rigid format, where deviation can mean elimination from consideration. But a good cover letter and effective follow-up can be of immeasurable help in selling a proposal or quotation.

A well-written cover letter will not sell a bad proposal or quotation, but it can elevate a good one to the top of the pile. A cover letter offers an additional chance to explain why you and your company are the right choices for the job.

Be sure to ask your customer or prospect for more information if you have questions. You can't write an effective proposal without having all the facts.

Proposals and Quotations. The key to getting the client to say "YES" is planning and preparation. What are the reader's needs? Have you considered what is most important to the client and emphasized those elements in your proposal or quotation? Is your proposal aesthetically pleasing (paragraphs not overly long, indents and underlines to draw the reader's eye to telling points)? Does it answer the key questions, What, When, How and How Much?

If your proposal can be stated in one or two pages, don't stretch it to three or four. The longest proposals don't win the job; the best ones do.

The prolific author, James Michener, corrected a reporter who had just called him "a great writer." Michener disagreed by saying, "I'm not a great writer, but I am a great editor." That's the best advice for writing winning proposals, quotations, sales letters, or any other correspondence. Take the extra time to review your first draft critically. Think about your reader and his or her objectives. Look at the structure of your proposal; does it invite readership?

A little extra time spent considering the form and content of your proposals and quotations will pay off in their acceptance.

Company Name
Address
City, State Zip

Date

Ms. Adrienne Bentley
Fox Pharmaceuticals
522 Orange Avenue
Franklin, TN 37064

Dear Ms. Bentley:

Will you let us save you $5,000? $10,000? $100,000?

We'll review every facet of your telephone system, including:

- toll and usage billing
- service and equipment
- pricing from Bell and other interconnect vendors

Then we'll develop a matrix of costs for your equipment and facilities by location, present current-value cash flow analysis for alternatives, and provide a complete report of short and long-term actions that will generate substantial savings and provide better services for your company.

The enclosed proposal outlines the details of what we'll do and how successful we've been at doing this for other companies. In fact, we guarantee you'll save no less than $5,000 a year as a result of our efforts.

I'll call after you've had a chance to review our proposal.

Sincerely,

Warren Vernon
VP, Sales

- A solicitation to prospects in the form of a proposal can be effective—when you're sure the company can use your services.

- Dramatize the key point of your proposal (savings).

- Summarize some of the key steps.

- State that you've been successful with other companies.

Company Name
Address
City, State Zip

Date

Mr. Huntington Daniels
Vice President, Operations
EquiBank Corp.
1145 Holden Avenue
Danbury, CT 06815

Dear Mr. Daniels:

Because of my work with various EquiBank departments and branches, I'm interested in submitting a proposal on the feasibility of consolidating some or all of your domestic business groups into one major data network. The ultimate benefits that should accrue to you include:

o Cost containment (your continuing growth precludes discussion of cost reduction)

o Enhanced responsiveness to business needs (critically important to an organization where minutes can mean millions of dollars)

o Higher quality of communication services

To offer a thorough proposal, I'll need access to your principal telecommuncations and operations managers for approximately 30 days. If you're willing to make them available, I'll deliver a proposal that could lay the cornerstone for your next 5-year strategic plan.

In the event you're not familiar with my work with EquiBank (and other financial conglomerates), I've enclosed a "backgrounder" for your review. I'd like the next step to be a meeting, so I'll call you early next week to see when such a session would be convenient for you.

Sincerely,

Stanley Danese, Ph.D.

- Enclose sufficient data to establish your credentials.

- Share your vision with a person who can act on it. A technical proposal, for example, may be lost on a CEO.

- Tell what you need to do a thorough job.

Company Name
Address
City, State Zip

Date

Mr. Stephen Anderson
Arcadia Manufacturing
418 Hampton Street
Fort Smith, AR 72904

Dear Mr. Anderson:

We have completed our analysis of your scrap removal requirements, and have put together a proposal to sharply reduce your expenses in this area. By installing our pneumatic conveyor to remove scrap glass cullets from your plant, you will:

1. Have a cash payback in only 2.14 years.
2. Earn a 3-year average ROI of 45.2%.
3. Receive an internal rate of return of 20.6%.

According to our analysis, approximately 42 tons of scrap glass must be removed each month. This is currently accomplished by six employees. We can help you do the job much more efficiently by replacing the workers with a pneumatic conveyor that will transport the cullets from the three sealers to the holding tank outside the plant.

The principle component of the conveyor system is a centrifugal high pressure fan with a filter for glass particles. The fan and additional peripheral equipment will cost $50,638, including installation and training. The breakdown of costs is on page five.

Thanks for your consideration. You'll find this system a tremendous addition to productivity and profits.

I'll call you next week to answer any questions.

Sincerely,

Norman Simon
Sales Engineer

- Use your cover letter as a concise summary of the overall proposal, particularly helpful when technical proposals are being read by non-technical managers.

- Whenever possible, list financial benefits.

- Advise that you will be following up to answer questions.

Company Name
Address
City, State Zip

To: Brigadier General Amos Flagson

From: David Bailey, Robert Moore

Date:

Subject: Response to TELCOMNET's Request For Proposal (RFP) TELC-7101, titled
Engineering Assistance for the TELCOMNET-Z Spacecraft Program

OBJECTIVE: Present and establish the outstanding resources LTI, Inc. will bring to the
technical issues relative to the development of the TELCOMNET-Z spacecraft.

THE PROPOSAL includes two volumes:
1. Technical and management proposal
2. Detailed price/cost proposal

LTI, Inc. is uniquely qualified to perform the TELCOMNET-Z Engineering Assistance tasks
in a timely, comprehensive, and cost-effective manner. LTI support resources include
extensive computational capabilities coupled with staff members who possess a combined
88 years of experience in spacecraft methodology and techniques, including:
BETACOM I and II
BT&T Comstar
GAMMA 3 Enhancement
KOLB/GFI Spacecraft
LinkTELCO

LTI STATUS: LearnTech International, Inc. (also registered as LTI) is a Delaware
Corporation, with principal offices in Wilmington. LTI was incorporated in 1983 and
maintains all business insurance requirements of the State of Delaware, including
workman's compensation, liability, property and loss, and comprehensive coverage. LTI
has no outstanding debt and owns all office equipment (including computers) with a value
in excess of $300K. Ownership is 50% minority.

- Follow the proposal style that is appropriate to that particular industry or sector.

- Specify the objective of the proposal, and spell out key supporting data.

Company Name
Address
City, State Zip

Date

Mr. Henry Lau
Dore & Foster Corporation
72 N. Allegheny Avenue
Madison, WI 53780   RE: F.08.104 Phase I, Reformatting of
                           Remittance Input

Dear Mr. Lau:

I once worked for a man whose motto was, "Never make the same mistake once." That's a bit of wisdom I'd like to invoke now.

It would be to our mutual benefit if you'd extend the deadline for the RRI proposal submission by an additional three weeks (to August 17). That gives us time to answer new questions that have arisen about the overall programming design. And it gives you the assurance that we'll have explored every possibility beforehand. An additional week now will avoid costly delays later.

Thanks for your patience and understanding. Both will help to insure that "We don't make the same mistake once." I'll call for confirmation of the extension.

Sincerely,

Martha Wedington

- An attention-getting opener is not a requirement for this sort of request, but it is a useful technique for creating a favorable feeling about you and the extension request.

- Explain why you feel the extension is warranted.

- Call for confirmation so you can have immediate feedback, and ask for written confirmation during the call.

Company Name
Address
City, State Zip

Date

Mr. James Sturmessner
Senior Vice President
Marketing Specialties, Inc.
9220 Baroness Road
Waco, TX 76767

Dear Jim:

We've reached the moment of truth. Your internal consulting team has recommended that we proceed with the new information base project, and your management committee was favorably impressed during the briefing on Tuesday. (A complete summary is attached.)

We'll proceed as soon as you sign the enclosed contract. We can then begin the process of upgrading your information and statistical capacity, with no disruption to current operations. That will translate into enhanced client reporting and analysis, which should, as you start to promote your new capabilities, result in significantly more clients.

If any questions remain, please call. We're anxious to do our part to help make MSI the number one marketing agency in the Southwest.

Regards,

Charles Otis
Vice President, Sales

Enclosure

- Even though this is a confirmation letter, it can't hurt to continue to "sell" the merits of the project. When someone is about to sign a contract giving you thousands of dollars, make him/her feel good about doing it.

Company Name
Address
City, State Zip

Date

Mr. Richard Goldstein
Areta Computer Peripherals
4200 Blackford Avenue
Akron, OH 44307

Dear Mr. Goldstein:

I'm delighted that I'll have the opportunity to present my Creative Listening Workshop to your employees. Based on the successes I've enjoyed with other leading companies, I think your employees will be pleased about it, too!

We've agreed that:

1. The workshop will be held in your training room on Tuesday, September 13, from 9:00 a.m. to 4:00 p.m., with a one hour lunch.

2. The cost is $1,600, including all course materials, handouts, and tests for up to 25 people.

3. Upon completion, students will understand the psychology of the communication process; identify barriers to listening and be able to overcome them; be able to separate fact from opinion; apply techniques of empathetic listening to help others work out their problems; improve their own problem-solving abilities.

Thanks for selecting Belgrade Associates to run this workshop for you. I hope you can find the time to sit in as my guest (I can always make room for the boss!).

Cordially,

Alvin Darwin

- Reinforce the buyer's decision to select your product or service.

- Outline the points of agreement.

- Thank the buyer.

Company Name
Address
City, State Zip

Date

Mr. Charles Sweeney
Devoe Manufacturing Co.
6700 Alverton Avenue
Harrisburg, PA 17110

Dear Mr. Sweeney:

We're very pleased to be selected as supplier of furniture for your new offices. We can confirm that the following changes in specifications are accepted:

1. Executive chairs will be the "Ergonometric Model 1600" with fully adjustable lumbar support controls.

2. Office partitions will be six feet high.

All else is as previously agreed (see confirmation, dated January 22). And we will hold the price as originally quoted, even with the changes.

A reminder: Please be certain we have your move date by May 1. We want to have the furniture available when you need it.

Sincerely,

Peter Lenz

- State that the changes are confirmed, and list each one.

- Reconfirm everything that has been agreed to previously.

- If there is a deadline to be met by the client, put it in writing to avoid future problems.

Company Name
Address
City, State Zip

Date

Mr. Dennis Autrey
Precision Electric, Inc.
River Site #3-08
Portland, OR 97251   File: 34.899
     Doc. I.D. FLMN142

Dear Mr. Autrey:

This is a confirmation that we accept your changes to PP&E/PEI contract 34.899, with one exception. The two new chiller controllers we originally specified were omitted from the agreement.

Since the existing controllers are not compatible with the new heating and ventilating system, the new controllers must be added to the job specifications. To save you the trouble, I've affixed a Change Order Estimate to this letter for your signature.

I'm not sure how we lost track of the chillers along the way but, however it happened, we have to have the new units if we plan to vent the facility.

Thanks for your quick action. As soon as I receive the signed COE, we'll start construction.

Very truly yours,

V. M. DiGiacomo

Enclosure

- Highlight any changes of specifications with as detailed an explanation as necessary.

- Be certain the client knows he/she must sign for the changes before work begins.

Company Name
Address
City, State Zip

Date

Mr. Peter Scales
International Engineers, Inc.
1475 Allerton Way
Grand Forks, ND 58206

Dear Mr. Scales:

I enjoy working with someone as thorough as you, even if it means spending a week on revisions. I think you'll be pleased to see that we've included all your recommended changes and that they resulted in a cost reduction of $12,800.

We added a series of pneumatic pressure tests and helium leak tests to assure the integrity of the indium gasket under room and cryogenic temperatures. But these procedures will cost only $1,400, so your net gain from the revisions is $11,400. Details are attached.

Thanks for your help. I'll call you by next Wednesday for your approval. (We can't afford too long a decision period if we're going to make your deadline.)

Sincerely,

Allan Woodson

Enclosure

- When asked to submit a revised proposal, briefly highlight what was changed, including pricing.

- If the prospect has been of help in the revision process, be sure to note it.

- Remind the prospect that a decision must be forthcoming to meet a tight deadline.

Company Name
Address
City, State Zip

Date

Mr. Russell Whitten
National Sales Manager
Jensen & Jensen Products
401 Fremont Avenue
Skokie, IL 60076

Dear Mr. Whitten:

We've done a number of sales presentations for FORTUNE 500 companies, and I think your idea for a combination live/animation sight and sound show has the ring of an award winner. But before we give you our complete proposal, I have a few questions that will affect pricing:

1. You want photos of a number of your locations in the presentation. Do these already exist, or will new location photography be required?

2. How insistent are you on using actual managers instead of actors? By the time you've gone through all the takes with amateurs, you really haven't saved any money.

3. Would you mind if I quoted the job with packaged music as well as original music? If price is a major consideration—as you've indicated—you can cut costs by letting me find inexpensive "needledrop" music.

Thanks for asking us to bid. We'll have our proposal to you within one week of receiving your answers.

Sincerely,

Paul Greene

- Advise the prospect as quickly as possible that you're interested in bidding.

- Be specific about your questions.

- Tell the prospect when to expect the proposal.

Company Name
Address
City, State Zip

Date

Mr. Robert J. McCartney
American Society of Professional Accountants
633 Avenue of the Americas
New York, NY 10020

Dear Bob:

I appreciate your considering us to develop the audiocassette version of
ASPA's Audit and Accounting Manual. I think you'll like our price of just
$20,000, which includes scripts, a professional accountant's time and
assistance, top-notch narration (male and female), studio, and direction.
Attached is a detailed quotation.

This six-tape series will be informative, enlightening, and enjoyable. I
think you'll really open a lot of people's eyes with what we're proposing.
It's innovative and attuned to the learning style of the new professional
accountant.

Thanks for letting us quote. I'm excited about the chance to work with
you and ASPA. I'll call you next week to discuss the project.

Very truly yours,

Josephine Soltoff

Enclosure

- Express appreciation for the opportunity.

- State the major points (benefits) of using your company.

- Don't be afraid to express your enthusiasm for the project.

Company Name
Address
City, State Zip

Date

Ms. Natalie Baumer
Mainsail Software, Inc.
121 E. Pennsylvania Boulevard
Idaho Falls, ID 83404

Dear Natalie:

As promised, I've put all my numbers together for receiving your inventory, warehousing, and fulfilling your orders. Now I can give you the complete quotation, which I've attached.

These costs are easily passed on to the consumer in the form of a modest shipping/handling charge. Also keep in mind that we make you look good with your customers because every order we receive will be shipped within 72 hours.

I'll call you by the 10th to review the quote, answer any questions and receive the assignment.

Cordially,

Harry Arost

Enclosure

- Quotations should be submitted when promised.

- Explain the benefits (the cost is passed on to customer, and the customer receives prompt shipments).

- Ask for the sale.

Company Name
Address
City, State Zip

Date

Mr. Timothy Harris
Allied Manufacturers
American & Tasker Streets
Orangeburg, SC 29116

Dear Tim:

I was pleased to see your management take such a strong interest in Quality Control Awareness training. Your continuing emphasis on training and motivation will always keep your company on top.

The enclosed quotation is based on these assumptions:

1. All full-time employees (including supervisors and mid-level managers) will receive the training.

2. There will be at least ten QCA teams trained.

3. The numbers of employees are based on the departmental breakdowns you provided me.

4. The estimated travel costs to our training site, as always, are contingent on the vagaries of the airline industry and its pricing policies.

Thanks for the opportunity to quote. We're looking forward to adding another "boost" to your organization's impressive record of achievement.

Sincerely,

Jennifer Saltz

Enclosure

• Remind the prospect that top management has a strong interest in the project.

• Detail the assumptions that went into the pricing.

• Never pass up the chance to give <u>honest</u> praise to the organization, and to demonstrate enthusiasm for the company and the project.

Company Name
Address
City, State Zip

Date

Mr. Gary Fisher
United Department Stores
1398 Walnut Street/Suite 800
Philadelphia, PA 19108

Dear Mr. Fisher:

Before you read the enclosed quotation for our high-power binoculars,
I'd like to remind you that my government has promised to maintain the
rate of the Won against the U.S. dollar. That means you have no
worries about exchange rate fluctuations—big or small—affecting your
purchase price.

I'll repeat: the prices shown on the enclosed quotation are <u>stable</u>. They
are guaranteed for the balance of the year by the South Korean
government. That means, of course, that you now have the opportunity
to purchase top quality at a low and stable price.

Thank you for your understanding. If you need any further clarification,
please call me or Mr. L.C. Kim, the Business Attache at our consulate in
Philadelphia.

Sincerely yours,

Anthony H. Yoo
Managing Director

- If there is a concern about pricing, exchange rates, stabilization policy, etc., deal with it
  before the prospect gets to the quotes. Otherwise, he/she may not believe your quotes can be
  trusted.

- Suggest names to call for further clarification.

Company name
Address
City, State Zip

Date

Mr. Dennis George
George and Kidder Associates
555 Kirby Avenue
Columbia, MO 65212

Dear George:

The quotation you requested for changing windows #319 and #450 to
4'x0" wide is attached. The hardware you've already received is fine, so
the pricing excludes the cost of new hardware. We'll simply furnish new
windows and frames.

A reminder: to avoid confusion, please have all changes and requests
for quotes go through your office. It's starting to get a little "crazy," with
three or four people calling us for every change or quote request.

Also, let me know how you want the billing handled. Is this separate, or
should I make it part of Job #220-14?

Thanks for selecting us as your primary suppliers. We'll work hard to
keep you satisfied.

Sincerely,

L.C. (Chip) Greenwood

- Tell the client what is and is not included in the quote.

- If there are billing questions, ask them.

- Thank the client for the opportunity to quote.

Company Name
Address
City, State Zip

Date

Mr. Gerald Rullo
Guardian International Corp.
1 Guardian Way
Williamsburg, Va 23185

Dear Mr. Rullo:

We think you'll find us uniquely qualified to oversee the coordination, scheduling and installation of the APR system 28 and V-Band Trading Turret to support your fax and telex machines as well as your other data requirements.

As specialists in the computer-managed voice/data field, we propose to:

1. Receive, test, and install all incoming telecommunication equipment and facilities.

2. Ensure the necessary power requirements and environmental conditions for correct operation by coordinating the architect, equipment vendors, and client resources.

Our normal rate for this service is $1,200 per week. But since the job will take approximately six months, we'll reduce the rate by 15%, for a fixed fee of $26,520. Out-of-pocket costs will be billed separately. Our detailed proposal is attached.

I'll call you in a week to discuss the details. After you review the eight successful installations we've completed this year (you can never be too current in this business), I think you'll agree that we are the team you're looking for.

Sincerely,

Dr. Stanley Greenleaf

Enclosure

- State the facts and the benefits to the client.

- Be specific about when you'll follow-up. Don't expect the client to come to you.

Company Name
Address
City, State Zip

Date

Franklin Dykstra, Commander
Support Engineering Department (83232)
United States Navy
700 Robbins Avenue
Norfolk, VA 23599   Preliminary E-28 Emergency Runway
                          Arresting Gear Review and PROPOSAL

Dear Commander:

Our preliminary review has uncovered the following:

1. The crank handle binds prior to engaging the latch, leading the operator to believe the latch has been engaged. This will cause damage to the arresting gear and can be hazardous to incoming aircraft.
2. To securely latch the crank handle in the lock position with latch FK 4392-1, the latch must be lifted with one hand and the crank moved into position with the other.
3. Beveling the edges did not improve performance.
4. The latch is unsuitable for locking the crank handle.

PROPOSAL
Therefore, we propose to redesign the latch so it locks the crank handle into position without being manually lifted. This can be accomplished inexpensively by securing the base of the latch to the sprocket and having the top portion hinged. Total cost for testing, tooling, and design is $4,283.00. The job will require no more than eight weeks, and we can begin immediately.

Thanks for your consideration.

Cordially,

Kurt Winterspoon
Vice President

- Clearly identify the proposal (very important with government proposals).

- Listing key points is easier to read than writing large paragraphs of copy.

Company Name
Address
City, State Zip

Date

Mr. and Mrs. David Whitsell
554 Pleasant Grove Avenue
Cedar Bluff, VA 24609

Dear Mr. & Mrs. Whitsell:

Here's our step-by-step breakdown for providing this year's Spring Clean-Up Service:

Step	Service
1.	<u>You</u> put on comfortable clothes, relax on your patio, and think about all the work we're saving you. While you're relaxing...
2.	<u>We</u> prune shrubbery in the beds around the house (front, sides, and back).
3.	<u>We</u> remove grass and weeds from the beds.
4.	<u>We</u> feed all shrubbery with super-mix fertilizer.
5.	<u>We</u> pick up and bag all debris.
6.	<u>We</u> apply 8 cubic yards of cedar mulch to beds.

You don't have to sit on your patio, of course. You can work around the house, visit friends or relatives, or do anything you want. By the time you come back, your property will look like a cover story for <u>Better Homes and Gardens</u>.

Please sign and return the copy of this letter. We'll be there in less than two weeks, for a cost of just $395.00. Thanks for selecting The Greenery.

Cordially,

Wallace Elliston

Agreed:

Date:

- While light in tone, this proposal sells the value of having an outside service perform a task that homeowners could do themselves.

- Don't assume the customer knows how much work is involved. Spell it out.

- The letter proposal can also serve as an agreement. That's one less piece of paper to deal with—and it makes getting a signature much easier.

Company Name
Address
City, State Zip

Date

Mr. Salvatore Piazza
Piazza Construction, Inc.
3206 Penn Center
Syracuse, NY 13219   RE: SYRACUSE MEMORIAL HOSPITAL
                            DOOR AND FRAME SUB-CONTRACT #44-553321

Dear Sal:

As you requested, here's our proposal for furnishing doors and windows for your hospital project. For the record, I guarantee meeting your delivery date, provided you accept this proposal by September 15.

We will inventory the entire order in our heated warehouse. That gives us an edge over other manufacturers because you have the flexibility to stage the job as your schedule dictates. All materials will be available at your request.

We propose to furnish the following (the full proposal is attached):

05023 Steel doors and frames	$28,740.00
05211 Flush wood doors	$26,192.00
05439 Steel windows (pre-glazed)	$9,549.00
05489 Finishing hardware (including installation of automatic door operators)	$3,819.00
TOTAL	$68,300.00

I look forward to doing another great job with you and Piazza Construction.

Sincerely,

Herb Mies

- Clearly identify the proposal.

- State any special qualifications and considerations.

- Remind the prospect that you've done successful work for him before.

Company Name
Address
City, State Zip

Date

Mr. Christopher Kenney
Allied Engineers, Inc.
4200 West Overton Road
Waltham, MA 02154   RE: Project 428Z13.805

Dear Mr. Kenney:

I appreciate your asking us to quote. Our projected costs are:

One (1) IEEE vertical flame test @ 215,000 BTUs	$400.00
Six (6) Certified Test Reports	$450.00
TOTAL COST	$850.00

The IEEE test will be performed at the Windom Wire plant in Elkton, MD. The reports can be delivered by noon next Thursday, if the job is let by this Friday. To meet your deadline, I'll need confirmation by Wednesday.

I'll check with you by Wednesday noon. Thanks again for selecting us to quote.

Very truly yours,

Albert Wheeler

- Clearly identify the project and the costs (don't make the prospect search).

- Indicate that a follow-up will occur.

Company Name
Address
City, State Zip

Mr. Rodney Crum
Fast Food International, Inc.
38 Western Highway
Sumter, SC 29152   QUOTATION: FFI
                       FRANCHISEE GUIDE

Dear Mr. Crum:

Here are the specifications and quotation for 100,000 copies of your 30-page guidebook
(trim size 8-1/2 x 8-1/2).

You supply:
- o Non-scannable art for six-page fold-out cover (25-1/2 x 8-1/2).
- o 11 halftones (to reproduce as duotones).
- o Mechanicals with screens, tints, and knockouts.

We supply:
     Color proof for front cover and bluelines for text.

Costs:

Print and bind (saddle-stitch) 5/2 cover plus 2/2 text	$17,771.00
Paper: 80# cover, 100# text	$23,781.00
TOTAL	$41,552.00

Terms: Net 30 days, F.O.B. Columbia, SC.

We can guarantee the paper price for only 90 days, which will give you an idea how
volatile the paper market is. By ordering now, you can hold the price and have the stock
in-house to avoid last-minute delays.

Thanks for the opportunity to quote. We'll do an outstanding job for you.

Cordially,

Mary Tomlinson

- Be sure to point out any pitfalls (irregular sizes, price volatility), and you'll avoid acrimony
  when it comes time to bill.

Follow-ups to Sales Calls 4

You've held the sales presentation. You've met the customer and made your proposal. The meeting has gone well and you feel you can take it easy. Wrong! This is the point at which inexperienced salespeople assume that the sale has been made and mistakenly take their eye off the ball. Quite often, the old cliche "Out of sight, out of mind" comes into play, with the result that the prospect loses interest and you lose the sale. What do you do to ensure that the customer buys? Be enthusiastic. Don't let there be a hint of a letup in personal interest because you believe the sale is in the bag.

After Contact. It doesn't really matter whether you're writing after a sales presentation or after submitting a proposal or sending a sample. The purpose of your letter is the same: to summarize key details and and highlight parts of the discussion that may need reinforcing. You're also creating a written record of your meeting, which can help avoid disputes down the road.

The follow-up letter can convince someone you're the right person for the job. It can remind a prospect that you've had similar successes. It can state a deadline or price with finality. It can stir someone to action.

Reaffirm your product's benefits. Point out favorable comparisons with your competitors without running them down, putting the emphasis on what you can offer that others can't. Point to success with other buyers. Set the stage for the next contact, the close.

After a Sale. It's good business to reinforce a customer's decision to buy. A letter after a sale is your ticket to repeat sales and enthusiastic customers.

Thank the customer for the sale. State your pleasure in having a successful relationship. Confirm quantities, prices, terms of payment or other details in a summary that shows your interest in your customer and in his or her needs.

Clarify the next step to be taken by the customer—the order to be sent, the specs to be changed, the approval to be obtained. Indicate exactly what you will do to smooth the path—make an appointment for installation, arrange a training seminar, extend the warranty.

Be specific with time and date designations—delivery two weeks after the signed purchase order is received, warranty on parts covers one year from the date of installation, etc. Allow the new customer to feel cherished and pampered because of your interest and foresight. Offer any pertinent addition to the sale that will keep your foot in the door and make you welcome to reenter.

Company Name
Address
City, State Zip

Date

Mr. Bert Bradford
Sales Buyer Magazine
1234 Primrose Path
Springfield, IL 62709

Dear Bert:

I enjoyed our meeting and the luncheon discussion that followed.

Here's the promised summary of where we are on the project we discussed. If you disagree with anything I've written, let me know by next Friday. Otherwise, I'll move ahead with art, copy, and contracts.

Book Club Opportunity

Neil Lawrence will confirm in writing that he will pay you the full membership fee ($14.95) for each of your readers who joins his Business Book Club. He'll give you complete details on reporting, coding, payment schedule, etc. He'll also supply all advertising negatives for use in your magazine. In return, you'll give him the ad space at no charge. If you make as much money on this deal as I think you will, you'll want to make this a regular monthly commitment.

I'll check with you once more before this program goes into effect. Once you see everything in black and white (or color, in this case), I think you'll realize what a positive addition it will be to your sales and profits.

Cordially,

Scott Brooks

- Demonstrate enthusiasm about the prospect and the meeting.

- Clearly summarize the key points.

- Indicate the action you will take as a result of the meeting.

Company Name
Address
City, State Zip

Date

Mr. William Crowell
Trinity State College Alumni Association
300 Old Main
Sulphur, LA 70663

Dear Mr. Crowell:

I'm disappointed that your committee decided not to co-sponsor a test advertisement in your alumni journal for our line of exclusive glassware. Our research shows that glassware with college logos is displayed prominently in alumni homes and offices. And, of course, glassware promotions can add substantial profits to your alumni fund.

Perhaps some of the statistics were omitted during your deliberations. Queen City College, for example, generated over $18,000 in glassware profits this year...and they have a much smaller alumni association than you do. New Caledonia Community College kicked off a library fund drive with the nearly $9,000 in profits they generated.

I'm going to put together an additional report, hopeful that you'll resubmit it to the committee. Everything points to a successful collaboration and considerably more dollars than any of your current programs are delivering.

I appreciate your support. You have much to gain by reconsidering this concept.

Cordially,

Marjory Robbins
Vice President, Sales

- Acknowledge the prospect's decision not to buy.

- Restate the value of your offer.

- Point out case histories that support your position.

- Send additional material to make your case.

Company Name
Address
City, State Zip

Date

Mr. Bart Johnson
Medical Association of America
535 N. Michigan Street
Washington, DC 20032

Dear Bart:

Thanks for the opportunity to present my ideas. As you work your way through the various concepts, please keep four things in mind:

1. Your investment ranges from zero to minimal cost. Either way, you generate <u>substantial new revenues</u>.
2. You retain full control of what is offered and said to your members.
3. Numerous other professional societies are already taking advantage of this joint venture program (including the National Institute of Accountants, the American Society of Science, and the American Law Association).
4. You make a major contribution to the education, well-being, and continued personal and professional growth of your members.

I trust you'll agree that's quite a combination! I'm looking forward to talking with you on "decision day" next week.

Sincerely,

Arthur Moses

- A timely follow-up will hasten the decision-making process.

- Enumerate key benefits and supporting data.

- Remind the prospect that there's a deadline involved.

Company Name
Address
City, State Zip

Date

Karl Melitz, Ed.D.
Alpha Business College
1611 Robinson Way
West Chester, PA 19380

Dear Dr. Melitz:

I've continued to give our proposal quite a bit of thought, particularly since it differs somewhat from your suggested model. Although I understand your desire for a customized speed-reading course for your students, I remain convinced that our generic speed-reading course is the most time and cost-effective solution.

To redo the entire course is not only expensive, I believe it's unnecessary. We've used the generic course with engineers, architects, stockbrokers, accountants, and virtually every other professional you can think of. If I thought for a moment that a customized course would enhance the learning, I'd certainly say so.

Please review our proposal in its entirety. When you complete it, I think you'll be as enthusiastic as we are about increasing the learning capacity of your students without "breaking the bank."

I'll call you next week to get your thoughts.

Cordially,

Lawrence J. Dougherty

- State your belief that your proposal fills the need.

- Remind the prospect that you've had successes in similar markets.

- Always present the opportunity for a follow-up call.

Company Name
Address
City, State Zip

Date

Ms. Amy Lobell
Kiss of Spring Products
1448 E. Route 29
Knoxville, TN 37928

Dear Amy:

I enjoyed getting to know more about you and your catalog operation. You've built an impressive sales record in a short period of time. And I'm convinced my products will help continue your growth in the upscale women's market.

As promised, I've enclosed two of our lead crystal perfume atomizers. One is for purse or travel, the other for display in bedroom or bath. Both styles are available for your Spring catalog and give you plenty of room for a sizeable mark-up (see the attached quantity price list).

Please keep these samples and observe the positive reactions of your friends and colleagues. Your catalog readers will react with equal enthusiasm.

Remember, these are new. By getting them into your Spring catalog, you'll be the first to offer them.

I'll call you by week's end to work out final details.

Cordially,

Jason Garfinkel
Enclosures

- Remind the prospect that you're delivering as promised, marking yourself as someone who can be trusted.

- Tying your product to the prospect's achievements is an excellent way to draw favorable attention to your merchandise.

- Sell your benefits (price, newness, availability, beating the competition to the marketplace).

Company Name
Address
City, State Zip

Date

Ms. Norma Cantor
Costner Personal Care Products
415 Rotary Center
Hamilton, OH 45020

Dear Ms. Cantor:

By now you've probably received the sampling of toothbrushes you requested. I urge you to compare the quality of our brushes to the brands you currently carry. You'll feel the softness of their bristles, and marvel at their extremely high quality.

All of us at Universal Brushware are excited about the possibility of your offering our products throughout your chain. Since we use the latest technology for manufacturing, we can produce high quality brushware products less expensively than anyone in the industry.

Thank you for your consideration. I'll call during the week of the 15th for your feedback.

Cordially,

Robin Bayliss

- Resell your product.

- Set the stage for the next call; tell the prospect when you will follow-up and stick to it!

Company Name
Address
City, State Zip

Date

Mr. Steven Lambert
Lucky Dollar Casino
Culbreath Street at the Boardwalk
Atlantic City, NJ 08403

Dear Mr. Lambert:

Whoever said "Silence is Golden" didn't know what he was talking about!

If you're serious about an August 1 deadline for delivering new uniforms for 600 employees, we need to talk—quickly. Costume design must be finalized, dates set for measurements (to avoid disrupting schedules), final pricing is still an issue, etc., etc.

I'd like to have your business, and I sense you'd like to work with us. (You said you called because of our reputation.) But I can't accept your account if I don't feel I can give it our best effort.

I've tried to reach you repeatedly since we met. I'll leave the next move to you. But for the record: If we don't have agreement by next Friday, I must—very reluctantly—withdraw my company from consideration.

I hope to hear from you.

Very truly yours,

Albert Barile

- This is a "last resort" letter. It can be very effective for getting the point across to someone with a serious procrastination problem.

- Make it clear that you want the business, but there must be ample time given to do it properly.

Company Name
Address
City, State Zip

Date

Ms. Estelle Camarillo
Canyon Office Works
900 E. Yorktown Plaza
Locust Grove, AR 72550

Dear Estelle:

You must be having so much fun with our All-In-One pen and pencil combo you forgot to give me your starter order!

These remarkable writing instruments are more than fun, of course. They're practical—you have a pen and pencil in one slim casing; they're economical—wholesale pricing is under $20.00 even for small quantities; and they're profitable—you can earn at least a 50% mark-up.

The All-In-One is perfect for everyone, but it has particular appeal to architects, engineers, accounting personnel, salespeople—everyone who has to do drawings or calculations in pencil, but also needs a pen to write letters, specifications, and orders.

I want you to get in on the first wave of buying. Mail the enclosed form, send in your P.O., or call me. I look forward to receiving your first order.

Sincerely,

Dan Josephs

P.S. If you need a few samples for your husband or kids, let me know.

- List the key points of a new product: price, uniqueness, profitability, etc.

- Remind the prospect who the market is.

- Ask for the order.

Company Name
Address
City, State Zip

Date

Ms. Carla Jennings
PSI Steel Corp.
1300 Clarkson Road
Carbondale, OH 45717

Dear Ms. Jennings:

I've enclosed, as you requested, a printout of large companies that use our motivational posters and booklets to boost morale and productivity (72% of the Fortune 1000!).

You'll also find a few pages of testimonials (there are many more on file). Two of my favorites are:

> "Pep talks from the boss leave me cold, but I look forward to the new Campion poster each week."
> Warehouseman, Anchorage AK

> "My employees used to roll their eyes when I spoke about absenteeism, loyalty, and productivity. I guess I was too heavy-handed. Now that I let your posters and booklets do the talking, the men seem to respond better."
> Foreman, Greensboro, SC

How about this for the icing on the cake: I'll give you a month's free subscription so you can watch the reaction of your employees. More than 15,000 companies say you'll benefit by trying the program. If you don't agree, we'll stop your subscription at the end of the free month.

Do I have your go-ahead?

Sincerely,

Leroy Platt

- Remind the client that you're responding to her request for information.

- Let the testimonials sell your product.

- If you can tie in a special offer, you have an even better opportunity for closing the sale.

Company Name
Address
City, State Zip

Date

Mr. Tyrone Bellamy
Southwest Oil Drillers
5600 Lamar Avenue
Houston, TX 77250

Dear Mr. Bellamy:

I'm a great believer in our grand old Texas saying, "It ain't braggin' if it's true!"

I've enclosed the list of happy copier users you requested. That's what makes COPIFLEX different from other office equipment dealers in the Southwest: our clients really _are_ happy, because we give them the service we promised when we made the sale.

For example, Sally Chapman called when Machine Technology's high-speed copier went down. Her boss had a presentation due within hours. We were there in less than one hour. Jerry Gold, from Landscaping Plus, called before he went out for lunch, and we had his copier ready by the time he returned.

We brag about our service and our clients brag about us. We may be the only copier company in Texas whose customers do the selling! I'll call you next week to get your reaction to our happy users. Thanks for asking.

Cordially,

Corey Wainwright

- Avoid the temptation to just affix a list to a note that says, "Enclosed is the list of users you requested." Every correspondence is an opportunity to sell.

- Personalize the list. Give an example of what to expect. Express confidence.

Company Name
Address
City, State Zip

Date

Mr. George Hammond
The Software Place
Venturia Mall, Level One
Venturia, ND 58489

Dear Mr. Hammond:

When you carry the FOLLOW-UP software package, you're also eligible
to become an authorized trainer. That means you'll receive customer
referrals from us, deeply discounted software for use in your training
classes, and the credibility that comes with our training certification.

Once you've been certified, you can conduct classes at your facility and
earn extra fees—in addition to your profitable FOLLOW-UP software
mark-up. And if you aggressively pursue corporate sales, you'll really
earn significant dollars by conducting corporate training.

The enclosed brochure explains our complete dealer training program.
It's a great opportunity for you to increase your sales beyond an initial
software purchase. And it all starts by becoming a FOLLOW-UP dealer.
If you can't wait for my FOLLOW-UP call next week, just dial 1-800-555-
0022 to get started immediately.

Sincerely,

Teresa Lever
Vice President, Sales

- Advise the prospect that training enhances product sales, credibility, and profitability.

- Suggest that the prospective dealer call for an immediate start.

Company Name
Address
City, State Zip

Date

Ms. Elizabeth Powers
Fortune Galleries
14 Westmont Street
Raleigh, NC 27669

Dear Liz:

Trade shows are tough work, but enthusiastic visitors like you make them enjoyable.

Thanks for spending time with us at Decorator's Expo in Atlanta. I enjoyed showing you our porcelain bowls, jars, and vases. And it was obvious that you thought they would have great appeal to your upscale customers in Raleigh and Charlotte.

On the off chance that you may have misplaced our literature (trade shows can be hectic), I've enclosed another catalog and price list for you. And as a show special, if you purchase any items by the 22nd, you can take an additional 15% off the listed wholesale price. I want you to see for yourself how your customers will respond to our pieces.

I look forward to talking with you soon.

Cordially,

Marvin Waxman

• Always remind the prospect where you met.

• Enclose a fresh set of literature. It's easy to lose literature at a show, and prospects often have no idea how to get in touch with you, or even what your name is.

• Tie in some sort of incentive to buy based on the show.

Company Name
Address
City, State Zip

Date

Mr. Wilson Norwood
Communication Research, Inc.
1 Executive Park Plaza
Grand Rapids, MI 49502

Dear Wilson:

Sometimes I think our "opposing" attorneys try to out-do each other. In any case, I can report—with relief—that the language has been settled and a deadline date established.

You should receive two copies of the agreement in about a week, but I wanted to give you a head start on preparations. I'm planning to send our team of experts to your lab on the 29th to begin working with your people. We think the study of Charge Sensitive Mode EBIC Microscopy will prove to be a valuable assist to your scientists.

I'm pleased that we were able to resolve our contractual differences. Now we can get on with what should prove to be breakthrough research.

Cordially,

Dr. Vincent Ingleston

- Confirm that the contract is accepted and that you are prepared to fulfill your obligations enthusiastically.

- Reaffirm that the service will be of great value.

Company Name
Address
City, State Zip

Date

Ms. Anne Marie Bonfiglio
Edison Technologies, Inc.
Southern Lakes Industrial Park
Drew, MS 38737

Dear Ms. Bonfiglio:

Before I turn the project over to our legal department, allow me to confirm the major details of the controlled substance abuse program we hope to administer for you:

1. CSI will evaluate employees who test positive for drugs and/or alcohol. Those employees who can be helped via counseling will be treated.

2. CSI will provide support to families who are undergoing counseling.

3. CSI will establish a 24-hour HOT LINE to answer any abuse or usage questions that your covered employees or their families may have.

Your work force is your most valuable asset, and we'll make yours better by helping you combat lateness, absenteeism, and accidents due to substance abuse.

You should receive our suggested agreement within 10 days. I'll call when it's ready. Thank you for considering us as your drug program administrator. You'll be pleased you turned to a knowledgeable outside source to handle this important program for you.

Sincerely,

Marshall Janewicz

- A follow-up letter of this sort is useful for confirming details before asking lawyers to draft an (expensive) agreement.

- Confirm key details, and indicate follow-up.

Company Name
Address
City, State Zip

Date

Mr. and Mrs. Morton Jaffe
32 Sandringham Terrace
White Sulphur Springs, WV 24986

Dear Mr. and Mrs. Jaffe:

Now that you've had a few days to enjoy your luxurious new whirlpool, you may be asking yourselves why you didn't get one long ago! Is it any wonder we call your model the "Tension-Easer?"

Thank you for purchasing your whirlpool at Elegant Baths. We hope you'll continue to think of us for all your bath and related needs. We appreciate your business.

Cordially,

Debbie Sabatino

- It's smart business to reinforce the customer's buying decision.

- Tell the customer you appreciate his/her business.

- Send the letter within a week of installation or purchase.

Company Name
Address
City, State Zip

Date

Mrs. Beatrice Colwyn
38 Brookhaven Street
Colts Neck, NJ 07722

Dear Mrs. Colwyn:

I understand that the living room set we delivered last week has several problems. I'm writing to reassure you that I am personally involved, and that you will be hearing from our repair team within seven days. They will either repair your sofa or replace it—whichever you prefer.

I promised you when you bought the "Andulusian Suite" from me that your satisfaction is our most important concern. Now we have a chance to prove that that is not just our motto.

I can assure you that within two weeks the matter will be settled to your complete satisfaction. After all, we want to serve you for all your future furniture needs.

Cordially,

Charles Dorian
Vice President

- Your reputation is your most important asset, so protect it every way you can.

- A letter from a top level official puts a customer's mind at ease when a product is received damaged.

Company Name
Address
City, State Zip

Date

Ms. Sharon Stempler
Atlas Office Furniture
488 W. Chester Avenue
Mansfield, OH 44906

Dear Ms. Stempler:

How was your awards ceremony? Were your record-breaking
salespeople pleased with their customized "Top of the Line" plaques? If
they're like most award winners, they were thrilled to be recognized and
delighted to receive a memento that properly reflects the magnitude of
their achievements.

Please remember us for all your gift, premium, and award needs. You'll
be equally pleased with our commemorative pewter plates and mugs,
fine crystal and porcelain, and original sculpture and watch collections.

Keep the enclosed catalog handy for your next special occasion. And if
you don't see what you want in the catalog, we'll create it for you.

Thank you for using Roman's Trophies.

Cordially,

Lionel Huggins

P.S. Please give my compliments to your art director. The design he
suggested for the plaques was a joy to execute.

- Show the customer you're interested in more than a sale. Inquire about the event for which
  your merchandise was used.

- Tell the customer about your other fine merchandise.

- It's a nice touch to pass along a compliment about some facet of the job (art direction).

Company Name
Address
City, State Zip

Date

Ms. Louise Fairmount
Training Specialist
Automated Engineering, Inc.
3275 Reston Boulevard
Silver Spring, MD 20910

Dear Louise:

Do you feel as good as I do about the "Dealing With The Government" seminar? I'd like to pat myself on the back, but I have to admit your new salespeople were great. That's as much fun as I've had training a group in a long time. They really demonstrated a willingness to learn. (Nice preparation on your part.)

As good as your salespeople are, you may have noticed one weakness that was apparent to me: they need work on briefing techniques. Much of their dealings with governmental agencies will be before committees, panels, groups of officers, etc. They have a solid grasp of what they have to do to prepare for a sales call, but I don't think they have the seasoning to know what to say, when to say it, and who to say it to.

I strongly recommend you propose this 2-day workshop to your sales management committee. Another $160 per person will put your young people head and shoulders above their competition.

I'll call to see if you agree.

Cordially,

Paul Turner

- Thank the client for having you perform the initial service.

- Be <u>specific</u> about why additional service is required; otherwise, you can be perceived as less than sincere.

- If this is a trial balloon, you may want to deal with the price issue up front to avoid wasting time.

Company Name
Address
City, State Zip

Date

Mrs. Rochelle Berg
3801 Clarendon Road
Madison, WI 53797

Dear Mrs. Berg:

Happy anniversary! The vacuum cleaner you purchased from us is nearly one year old.

We're sure you've already had lots of rugged use from it (it's one of our top-selling models), and we expect you to have many more years of reliable service. But we wanted to remind you that the manufacturer's warranty runs out on the anniversary date.

Vacuum cleaners are about as well-built as an appliance can be, but they often run afoul of paper clips, bobby pins, nails, and other hard-to-spot impediments that can cause major trouble. That's why we urge you to take advantage of our owner protection plan. A small payment now can save you a major repair bill later.

Please review the enclosed service agreement, and return it with your payment for 100% protection (parts and labor). If you have any questions, call me at 608-555-5678. This offer is extended for 30 days beyond the anniversary date and is then withdrawn. So sign up by June 6—while you're still eligible.

Sincerely yours,

Kurt Reifsnyder
Service Manager

- Reconfirm the customer's smart buying decision.

- Extend new protection with a deadline date. No deadline means inaction.

Company Name
Address
City, State Zip

Date

Ms. Barbara Horton
Cartech Oil, Inc.
213 Eleventh Street
Shreveport, LA 71162

Dear Barbara:

Thank you for your faith in our SUCCESS! software. You're going to get the centralized access to sales reports that prompted you to purchase our program, along with an added bonus: increased sales.

Many studies show that well-organized salespeople are the ones who generate the most sales. That's why it's so important your salespeople learn how to use SUCCESS! properly. And that's why we want to train you—or someone you designate—on every facet of this program. You will then be equipped to conduct classes for your salespeople, training them before they develop bad habits or misconceptions about SUCCESS!

The attached sheet outlines our intensive 3-day workshop, a $495 course that we want you to attend as our guest. That's our way of showing appreciation for your business and to help you make the most of your purchase.

Please call me by May 10 to let me know if you'll be joining our June class.

Cordially,

H. L. (Hank) Lester

- Thank the client for the purchase.

- An offer of training free or at a reduced rate makes the client happy because he/she receives a bonus.

- Training develops a bond between the customer and the company. The result is a satisfied customer who keeps buying.

Closing the Sale 5

There are lots of great presenters; there are only a few great closers.

The closers are the ones who use everything at their disposal to make the sale. They write letters, they use the phone, they take prospects to lunch, they give them samples to test. Great closers use their people skills to size up others. They know how to qualify a prospect to be sure he or she has the authority to purchase, and they know how to position themselves for the sale.

A closer can demonstrate the value of a product or service; a closer understands that when someone says "Your price is too high" he or she is ready to negotiate a sale. A closer knows how to keep a conversation going, how to use questions, how to handle complaints with a "Yes, but..." and keep on going.

A closer has an arsenal of answers that prod the customer to the point of sale. "How many do you think you need?" presumes the sale is made and only quantity is left to be negotiated. "Which color do you prefer?" works similar magic. The most important technique, of course, is to ask for the sale. If you don't, someone else will.

Here are some suggestions for closing the sale.

Inducements. These are your bag of tricks, not only to get someone's interest, but to get the sale. Can you offer an introductory special? A one-time-only offer? These can help you break the ice, even if they're not giant profit producers for you. Do what it takes to get the customer to say "Yes" once. He or she will say yes again.

Do you have a supply of testimonials? You have plenty of people who are happy with your product or service. Get them to put it in writing. People love success stories. Use your current clients to get new clients.

Free Trial! Satisfaction Guaranteed! No-Risk, No Obligation. These are the words that any new prospect needs to hear to take a chance on something new to his or her company. Almost all mail order ads offer these inducements because they work.

Product demonstrations can be of immense value. They show off your product in a controlled environment, and they can often be combined with a visit to your plant where you can present your company and support team.

Overcoming Objections. Top salespeople know that if you haven't made a sale, you simply haven't found the key benefit that will overcome the prospect's objections. It's always there, they say, but it's up to you to find it.

The objections covered in this chapter are no different from objections you meet on a face-to-face sales call. In some cases, the responses may be more effective when presented on-the-spot. In other cases, they show thought, concern, and research on your part, and are more appropriate when offered in a letter.

This chapter offers numerous examples you can build into your own negotiating/selling arsenal. You'll find responses to comments such as, "Your product is too cheap (in other words, it can't be any good)," and "Your product is too expensive." You'll learn how to counter a stall by adding a sense of urgency.

There are stories and vignettes that illustrate the folly of some objections, and classic strategies to brush aside some of the more classic objections (business is bad now; maybe next time; I always do business with "X"; I had a bad experience with your company).

Do you remember one of the more successful advertising campaigns of the last twenty years: "You don't have to be Jewish to enjoy Levy's rye bread?" Well, you don't have to be a salesperson, in the technical sense, to profit from this group of letters. They have value to you in meetings, negotiations, virtually any persuasive situation in which you find yourself. "Closing the sale" is a phrase that means getting what you want.

Company Name
Address
City, State Zip

Date

Mr. Christopher Wagner
Sip 'n Sup Food Stores
906 N. Second Street
Tacoma, WA 98430

Dear Mr. Wagner:

I appreciate the time you gave me on the phone. I was very interested to learn about your expansion plans for the next three years.

As I mentioned, Super-Market Designers has twenty years of experience designing interiors for some of the largest chains, including Giant Foods, Star Markets, and Value Grocers. Our computer-aided design for traffic patterns has helped increase gross sales per square foot by 15% to 45%. And our service costs no more than you would pay for ordinary designs.

I look forward to meeting you next week when I'll show you a videotape of some of our installations. I'm confident you'll be impressed with the extremely handsome design of the stores and their equally impressive sales figures.

Cordially,

Charles De La Croix
Vice President

- Build credibility with success stories.

- Successes that are most convincing are those in the prospect's industry.

- Whenever possible, reinforce your comments with additional support (references, surveys, etc.).

Company Name
Address
City, State Zip

Date

Ms. Viola White
Keystone Products, Inc.
222 Algonquin Road
Poughkeepsie, NY 12610

Dear Viola:

I've given a great deal of thought to what you said about buying an "off-the-shelf" performance appraisal training system. I'm more convinced than ever, however, that a customized system would be particularly effective for your company for the following reasons:

o It allows each department, and each level within each department, to be evaluated more accurately than off-the-shelf systems provide.

o Our customized training programs keep pace with the changes in your company, so the system is always up-to-date.

o Customization is done by our staff, which avoids tying up your personnel department.

Before we meet again, you might like to contact three people (see attached) for whom we've recently implemented customized performance appraisal training. They're all from organizations as large and complex as your own. They'd be happy to tell you why they opted for customization over packaged training.

I'll call you next week to discuss implementation.

Cordially,

Ellen Dickinson

Enclosure

- Since it's a "given" that customization is more expensive, give specific examples of how its benefits more than outweigh the additional cost.

- Stress that the customizing won't tie up their personnel.

- Provide references from the same size or type of organizations.

Company Name
Address
City, State Zip

Date

Mr. Lawrence Gormsley
Regal Restaurant Supply
58 W. Tucson Street
Fayetteville, AR 72701

Dear Mr. Gormsley:

There's an omission in your restaurant equipment catalog (and probably in your profits, too!). You forgot to include our patented "Collapsaway" coat racks that work equally well in small cloakrooms and large banquet halls, giving you 100% market coverage.

Please review the enclosed brochure. Then take advantage of our 20% OFF WHOLESALE introductory discount! We want you to see for yourself what our portable coat racks will add to your sales.

I'll call you next week to answer any questions, and to help you select the racks for your starting order.

Sincerely,

Peggy Werbock
Sales Director

- A special offer is hard to resist, but is particularly compelling for a new customer.

- Be sure to sell your product or service in addition to the special offer itself. A good deal on a product that's not wanted isn't going to excite a prospect.

Company Name
Address
City, State Zip

Date

Mr. Adam Pilsner
11 Partridge Lane
Short Hills, NJ 07078

Dear Mr. Pilsner:

<u>Great news!</u> I just received approval from our gallery owner for you to take the Andre Matan oil painting home for a two-week free trial. She even waived a security deposit on my recommendation.

Now you'll have the opportunity to become comfortable with this beautiful impressionist art. I think you'll find the Matan will be a focal point in your home. I know you're the one who has to decide, but watch the delighted reactions of your visitors to this very special painting.

If at the end of the two week period you decide you can't part with it (that's my bet), just let us know, and we'll bill you. You can make time payments if you wish.

Thanks for being so persistent about "trying it before buying it." I'm glad I was able to help.

Sincerely,

Mandy Tinkers

- Share a sense of excitement with the prospect when you've arranged for something "out of the ordinary."

- Reinforce the value of the merchandise to be previewed.

Company Name
Address
City, State Zip

Date

Mr. Robert Nowicki
Office Manager
Fortress Enterprises
1200 W. Adirondack Avenue
Chatanooga, TN 37421

Dear Mr. Nowicki:

Do you recognize the enclosed report that I've labeled Exhibit I? It was produced by your marketing department and distributed to a number of clients. I think it does a reasonably good job of telling your company's story.

Now look at Exhibit II. Your marketing department asked me to show what my desktop COLORaid copier could do to make the same report a bit zippier. What do you think? The marketing people can't believe it...but there it is. Look how vivid the same black & white charts are in color...how headlines and key points jump off the page.

I'd like the opportunity to demonstrate the COLORaid copier—in your office—to show you how easy it is to operate, and give you an idea of how inexpensive it is to create sparkling color copies. Think of the time and money you can save by having in-house capabilities.

Your marketing manager, Bill Blount, asked that you review the COLORaid for possible purchase. When would be a convenient time for a demonstration? I'll call to get your schedule.

Sincerely,

Harris Benson

- "Before and after" is an irresistible lead-in to a product demonstration. Show your work against someone else's.

- Suggest ways that the new product will help the client.

- Ask for an appointment to demonstrate the product.

Company Name
Address
City, State Zip

Date

Ms. Carole Slayton
Coronet Tool & Die Works
8900 E. Wayfarer Avenue
Canton, OH 44707

Dear Ms. Slayton:

Picture this: your fellow exhibitors are in work clothes, they're sweating, and they're struggling to get their booths set up in time for the grand opening.

You, on the other hand, walk in with every hair in place, cool and collected, and dressed for the ribbon cutting. You walk over to a black box in your booth, undo the single strap, and push a red button. Within just 30 seconds, your booth has completely opened and locked in place. You're ready for show biz!

Don't you feel really special when you're the first in the field to have something new? Sure, in a year or so as word gets around, <u>everyone</u> will want to use the DANVILLE INFLATABLE DISPLAY. But right now you have the chance to enjoy that heady experience of being first.

We haven't heard from you since you sent for literature, but with the fabrications show coming soon, it's time for you to get serious about making your next booth a DANVILLE INFLATABLE DISPLAY. As a reward for being "first in the field," we'll take 20% off the already low price.

I'll call you next week to get a shipping address.

Cordially,

Morton Siegel

- This is an emotional sell. We all like to be first at something. Try to recreate that feeling.

- Offer a discount to force a decision.

- Suggest a follow-up call to get the order.

Inducement to Buy, Confirmation of Points of Agreement (5-07)

Company Name
Address
City, State Zip

Date

Mr. S. J. Warren
Covington Telecommunications
2000 S. Route 48
Brunswick, GA 31520

Dear Mr. Warren:

Based on what I feel was a <u>very</u> productive meeting, here are the elements of the job control file we will convert to a computer program:

1. Job requisition
2. Change order
3. Creative assignment
4. Creative dimension sheet
5. Request for quotation
6. Package quotation sheet
7. Service agreement
8. Creative assignment authorization
9. Job schedule
10. Job detail sheet
11. Purchase order requisition
12. Purchase order revision

Upon completion of this work, everyone on your staff will have access to what is going on, at any time, on any job.

I'll call to confirm that our understanding matches yours. We're looking forward to moving ahead with this project.

Sincerely,

Bert Dorsey

- Summarize the key points in an easy-to-follow manner.

- Advise that you will follow up with a phone call.

Company Name
Address
City, State Zip

Date

Mr. Meyer Linton
Billig Transportation, Inc.
3428 Brick Road
Albany, GA 31708

Dear Mr. Linton:

I obviously didn't do a great job making you understand that you're up against an unyielding government deadline. If you don't have a <u>workable</u> drug plan in place by December 10, you run the risk of being subject to enormous fines, penalties, and disruption of your business.

Here are just six important questions to which you need to be able to answer "yes." One "no" can invalidate even the best-intentioned drug compliance plan.

1. Are you providing gender-oriented, trained Collection Site Personnel?
2. Do your specimen collection procedures follow HHS guidelines?
3. Are you familiar with chain of custody documentation?
4. Are you using a qualified MRO?
5. Are you using a laboratory that is NIDA certified?
6. Are you prepared to maintain documentation in a limited access, high-security manner?

I rarely disagree with a customer, Mr. Linton, but you don't have time, as you suggest, to think about it. You must act now or run the risk of the government shutting down your business. Let us administer your drug awareness/compliance plan for you correctly.

Sincerely,

Carmen Viola
Program Administrator

- One way to deal with an objection is to create a sense of urgency, fraught with serious implications of what may happen while the prospect "thinks about it."

- List the obstacles that must be dealt with.

- When using this approach, be sure the situation warrants it, or you'll get the reputation of the person "who cried wolf."

Company Name
Address
City, State Zip

Date

Mr. Martin Lavin
Peabody Merchandise Corp.
320 N. Avenue of Commerce
Muncie, IN 47302

Dear Mr. Lavin:

As a young boy, I learned a valuable lesson from the owner of a grocery store. Each week he put most of his shipment of oranges in what he called a "dump" and sold them at 12 for 39 cents (it was a long time ago!). He would buff the other five or six dozen, carefully place them in a showcase, under lights, and sell them at 12 for 59 cents.

The moral of the story?
Just because something's more expensive,
it isn't necessarily better.

I know you've been wondering how I can supply mailing boxes at about 20% under your current prices. But instead of spending so much time trying to figure out why I'm "so cheap," as you put it, you should be asking your current vendor why he's so expensive!

Quality-wise, there's very little difference between us. Price-wise, it's a different story. From hints you've dropped in the past, you need more than 400,000 12x9x3 boxes a year. By switching to our boxes, you'll save around $20,000 a year—money that goes right into the profit column.

It's your choice, Mr. Lavin. Do you want oranges at 12 for 39 cents or 12 for 59 cents?

Sincerely,

Samuel Colombo

- To sell price as an inducement, you must stress that there is no loss in quality.

- Highlight key points.

Company Name
Address
City, State Zip

Date

Mr. Julio Rodriguez
Siesta Sleepware
329 San Miguel Avenue
Las Cruces, NM 87544

Dear Mr. Rodriguez:

Did you hear the story of the two shoe salesmen who were sent into the Australian bush? One sent a wire that he was returning immediately. "Impossible to sell shoes. Everyone is barefoot." The other sent a wire with a giant order. "Prospects unlimited. No one here has shoes."

Does that sound familiar? You've been taking the first salesman's attitude about our Lady Austin silk pajamas. ("Impossible to sell. Too expensive.") But the reason they're selling so well is <u>because</u> they're expensive.

Every woman wants silk pajamas, and every man wants her to have them. In fact, men are the major buyers of this product. They make exciting, romantic, sexy gifts.

Why not let your customers judge for themselves, Mr. Rodriguez? Valentine's Day is only a few months away. I'm willing to bet our future business with you that our silk pajamas will make this Valentine's Day your most memorable.

When I call next week I hope to hear you say, "Prospects unlimited. Siesta prepares to break sales records."

Sincerely,

Benton LeMoyne

- A joke can make your statement for you in a nonthreatening manner.

- Don't apologize for price, particularly when your product is of high quality.

- Select the <u>time</u> you write. Tie in your approach with a buying holiday to get best results.

Company Name
Address
City, State Zip

Date

Mr. Michael Strait
Lawrence Cameras, Inc.
990 N. Rockdale Street
Rochester, NY 14694

Dear Mr. Strait:

I asked three of my best clients how they would answer your objection that our cellular phone service costs too much. Here's what they said:

> "I found that using your phone service allows me to set up far more sales calls. And the more calls I make, the more I sell!"
> George Mason, Sales Representative
> National Encyclopedia

> "When I'm on the road, being able to talk to customers from my car makes me far more productive. I can't believe how much more I'm accomplishing now that I have your cellular phone service."
> Basil Strickland, VP
> International Brands

> "Having the ability to make calls from my car is worth every penny your service costs. It gives me the ability to respond to our accounts far faster than ever before."
> William Patterson
> Franklin Engineering

Let me install a phone in one of your salesmen's cars, Mr. Strait, and I'll show you how to increase your sales dramatically.

Sincerely,

Susan Finlay

- The best way to counter "too expensive" is to have clients who pay the money explain why they do.

- Try to force an opportunity to demonstrate how good you are (but don't cut price!).

Company Name
Address
City, State Zip

Date

Mr. Anthony Boniface
Bradley Insurance Group
1112 W. Overton Street
Newark, NJ 07101

Dear Mr. Boniface:

The railroad barons laughed at the thought of people flying all over the world. Impossible, they said. So they stayed with their tried and true product. Now the railroads function only because of government largesse.

The carriage and buggy manufacturers sneered at the horseless carriage. They plunged into oblivion when Henry Ford took advantage of their failure to stay current with the times.

I'm not about to say that Bradley Insurance will cease to exist if it doesn't switch to the new generation of HTMR mini computers. But I will say that your major competitor has been working with the HTMR for six months and can now generate reports, records, marketing and actuarial data in half the time it used to take . We estimate they now have nearly three more months of computer time available per year, allowing them to handle more clients, give better service, and operate at a far better cost efficiency.

I'd like to show you why you should never be too satisfied with the present. You need to see the HTMR in action to get a feel for what it can mean to you...and your ability to compete profitably. I'll call you next week to set up a demonstration.

Cordially,

Ronald Kovacks

- A prospect will react to a competitor's apparent edge—if you can provide facts.

- Strongly suggest a demonstration.

Company Name
Address
City, State Zip

Date

Ms. Betty Henning
Tri-State Art Supply
State Street Mall
Pontiac, MI 48053

Dear Ms. Henning:

Would you like to do yourself and your boss a giant favor? Show her the enclosed article from Art Dealer News.

Before you pass it along, take a look at the chart at the bottom of page 1. You'll see that our poster board is #2 in the country and still climbing while yours is losing market share.

Do you know why Luxor is moving up while your current brand is moving down? First of all, Luxor Papers offers the largest dealer profit of all paper companies. Secondly, our quality and texture can withstand any medium. And thirdly, a survey of end users shows that ours is the preferred brand. (I've enclosed a copy of the research.)

I suggest you tell your boss about how Luxor papers build store profits, and then show her the article. You'll make yourself look good, your customers will be happy with upgraded quality, and your store will make more money.

Sincerely,

Francis Largent

Enclosure

- Trade journals, business magazines, and newspapers are useful sources of supporting data. Find statistics that support you.

- Give your contact a good reason to sell his/her boss on your product.

Company Name
Address
City, State Zip

Date

Mr. Adam Hardwick
The Bag Boutique
72-08 Seneca Avenue
San Francisco, CA 94149

Dear Mr. Hardwick:

Sorry to hear that business isn't what it should be, but we're going to do our part to make it better!

I discussed your problem with my sales manager, and now I know why he's the boss. Here's his "Get Adam Hardwick's sales going" plan of attack:

1. We'll ship six dozen (assorted) of our best-selling handbags to you <u>immediately</u>. You haven't been buying new inventory, so this will give your store a fresh look.

2. Since these bags turn over faster than any others, you'll start to generate new sales, giving you much needed dollars.

3. And because you have a good credit rating, we'll extend <u>60 day terms</u> on this order! By the time the bill is due, you'll have made your money back.

Send me your purchase order as soon as possible, and we'll help you turn around your sluggish sales!

Sincerely,

Charlie Pressman

- Clients like knowing that you think enough of them to talk to your boss about their account.

- Even if you don't succeed in moving accounts with this approach, they will remember that you tried to help.

- Ask for the order.

Company Name
Address
City, State Zip

Date

Mr. Herman Reiss
Stanton Jewelers
1319 E. Taunton Boulevard
Ocala, FL 32672

Dear Mr. Reiss:

The day after I returned from visiting you, I was notified of an immediate 10% price increase in our series 1300 costume jewelry (see enclosed price list).

I know you didn't want to talk business until my next swing through Florida, but you still have a "window of opportunity" to put in one last order under our old pricing. My boss said all orders from current customers received by the end of this month will be honored at the old pricing schedule.

Please call or fax your order to be sure we receive it on time. We can't extend this offer beyond the end of the month.

Cordially,

Paul Rumsey

Enclosure

- Demonstrate how a delay will cost the prospect money.

- Create a sense of urgency by giving an absolute cut-off date for ordering.

Company Name
Address
City, State Zip

Date

Mr. Tracy Stoner
Harris Toy and Game Emporium
901 N. Stephentown Street
Boston, MA 02287

Dear Mr. Stoner:

It was nice chatting with you about the Red Sox' prospects for this year. After we hung up, I thought about how right you were in needing the correct mix to go all the way—and how much that same thinking can be applied to adding my line of unique games to your shelves.

In baseball, not everyone is a home run hitter. In fact, there are very few home run hitters. In business, you might hit an occasional home run, but it's the singles and doubles that usually score the runs.

You may not get many requests for my products because people don't ask for things they don't see. But when your customers do see them, these unusual games will turn over consistently for you. They'll provide steady profits because they are real crowd pleasers. They'll also help you attract a more upscale audience, giving you a chance to knock in a few more runs.

I'll stop by within a week or so to show you a few samples. Maybe I'll make it at the end of the day, and we can stroll over to Fenway and catch a game.

Cordially,

Ralph Fitch

- Mention that your products will widen the appeal of the store's regular line, and that they'll add to overall profitability.

- Avid sports fans are sure bets for sports analogies, which can work better than pure dollars-and-cents logic.

Company Name
Address
City, State Zip

Date

Mr. Alexander Shuman
Ship It Fast
66 East Brickton Street
Mobile, AL 36608

Dear Mr. Shuman:

About a month ago, a local supermarket shifted some items next to the bread section. Yesterday, I asked the store owner why he made the change. He grinned and told me his bread sales had gone up nearly 20%, and the "new" items—peanut butter and jelly—had jumped by 70%!

He said that for years his distributor had told him to move the spreadables next to the bread, that one feeds sales of the other. But he had "never done that before," and was content with his regular profit. It was only when sales were dropping that he finally tried something new.

You'll see a similar sales surge by adding wrapping paper and greeting cards to your shipping store. An impulse table at the counter virtually guarantees people will ask you to wrap their gifts and/or include cards before shipping them. You'll also get new business from shoppers at the gift store next door once they know you can take care of their needs (we'll give you the <u>exclusive</u> for your neighborhood).

Try it, Mr. Shuman. Instead of saying "I've never done that before," you'll soon be saying "I don't know why I never did that before!" Send in a test order <u>now</u>. You'll have your cards and wrapping paper in time for the holiday rush.

Sincerely,

Les Bloch

- Illustrate the advantages of trying something new.

- Explain why your product will work in a given situation.

- If your product has a seasonal application, send your letter to arrive in time for seasonal buying.

Company Name
Address
City, State Zip

Date

Mrs. Leia Norris
Central Opticians
900 W. Brundage Avenue
Charleston, WV 25317

Dear Mrs. Norris:

I value loyalty. It's one of our nobler traits. Your reluctance to buy eyeglass frames from anyone other than George Coulter speaks volumes about you.

But I'd like to <u>add</u> to your line, not subtract from George's. You must know how hot our "California Casual" frames are with teens and young adults. You should be getting a piece of those profits, as well as the steady business that your regular line provides. Think what your business can do with a dramatic new appeal.

There's a new mall opening about ten miles from you, and it includes The Frame Place. Don't force the young people of your community to go there for glasses. If you do, your loyalty to George may not mean much because your future customers will be getting fitted at the mall.

Stay loyal to George. But expand your thinking to include loyalty to your own longevity. Add "California Casual," and we'll give you our sparkling new impulse display (a $100 value!) as a "Welcome to California" bonus!

Looking forward to earning your loyalty.

Cordially,

Jeffrey Dickey

- Acknowledge loyalty, but promote good business judgment.

- Don't hesitate to mention the threat of competition (fear is a powerful motivator), and future consequences.

- Offer some form of incentive to get the prospect started.

Company Name
Address
City, State Zip

Date

Mr. Bradley Hughes
Associated Grocers
950 American Avenue
Butler, PA 16001

Dear Mr. Hughes:

May I be up-front with you? All I've heard since I've come to this company is, "Don't waste your time trying to do business with Brad Hughes. He's got it in for us."

When I asked my boss what the problem was, he said, "I really don't know. Hughes was angry with us when I joined the company." So I asked our president, and he said the same thing. I made one more try with Ty Everett, who's been here since the Civil War, and he said, "I never knew, but if you find out, let me in on it."

Mr. Hughes, I wasn't here when you had your problems with the company. Neither was the sales manager or the president. A lot of years have passed since whatever happened happened. We've grown, we've improved, we have a lot of people you'd enjoy working with. More important, we have the <u>leading line of frozen bagels in the business, and your stores are losing money and customers without it</u>.

It's time to start a new relationship. I'll call on Friday to schedule a meeting date. You have no idea how much I'm looking forward to meeting you.

Sincerely,

Janet Haverton

- Putting a foolish situation on paper can help the prospect understand how little sense it makes.

- Make it clear that the prospect is losing money by carrying a grudge.

- Ask for a meeting.

Company Name
Address
City, State Zip

Date

Mr. Roy Atkins
The Hawthorne Company
40 E. Franklin Street
Carson City, NV 89705

Dear Mr. Atkins:

I've regretted things I've done in the past. You probably have, too. And so has my company, particularly for keeping my predecessor on board as long as they did. He had a facility for alienating too many good customers.

But that's past history. I'm new, I'm eager to work with you, and I'm excited about what we have to offer you: new sales and profits for your premium division.

Can we look ahead together, Mr. Atkins? I'll call you for an appointment. We have to make up for lost time.

Cordially,

Jay Gould

- Dismiss the past and look to the future. Don't dwell on what may or may not have been said by your predecessor.

- Tell the prospect to expect your call.

Keeping the Customer Buying 6

Some people call it servicing the account; others call it smart business. Whatever you call it, keeping the customer buying is the lifeblood of any business.

There's no customer like your current customer. A direct mail company, for example, may rent its regular customer list for $70 per thousand names. It may rent its "hot-line" names—customers who have purchased in the last three months— for $100 per thousand names. Mailers are happy to pay the premium because they know they will sell more to a recent customer than to someone who has not bought in a while.

It costs a lot of money to acquire a customer. Once you have made the acquisition, your future profitability may very well depend on keeping that customer buying. A business that continually resells its customers is a business that prospers and grows.

What methods can you use to keep the customer buying? First, you can say "thank you" in a number of ways. Some companies offer customer appreciation awards: plaques, certificates, donations to charity in the name of the customer. All say "we want you to keep buying from us, and we will continue to reward your good judgment."

Some large-ticket merchandisers offer cash rewards for bringing in new customers. They know how effective a referral can be, and how the recipient of the cash incentive will be prone to buy from them again. Clothing stores, automobile dealers, candy stores, book stores, and many other kinds of retailers thrive on repeat business. They keep extensive files on their customers and use every possible occasion to notify them of special events, customer appreciation sales, bonus discounts, preview parties, etc.

Smart sellers offer discounts and incentives to existing buyers. They want to encourage their customers to buy because statistics show that people who have bought from you before are likely to buy again and again—if you give them the opportunity.

If an individual buys a book from you, that individual should receive a package insert or statement suffer with the book, selling another book. If someone purchases flowers from you, a letter or announcement with special customer offers should be sent to that buyer before every major holiday or event. That buyer already knows you. He or she will buy from you again if you provide a reason to.

Many people stay with a company because that company does a good job for them and services them well. It doesn't always matter that another printer can do a job less expensively; it may not be a factor that another manufacturer can turn a job around faster. People prefer to stick with a reliable vendor rather than change. All you have to do is keep that customer happy.

Did you put on a new customer service rep to service one of your accounts? Tell the customer about it! Don't hide the news that you are giving him or her preferential treatment. Always emphasize how important the account is and the kind of special handling you're offering.

Another way to keep your customers buying is to offer them a chance to buy something that is only available to good customers. Special merchandise and quantity pricing are both ways to reward good customers.

Your current customer is your best customer. As the old song from the great musical <u>South</u> <u>Pacific</u> said, "Once you have found her, never let her go." She—or he—will help make you successful.

Company Name
Address
City, State Zip

Date

Mr. Charles Brookins
Pace Electronics
420 West Norriton Street
Orem, UT 84058

Dear Chuck:

My company has a tradition that's grown with the years. And you've just become a part of it.

Among all our customers, you've shown the largest percentage increase in purchasing this year. I like to think I do a nice job of regularly demonstrating how much I appreciate your business, but the company will go one step further.

<u>We will contribute a $1,000 check
in the name of Pace Electronics
to any charity you designate.</u>

After you name the charity, I'll hand-deliver a handsome plaque for your office, commemorating the event. It will serve as a reminder that good things happen when you purchase from us.

Thanks for your business. I'll call to find out which charity you've selected and when you can join me for lunch.

Regards,

Lanny Payson

- Tell the customer why he has been singled out for an honor.

- Explain what will happen as a result of the award (don't embarrass the client with a personal award; it may be misconstrued as a kickback).

- Follow up with a call and a visit.

Company Name
Address
City, State Zip

Date

Mr. & Mrs. Jack Finch
42 Morning Glory Drive
Oak Grove, MI 48057

Dear Mr. and Mrs. Finch:

In less than one month your automobile will be 36 months old, and its value for trade-in on one of our brand new models will never be greater!

I want you to continue to get the most for your automobile dollar, so call me today to:

1. See our complete selection of great new cars.

2. Use the $1,000 rebate check we've enclosed with this letter to purchase any new car with a sticker price of $10,000 or more. (The new version of your model is a knockout!)

Think about it: Top trade-in value, a wide selection to choose from, and a $1,000 rebate on most models waiting for you. All signs point to "GO." I'll call to set a date to review how you will get the most for your money at Oak Grove Motors.

Sincerely,

Bob Steele
Sales Manager

• Go through your customer records to recognize anniversaries. It makes the customer feel you care.

• Emphasize any fact that will prompt action ("the value of your 36-month old car will never be higher").

• Ask for a firm appointment.

Company Name
Address
City, State Zip

Date

Mr. Richard Grossman
132 Squire Lane
Columbus, IN 47201

Dear Dick:

It's been nearly a year since you purchased your automobile from us. We appreciate your business, and we invite you to take advantage of our special cash offer for referral business. If you bring in the enclosed coupon before the expiration date, you can earn yourself $50, $100, or more.

All you have to do is write on the back of the coupon the names and phone numbers of people you think might be interested in a new or used truck or automobile. For each one who buys from us, you'll receive $50 in cash.

While you're here, I'd like to show you our wide selection of great new cars. As you already know, we have the best prices and the best service in our area! And now, we have a great new cash referral program for you, as well!

Don't forget—the coupon expires in three weeks. So bring it in <u>soon</u> to be eligible for your cash awards!

Sincerely,

Travis Wayne

- Buyers are likely to know others who might be interested in your products.

- Coupons are traffic-builders, so use a cover letter to illustrate their value.

- Encourage the prospect to act by including a time limitation on your offer.

Company Name
Address
City, State Zip

Date

Mrs. Lena Haugen
76 Spirit Drive
Gulfport, MS 39505

Dear Mrs. Haugen:

Congratulations! Your house is now termite-free.

You've seen, first-hand, why so many people in your neighborhood work with us on a continuing basis. We're efficient and successful. We suggest that you now consider our monthly preventive service. During each visit, your home will receive a spraying for common pests plus a thorough search for hidden problems, such as seasonal infestations.

I've enclosed our standard service contract for your review. It's inexpensive, particularly when you consider what we can save you. It's convenient—you pick the day and approximate time of our service call. And for the next 30 days we're offering a 10% discount as a "thank you" for selecting us for your termite work.

Thanks for choosing Slug-a-Bug. We're looking forward to protecting you on a monthly basis.

Cordially,

Mayer Morrison

- Remind the customer that you've just completed a successful job for him/her and are used by neighbors.

- Enclose a contract/agreement to take advantage of impulse buyers.

- Offer an incentive (discount, etc.) to close the sale.

Company Name
Address
City, State Zip

Date

Ms. Rosemary Lane
Lane Interiors
488 Robinson Street
New York, NY 10011

Dear Ms. Lane:

I just received your first repeat order for our reproduction schoolhouse clocks. Thank you. As I indicated when you placed your starter order, our clocks are big favorites with discriminating buyers.

Before I fill your order, I want you to be aware of a special pricing policy for repeat buyers. If you order $2,000 or more of our clocks—in any combination of styles—and take them all in one shipment, you may deduct 20% from our wholesale price!

You've already seen how well our clocks are received, and this special pricing gives you the opportunity to experiment with other designs and models. My experience is that our novelty line, including the "clear dial" and "numberless" models, sells very well with an audience that appreciates unique styles.

Please call me before your scheduled shipping date of the 18th if you want to take advantage of our volume buyer discount plan. And thanks again for your business.

Cordially,

Newt Granville

- Acknowledge a repeat order. The buyer appreciates the personal touch even when you're not courting him/her.

- Clearly define your discount offer, and suggest reasons why it makes sense to buy in larger quantities.

- Force action with a deadline.

Company Name
Address
City, State Zip

Date

Mr. Jack Engblom
The Normandy Group
11 W. Olmsted Street
Dallas, TX 75220

Dear Jack:

You've reached our "valued customer" status. That's an honor accorded only to a select few.

It means that we recognize the very special needs related to your volume and customization requirements. You need access to design and manufacturing information, estimated delivery times, open-to-buy status, and dozens of other details that call for fast, accurate answers.

To be sure you get the data you need within minutes of your asking, we're assigning you your very own <u>Customer Service Representative</u>. Julie Rheingold will monitor your orders, review them with manufacturing, art, traffic, etc., and keep me up-to-date on your activity while I'm out of the office. Her direct dial number is 555-8971.

Julie will call you next week to introduce herself. She's a bright young woman who has been trained for the last three weeks on every facet of your account. I'm sure she'll do a wonderful job.

I appreciate your business, Jack. We all do.

Sincerely,

Russell Jamison

- Tell the customer he/she is unique.

- Explain how you will handle this account to better accommodate the customer's requirements.

- Express your appreciation for the business.

Company Name
Address
City, State Zip

Date

Mr. Gordon Cornell
Tillotson Speaker Corporation
1384 W. Morrison Drive
Chicago, IL 60664

Dear Gordon:

I think our publisher was an alchemist in an earlier life. He can turn virtually anything into gold, including your advertising budget! Here's what he's authorized me to offer you in our upcoming July Buyer's Guide issue:

1. Inclusion of your logo on our special gatefold cover. That means our 200,000 regular readers and 45,000 bonus distribution music show attendees will see your name on the front cover of the industry's leading magazine!

2. A four-color product release in our magazine for any product you choose, giving you even more exposure, impact, and leads.

3. A four-color "As Advertised In Stereo Sound Magazine" blow-up of your regular ad for display in your booth.

That's at least $20,000 worth of free exposure that's available to you as a 12x contract advertiser! You can earn those incentives by (a) expanding to a 12x contract for the balance of this year, or (b) committing to a 12x contract for next year.

Let us turn your advertising budget into pure gold by delivering the audience, the incentives, and the discounts that pay off in more sales and happier dealers. I'll call you next week for confirmation.

Cordially,

Bill Schaeffer

- By personalizing a standard offer, you can make the client feel appreciated as an individual.

- Be specific about the incentives and what the client must do take advantage of them.

- Follow up.

Company Name
Address
City, State Zip

Date

Mr. and Mrs. Charles Somers
529 Atkinson Drive
Asheville, NC 28806

Dear Mr. and Mrs. Somers:

The holidays are now behind us, and warm spring breezes are preparing for their annual visit to the most beautiful beach in America. This seems a perfect time to show you how much we appreciated having you as a guest last year.

We're offering a Customer Appreciation Weekend Getaway (May 1-3) that will reintroduce you to the beauty and calm of Williamstown Island. We have special events planned, including a country hoe-down, an old-fashioned beach barbecue, and a bicycle tour of the historic section.

You'll be housed in our newly renovated West Wing and enjoy an ocean view that is guaranteed to lower your blood pressure. With the enclosed Customer Appreciation coupon, your room rate is only $49.95 per night (a $40 saving per night!), double occupancy, including all Spring Getaway events.

We're looking forward to seeing you again.

Cordially,

Barry Marconi
Manager, Beach Inn

- Tell your customers you appreciate their business. Everyone likes to be told he's appreciated.

- If possible, offer a tangible "thank you" in the form of a gift or discount that keeps the customer coming to your establishment.

TREAT YOURSELF
TO EXQUISITE CRYSTAL SERVING PIECES...

JUST FOR USING DUNDEE COUNTRY BUTTER!

What an opportunity! Enjoy your favorite brand of butter, and treat yourself to genuine Irish Crystal at the same time!

On each one-pound bar of butter, you'll find a valuable proof of purchase seal. Cut out as many as you need, tape them as required to your DUNDEE IRISH CRYSTAL order form, and you'll have a magnificent crystal butter dish, salt and pepper shaker, or water pitcher in no time! Wait 'til you see the reaction of friends and relatives.

Send the coupon below to receive your official IRISH CRYSTAL. Then think about these unbelievable values:

	Retail Price	Your Price
IRISH CRYSTAL BUTTER DISH	$19.95	5 purchase seals plus $5.00
IRISH CRYSTAL SALT & PEPPER SHAKER	$29.95	10 purchase seals plus $5.00
IRISH CRYSTAL WATER PITCHER	$39.95	15 purchase seals plus $5.00

Treat yourself to Dundee's Creamy Country Butter and Irish Crystal serving pieces.

Offer expires November 30, 1991

- On-package promotions can spur continued buying, particularly when there's a direct tie-in with the product (butter dish with butter).

- Demonstrate the value and savings.

- Be sure to capture the names of respondents. They will be good prospects for future promotions.

Customer Relations 7

Dale Carnegie's <u>How To Win Friends and Influence People</u> is a publishing phenomenon that has spanned seven decades. More than 15,000,000 copies have been sold and there's reason to assume that the next seven decades will see another 15,000,000 copies sold. His advice remains timeless.

In his book, Carnegie disclosed what he called "The Big Secret of Dealing with People." He pointed out that at some time during our lives we will gratify all of our wants, with one exception: the desire to feel important. And that's the key to succeeding at customer relations. If you can make the customer feel important, you're almost assured of keeping your customer happy and buying.

Letters are wonderful vehicles for expressing appreciation for your customer. It's a terrific feeling to open a well-written letter that says "I appreciate you." You can show your appreciation through discounts, bonuses, or with the sincerity of your words. Showing appreciation is so unusual today that it will make you stand out from the crowd.

Compliments. If you pay attention, you'll find lots of opportunities to compliment your customers on various facets of their business. Was a client quoted in the newspaper or interviewed on television? Take the time to compliment him or her on (1) being recognized and (2) saying something of value. It isn't just good business, it's common courtesy. Do you read industry newspapers, newsletters, or journals? Do you keep your eyes open for news about your clients? If you do, you'll find many opportunities to offer compliments and congratulations. And you'll be appreciated in return. One caveat: Be sure your compliments are honest.

Nothing's as transparent as a compliment that isn't sincere.

Thank Yous. There are lots of ways to say "thank you" creatively. Unfortunately, most of us never take the time to try. You can make yourself so much more interesting by rephrasing your openings. For example, instead of saying "Thank you for the suggestion about changing packaging..." try "Thanks largely to your advice, we've switched from...." Instead of the traditional "Thank you for the letter of commendation you sent to my superior..." try "When I received a copy of your letter to my boss, I felt like I'd won the lottery!"

Put your personality into your letters. Say thank you with a flourish that says you mean it. Don't just write the first thing that comes to mind. Let the emotion that makes you a great persuader come through.

Meetings and Appointments. Meetings are the life-blood of the sales effort. Take the time to treat them with the importance they deserve. If you can't make a meeting, or are late, be quick to apologize—and do it sincerely. Upcoming meetings should be confirmed, particularly when the meeting requires special planning or was set up far in advance.

Requests. Making requests of customers and associates demands the same selling techniques that pervade this entire book. Demonstrate how responding to a request will benefit the other person, and express appreciation for the favor.

Changes in Business. When you change prices or items in your product line, tell your customers in the most positive way. Changes in sales personnel, management or the name of your company all present situations that give you the opportunity to resell your major strengths.

Apologies for Problems with products and services. There's an old adage that says, "Show me a person who makes no mistakes, and I'll show you someone who does nothing." In business, things go wrong. We strive for excellence and try to minimize errors, but mistakes happen, and we should be prepared to deal with them. The way you respond often will make the difference between keeping or losing an account. Don't be defensive. A light touch and honest effort will keep your customer buying from you.

Handling Complaints. A justified complaint is easy to deal with. Admit your mistake and tell the customer how you are rectifying it. Unjustified customer complaints, however, present the most difficult kind of letter to write because you have to do something you don't ever want to do: tell the customer that he or she is wrong. The key is being positive. Instead of saying "The order was late because you neglected to include the model number on your order," say something like "You can avoid future delays by including..." Instead of scolding, you're instructing.

You can tell someone you're sorry they're upset without backing down from your position. Put your own ego aside and think of the situation from the customer's perspective. And never embarrass a customer if you want that person to buy from you again.

Company Name
Address
City, State Zip

Date

Mr. Charles McReady
Vice President
Little, Page, Weaver and Robinson
One Liberty Place
Philadelphia, PA 19103

Dear Chuck:

It's nice to know that good things happen to good people. No one deserved that VP title more than you. You've been a major force in the rapid growth of your agency, and I'm happy you've received the recognition you so richly deserve.

It's a pleasure doing business with you. Congratulations and continued success.

Regards,

Helen Traitz

- Always acknowledge, in writing, a prospect's success. It has more permanence and impact than a passing remark.

Company Name
Address
City, State Zip

Date

Mr. Glen Goodman
Wilson Dairy Products
10 Fall River Plaza
Fredonia, WI 53075

Dear Glen:

I have mixed feelings about your taking the new job at Galloway Dairies. On the one hand, I'm happy for you. You were doing a heck of a job at Wilson, so it must be a terrific jump, in terms of compensation, for you to go to Galloway. Congratulations!

On the other hand, I hate to lose you as a client. At Galloway, you'll be dealing with Frank Bauer. As much as I hate to admit it, Frank will give you the same kind of outstanding service that I like to think I did.

When you have the opportunity, I'd appreciate some information on your replacement at Wilson, along with an introduction.

These last seven years have been wonderful, Glen. Thanks for the business and the friendship. Here's to your continued growth and success.

Sincerely,

Gordon Cambria

- If the client leaves, be sure to congratulate him/her. You may cross paths again.

- Ask for an introduction to the replacement.

Company Name
Address
City, State Zip

Date

Mr. Barton Rossiter
Oracle Technologies, Inc.
72 Cross Keys Bridge
Tempe, AZ 85282

Dear Mr. Rossiter:

Congratulations on the flattering feature article on your company in today's Tribune business section. I thought your comments about corporate responsibility to the community were courageous.

You may recall that we met briefly when you were with G.P. Ridley. We said that we'd talk again in the future. Now that I have considerably more insight into your corporate philosophy, I think the future has arrived. As executive vice president of one of the area's leading public relations firms, I have a number of ideas that pertain specifically to your business, and I'd like to share them with you.

I'll call you this week to arrange a time to meet. I look forward to seeing you again.

Sincerely,

Edwin Cunningham

- Referring to a quote or news story is a good way to approach a prospect.

- Newspapers and magazines are great sources of leads.

- Don't oversell in the letter since it is meant to praise the prospect.

Company Name
Address
City, State Zip

Date

Dr. Kent Anacorte
Burlington Wellness Center
559 Glen Cove Boulevard
Erie, PA 16546

Dear Kent:

If clothes make the man, then the office makes the company. Congratulations on your impressive new facility.

Did you use a decorator? If so, would you be willing to share the name? I'm looking for a new office myself, and I'd like to make it as comfortable, yet elegant, as yours. I've never seen a desk quite as lovely as the one in your office. Is it made of rosewood?

I've always enjoyed calling on you. Visiting your beautiful office just increased the pleasure! Great job.

Cordially,

Mary Ann Quinney

- A new office is a source of pride to any businessperson or professional. Don't pass up the opportunity to pay a justified compliment.

- If you've personally visited the facility, point out something specific (which will demonstrate that you really looked around).

Company Name
Address
City, State Zip

Date

Ms. Diane Bartlett
Yorktown Dental Supplies
380 22nd Street
South Bend, IN 46628

Dear Diane:

It's no wonder Yorktown has grown by leaps and bounds. Everything you do is so promotional, yet professional. Your new catalog is really special.

I was so impressed that I've enclosed a form for a national catalog competition. I'd love to see you get the recognition you deserve. I'm certain you'd take top honors in the professional catalog category.

Whatever you decide, congratulations. You've set a new standard for the industry. I'm proud that our precision instruments are a part of it.

Cordially,

Doug Renker
Vice President, Sales

- Customers appreciate compliments on their advertising. A catalog is a major undertaking and usually a source of pride to the producer.

- If the catalog is particularly special, say so and explain why.

- Comment on the inclusion of your own products.

Company Name
Address
City, State Zip

Date

Mr. Anthony McFadden
Alpha Brands, Inc.
1200 West Dinwiddie Street
Tysons Corner, VA 22180

Dear Tony:

I saw you in an entirely new light last Thursday evening, and was I impressed! As a direct result of your stirring speech on volunteerism, I've just signed up to assist in a local hospice program.

I've always admired your one-on-one persuasive powers; now I know they're equally impressive when you're in front of a group.

Thanks again for inviting me to attend. Let me know when you're speaking again; I'd like to bring Linda along. I told her she has a treat in store.

See you soon.

Cordially,

Alan Kirkland

- Tell the client you attended and enjoyed hearing him/her.

- If you were moved/motivated/informed by the speech, explain how. Keep it sincere.

- Thank the client for the invitation.

Company name
Address
City, State Zip

Date

Mr. Theodore Galvin
Stoneybrook Research Center
1200 Kennewick Avenue
Groton, MA 01471

Dear Ted:

I remember a quote from a European literature class that claimed "a modest man has everything to gain." If that's correct, then you have a bonanza in store for you!

How in the world could you let me sit through a meeting and lunch and never mention that you received the Father of the Year award from the county's Council of Churches? I'd be running around telling everyone if I had received it (which is just one reason why I never will!).

Congratulations, Ted. Obviously, you're not only a great guy to work with, you're a great guy to live with. I'm happy for you and your family.

Cordially,

Dan Custis

• Share your client's joy. Whenever you discover something positive, use it as an opportunity to correspond. It's appreciated.

Company Name
Address
City, State Zip

Date

Ms. Evelyn Berger
Ritter Industries
811 Winding Way
Columbia, MO 65201

Dear Evelyn:

When I received a carbon copy of your letter to my boss, I felt like I'd won the lottery!

Thanks for saying so many nice things about me. It's a great source of pride to be described as an extension of your staff. In many companies, a salesperson is regarded as an outsider; you make it possible for people like me to contribute because you invite comments and participation.

I appreciate your kind words, and I'll try to do the kind of job that makes you want to say them again.

Kindest regards,

Patrick Norden

- Always thank a client or prospect for a favor or compliment.

- If appropriate, return the compliment.

Company Name
Address
City, State Zip

Date

Mr. Douglas Leithgow
Harrison Binders
4256 Edgewood Avenue
Lincoln, NE 68599

Dear Doug:

I received a call from Janice Wirth, and she really seemed enthusiastic about meeting me. I'm not sure what you told her, but whatever it was, it worked!

Thanks so much for making this meeting possible. You're a man of your word. In appreciation for your help, I think I can convince my boss to give you an additional break or two. He'll probably make you an honorary member of our sales team.

This is the best kind of deal, Doug. By helping me, you've probably helped yourself, too. Thanks a million.

Regards,

Earl Jenkins

- A healthy sales/client relationship will always lead to additional sales. Be sure to acknowledge any help in writing.

- If it's reasonable to do so, hold out the promise of a "reward" for the help.

Company Name
Address
City, State Zip

Date

Mr. Seth Beverly
Chairman of the Board
U.S. Motors
One Winding Way
Detroit, MI 48234

Dear Mr. Beverly:

Please accept my compliments for the supportive role you played when our firm held the initial Person-to-Person training session at your company. I've had high level executives in our sessions before, but it's a rarity when they can resist the temptation to dominate.

You allowed your managers to express doubts, raise questions, and honestly participate in a frank discussion covering numerous sensitive topics.

You demonstrated the leadership style that other executives rarely see. Your willingness to participate as a co-equal will make this top-down program successful at each level.

Thank you for giving your time. It will pay off in a big way.

Cordially,

Richard Blender
Vice President, Training

- Time is our most valuable commodity. When someone gives it to you, it merits written acknowledgement.

- Articulate the value of the time given.

Company Name
Address
City, State Zip

Date

Mr, Judd Breaker
Crown Vinyl
One Calvert Plaza
Bangor, ME 04401

Dear Judd:

You're not just a great customer; you're a terrific guy. Thanks so much for your time and consideration during our visit last week.

I really appreciate your appraisal of Jonathan's abilities. I agree that he is a young man of exceptional talents, but it's nice to hear it from a client. We're strongly considering putting him on our "fast track" sales management program, and your feedback gives him another boost up the ladder.

If Jonathan makes it into the program (about 99% certain after your assessment), I'll tell him he owes you lunch. Thanks again.

Cordially,

Hal Leland

- Your clients are often great "sounding boards." To keep this information source flowing, be certain you respond promptly with "thank you" letters.

- Give the client a sense of satisfaction by telling him/her how the comments will be acted upon.

Company Name
Address
City, State Zip

Mr. Ellis Tobin
Allied Distributors
10 Boonton Road
Kansas City, MO 64145

Dear Ellis:

By the time you read this, we will have incorporated many of your suggestions into the development of our new billing system. I think you'll really be pleased to see the improvements over the old one. I've given it a test run myself, and I can assure you that all the invoicing problems you've experienced over the years have been eliminated, thanks in large part to your input.

I'm so pleased that you threw yourself into this project and were so sharing with your straightforward, insightful comments. Thank you!

Kindest regards,

Harold Pressman
President

- If you ask someone for help, acknowledge the contribution.

- Mention specifically what you did to follow-up on the suggestions.

- Express your enthusiasm and appreciation.

Company Name
Address
City, State Zip

Date

Mr. Hans Milton
Plymouth Groceries
22 Penn Acres Industrial Park
New Canaan, CT 06840

Dear Mr. Milton:

Thanks largely to your advice, we've switched from hand tying our meats to using flash netting. Although it's a bit more expensive (due to the need to bone guard before vacuum sealing), the increase in sales has more than made up the difference. The product is now much more appealing to the consumer.

Thank you for your very astute advice. You've made a terrific contribution to us and our other customers. In return, I advise you to stock up on your next order: I'm giving you a 10% discount as my way of showing appreciation.

Have any more hot tips?

Sincerely,

Hal Fenwick

- Explain to the customer how you incorporated his/her advice into your business. (If you didn't use it, say "thank you" anyway. People want to be acknowledged.)

- If the advice was of value, offer something tangible in return.

Company Name
Address
City, State Zip

Date

Mr. Alan Haney
The Parker Group, Inc.
1100 West Patterson Avenue
Idaho Falls, ID 83415

Dear Alan:

I can't wait until you start sending me large commission checks...
because that will mean I'm bringing you large orders! That's the best
way I can thank you for the opportunity to represent your firm.

Speaking of opportunities, positive answers to the following questions
will help insure that we have lots of them:

Are you willing to gold-emboss an organization's logo on
your binders? In other words, a private-label program?

Will you make available—at no cost—your promo
materials for use by a client? Negs, artwork, etc.?

I have a number of calls scheduled on your behalf next week, so I'd
appreciate a prompt response (call or fax). At least three of my
accounts are prospects for private labelling and that means large
volume!

Again, thanks for the opportunity. I'm going to prove how right you were
in giving me your account!

Cordially,

Peter Drocort

- Always express your appreciation in writing. Tell the client about the wonderful things that will happen to him/her because you were given an opportunity.

Company Name
Address
City, State Zip

Date

Ms. Claire Robinson
Liganier Industries, Inc.
1 Liganier Way
Burlington, VT 05405

Dear Ms. Robinson:

I was very pleased to learn from our sales manager, Jill McLatchey, that you've decided to host your upcoming national sales meeting at The Harbor Inn.

Your sales people will be delighted with the fine service, excellent food, wide range of sports activities, and other amenities—all located in a magnificent oceanfront setting. I'm confident that your sales meeting will be one your sales professionals will remember fondly for a long time.

Jill will be in touch shortly to discuss your meeting, banquet, and accommodations requirements. If there's anything else that you need, please feel free to call me directly at 802-555-5800.

Thanks again. The entire staff is looking forward to serving you.

Sincerely,

Marlin Faucher
Vice President, Sales

- It's a nice touch to have the manager send a personal thank you. It shows the client that your organization considers him/her important.

Company Name
Address
City, State Zip

Date

Ms. Meg Wolf
GBA, Inc.
5720 W. Oregon Avenue
Pasadena, CA 91126

Dear Meg:

How did you do it? I can't believe you talked your retail division into reopening bids to give me a shot.

Thank you so much! I really appreciate the vote of confidence in me and my company. (I know you stuck your neck out to help.) In return, I'll give your retail group the kind of service, product, and dedication to detail that prompted you to recommend their reevaluation.

I owe you one.

Regards,

Ken Braxton

- If someone does you a good turn, don't make your "thank you" read like a will. Say it in writing the way you'd say it in person; with enthusiasm and feeling.

- State what the favor was and how it will pay off.

Company Name
Address
City, State Zip

Date

Mr. Irvin J. Howell
Arnold M. Blaustein Management Academy
1050 Kennesaw Road
Alexandria, VA 22318

Dear Mr. Howell:

I appreciate the time you gave us during our visit last week. Your facility is impressive, and your staff seems remarkably committed and enthusiastic.

We'll talk again after you've completed your review of our training materials. I wanted to remind you that we can supply programs to your various centers for under $25 per pupil! That represents an unusual combination of quality and economy.

Again, thanks for the meeting and the consideration. I'll call at the end of the month.

Cordially,

Peter Hollander
Sales Director

- Always show your appreciation in writing. (The prospect may use it to his/her own advantage with a superior.)

- It's okay to be enthusiastic, as long as you don't overdo it.

- Remind the prospect of your key selling points.

Company Name
Address
City, State Zip

Date

Ms. Courtney Markham
The Westerly Group
1057 Industrial Boulevard
Rapid City, SD 57709

Dear Ms. Markham:

Your response to the advertisement in <u>Premium and Marketing News</u> for our pre-inked
stamps may open a profitable new sales avenue for you.

Children occupy themselves for long stretches at home by using our "Cuddly Animals"
stamps. Teachers use our educational stamps to reinforce basic concepts, such as
alphabet learning. Adults can use over 500 business-oriented stamps to make their office
lives less complicated.

Our pre-inked, no-mess stamps are compact and easy to carry. They're non-toxic, won't
dry out, can be used more than 5,000 times, and their plastic housings prevent ink from
getting onto hands and clothes.

Please review our enclosed catalog. Note that we have attractive, colorful display cases
for retail selling, and that all office stamps are available in English and Spanish.

I'm rushing you samples under separate cover. The sooner you place your first order, the
sooner you can start to generate new profits.

Sincerely,

Bruce Crenshaw
VP, Sales

Enclosure

- Remind the prospect what he/she responded to.

- Stick to the product(s) about which the prospect responded.

Company Name
Address
City, State Zip

Date

Mr. Joseph Wilson
MAXI Food Distributors
1093 Norwood Avenue
Pikeville, KY 41503

Dear Joe:

You and I have always agreed that vehicles—particularly refrigerated trucks—are only as good as the service they receive. That's why I share your disappointment about the servicing of your unit #3003 last week.

I appreciate the suggestion that we can do better. Of course we can, and we will. When you bring #3003 in for its 100,000 mile service, I'll see to it that we fix the oil leak and replace the exhaust system. For the life of me, I can't understand how those two items were overlooked.

We've serviced your trucks for many years, Joe, and I can't remember too many times (ever?) when you've been unhappy with our service. Thanks for pointing it out; I'll personally check to be sure you get the kind of attention you've come to expect.

I appreciate your business.

Yours truly,

Al Ciliberti
Service Manager

- Always project appreciation that you've been told about a problem. It enhances the service image.

- Tell the client what will be done.

- Remind the client of your history of outstanding work and that you will continue to perform at a high level.

Company Name
Address
City, State Zip

Date

Alvin Cutler, Ph.D.
LDI Technical Centers
35 Mall Road
Chicago, IL 60604

Dear Dr. Cutler:

I know you have confidence that our project team has the technical
know-how to subcontract this project for you. I simply didn't realize you
wanted each item broken out in detail.

Within five days, I'll have a new report in your hands with the following
tasks clarified:

- Testing all equipment and software
- Customization of software
- Implementation plan of competitive text retrieval systems
- Troubleshooting

I appreciate your prodding us to make the Steiglitz report as thorough
as possible. You'll have the revision by next Tuesday. And you'll be
reassured that we're the group to execute the contract for you. Thank
you.

Sincerely,

Steven Fischer

- Agree that you could do better, but reaffirm that you're the person for the job.

- List what you will do to be better.

- Thank the prospect for helping you give him what he wants.

Company Name
Address
City, State Zip

Date

Mr. Sterling Joyce
Chase, Marley, & Ebbets
8 West Oak Street
Gary, IN 46474

Dear Sterling:

No wonder everyone respects you. You have a generous way of "spreading the word."

I just concluded a meeting with Vince DeCarlo, and it looks like we'll do business. He said you recommended me because of the way I handled the Quality One public relations campaign for you last year.

You know my business philosophy for all projects—give it everything you've got! I did it for you, and I'll do it for Vince.

Thanks again for your kindness. I'm sure I'll have a chance to repay you somewhere down the road.

Kindest regards,

Jeffrey Horowitz

- Recommendations are important to any business and deserve more than a perfunctory "thank you."

- Mention the person who recommended you by name.

- Suggest some form of repayment.

Company Name
Address
City, State Zip

Date

Dr. William Ridgeway
Internist Associates, Inc.
11-22 Sandy Springs Way
Marietta, SC 29661

Dear Dr. Ridgeway:

You've joined a <u>very</u> select group of doctors who have switched to the technologically superior Douglas X-Ray 2000 system.

Your purchase marks you as someone on the leading edge of internal medicine. The enclosed certificate is an excellent way to display to your patients your commitment to their well-being.

Thanks for choosing Douglas's award-winning instruments. I'll call in a few weeks to see if you have any questions about your warranty or other fine Douglas products.

Cordially,

Ellen Flanders

- Customer service letters keep the contact alive. Reinforce the wisdom of the buying decision, particularly when the purchase is in the thousands of dollars.

- Extras count. A "certificate of commitment" advertises your name and is a constant reminder of your service.

- Don't stop selling. Be supportive, and be available when the next buying decision will be made.

Company Name
Address
City, State Zip

Date

Mr. Todd Alpern
Grand Designs
17 W. City Line Avenue
Chicago, IL 60667

Dear Todd:

Your attendance at my company's muscular dystrophy fund-raiser
helped convince many of our clients to attend. But your generous
pledge on behalf of your company was more than we could have hoped
for. You started a chain reaction of new pledges and helped turn what
is normally a moderately successful event into a smash hit.

Thank you from me, Jim Lovette (my Vice President), and Henry
Kaltenhof (our President and Chairman). Since this was my year to
chair the affair, you made me look particularly "heroic" in the eyes of the
people who count. I'm not sure how to thank you for your
participation...but knowing how much your contribution meant to
muscular dystrophy sufferers should give you a great deal of
satisfaction.

You've paid me a wonderful compliment, Todd, by your participation,
and I'm very grateful. Thanks again.

Regards,

Ted Parkes

- Thank the client for attending, and reinforce that his/her attendance was very important to you and your cause.

Company Name
Address
City, State Zip

Date

Ms. Aubrey Carroll
Redding Products Ltd.
1840 Carillon Road
Wilmington, DE 19876

Dear Ms. Carroll:

After "spinning my wheels" for a number of years with your predecessor at Redding, I have a feeling of confidence now that you've entered into the equation. Admittedly, I don't know you very well yet, but your enthusiasm is catching. I sense that you're going to make things happen.

I'm doing my part. The deluxe desk calendar I've enclosed will be a profitable addition to your business catalog...and a treasured resource in your office. It's not only an excellent way to keep yourself on schedule, it's full of intriguing facts, figures, and useable quotes. Keep it in your desk drawer or it may "take a walk" when you aren't looking—everybody wants one!

Good luck with your new job. I think you have an entrepreneurial fervor that will pay large dividends for your catalog operation. I'm looking forward to working with you.

Cordially,

Christopher Connor

- Enthusiasm is an asset. If you meet someone who has it, comment on it.

- Display your own enthusiasm with an energetic letter. If you're enthusiastic about your own product, others will be, too.

Company Name
Address
City, State Zip

Date

Ms. Lorna Jordan
Springhouse Electric
3000 Roaring Brook Road
Saddle Brook, NJ 07662

Dear Ms. Jordan:

It's rare to have a client take the time and effort to provide such a detailed evaluation of a product design. I'm taking your evaluation as a compliment. I can't imagine you'd spend that much time on something you didn't think had merit. Thank you.

I've submitted your evaluation to Engineering for a review and report. They're excited about working with a client who knows how to throw a challenge at them. Believe me, it doesn't happen all that often.

As soon as I get Engineering's comments, I'd like to meet with you again and bring Sam Archer along. That will be helpful in saving back and forth time between our companies, plus I think you'll like Sam. He's a terrific engineer and a great person to work with. If you decide to use our services, he'll head the project team.

I'll give you a call as soon as I hear from Engineering. Again, thanks.

Sincerely,

Bryce Randolph

- Compliment the prospect for taking the time to do a thorough evaluation.

- Advise the client that his/her evaluation is being thoroughly reviewed.

- Tell the client what will happen as a result of the evaluation.

Company Name
Address
City, State Zip

Date

Mr. Jeffrey Hodder
Sterling Diagnostics
3813 Sandy Ridge Road
Manhattan Beach, CA 90266

Dear Jeff:

I can't tell you what a treat it is to write to you on stationery with our new address, particularly since your business is largely responsible for our expansion to the new location.

Our move has been fueled, in part, by the continuing business from your company. We've added a dispatcher to handle and track your shipments, and we've added another full-time clerical person to process the paperwork. They would have had to sit in the hallway in our old building.

<u>Please note our new address.</u> (I've sent a change of address announcement to your secretary.) When you decide to make one of your periodic visits, take Old Mill Road South to Delaware Avenue, make a left, and go one-half mile. We're the two-story red brick building on your right.

Again, Jeff, thanks for your business. We'll be able to continue our high standards of warehousing and shipping for you because of the move.

Sincerely,

Julian Bender

- Although there's nothing wrong with sending a standardized announcement to your client list, a personal letter adds a particularly classy touch.

- Tell the client that you appreciate the role he/she has played in your growth.

Discount Coupon to Customer for Filling Out Survey (7-27)

Office of the President
Company Name
Address
City, State Zip

Date

Mr. Wesley Santee
960 Corona Place
Belle Fourche, SD 57742

Dear Mr. Santee:

Did we succeed in making your stay at the Chicago Aurora a pleasant one? If we did, it's because feedback from guests such as you made it possible.

We need to know what was special about your stay and what—if anything—wasn't. The point is, we work at making ourselves the best, and we need your help to maintain our superior quality.

If you'll take a few moments to complete and return the enclosed survey, we'll send you two coupons in return: One will be for a 10% discount on your room during your next visit to any Aurora; the second will be for a complimentary cocktail.

You have my assurance that your reply will be kept strictly confidential... but it will be carefully scrutinized by us to make your next visit even more enjoyable.

Thanks for your patronage. We value your business.

Sincerely,

Sheldon Reid
President

- Surveys are excellent vehicles for getting feedback from customers. If you include an incentive to complete it, you will get a significant return.

- A letter from the President (even if it's computerized) will draw favorable response.

- Thank the customer for his/her patronage.

Company Name
Address
City, State Zip

Date

Mr. Myron Dayton
Meteor Technologies
48 East Blue Creek Road
Birmingham, AL 35247

Dear Mr. Dayton:

Following up on our phone conversation, I look forward to meeting with you and your strategic planning staff on Thursday, April 1 at your office. I appreciate your arranging to have a 35mm slide projector and screen in the conference room for me to use during the presentation.

One other request. Do you think it's possible to have Ed Meisman attend as well? Since he will be signing off on the project, it would be helpful to have him see my presentation.

I'll touch base with you a few days before the meeting to reconfirm.

Cordially,

Lynnette Straughn

- When setting up a meeting in a prospect's office, make sure everything you need will be available—including, if possible, all the people who will be making the buying decision.

- Meeting details should be confirmed in writing, especially if they require special equipment.

- Reconfirm meetings that are set up way in advance.

Company Name
Address
City, State Zip

Date

Mr. Benjamin Carrington
Logan Financial Services, Inc.
9020 Franklin Parkway
Aurora, CO 80044

Dear Mr. Carrington:

Now that I finally have an appointment with you, I can understand why some teams make the playoffs—then fall flat on their faces. They're so excited about getting there, the game becomes secondary to the event!

I promise that won't happen with our "event." I have a great deal of information to review with you about the success of our current franchise operations and why we'd like to create a new joint ventured franchise with you.

For the record: We'll be meeting at 11:00 a.m. in your office on February 21. As you suggested, your secretary will handle lunch reservations. I'm looking forward to it.

Very truly yours,

Peter Matthews

- Try to convey a sense of appreciation and anticipation about your meeting. You can transfer your sense of enthusiasm to the prospect, and make him/her feel good about setting it up.

- Clearly state the pertinent details. Where. When. Why. What. Even who will make lunch reservations. Leave nothing to chance.

Company Name
Address
City, State Zip

Date

Ms. Judi Conyers
Kelso Architects and Builders
1262 Imperial Plaza
Columbia, MO 65211

Dear Judi:

During our last conversation I may have mentioned I was about to become "big brother" to a sales trainee, fresh out of college. As you could probably tell, I wasn't thrilled about having a "sidekick," particularly one half my age.

Much to my surprise, Alene McGrath is bright beyond her years, is a highly motivated salesperson, and has a hungry look that is usually reserved for the people striving to reach the top of the ladder. In other words, I like her.

Would you mind if I brought Alene to sit in on my presentation to your marketing committee next week? In fact, I might actually give her a cameo role to see how she holds up under questioning. My guess is she'll impress us both.

Thanks for your consideration. I'll check with you prior to the meeting.

Cordially,

Mike Bullard

- Most people have no problem with your bringing an associate to a meeting, but it's considerate to ask.

- Tell your client in advance if you plan to have the associate participate or just observe.

- You're asking the favor. It's up to you to follow-up.

Company Name
Address
City, State Zip

Date

Mr. Edward Volksmann
Carstairs & Company
706 Edmunds Avenue
Oklahoma City, OK 73149

Dear Ed:

I vowed never to get a car phone. But after missing our meeting and having no way to tell you I was stuck on the turnpike, I've changed my mind.

If you're willing to reschedule, I'd like to make it up to you with lunch at La Buca. I'll be back in town during the weeks of the 19th and 26th, and I'm totally at your disposal.

I have some terrific ideas about expanding your product line. And the most amazing story to tell about what I went through trying to reach you.

Thanks for your indulgence. I'll call to confirm dates with you.

Regards,

Pat Cummings

P.S. Do you have any recommendations on car phones?

- Instead of avoiding the reason for the missed appointment, use the incident as a conversation piece, and even as a "tease" ("I have the most amazing story to tell").

- If you're comfortable with humor ("Do you have any recommendations on car phones"), it's a nice device for softening the missed meeting. If you're not, avoid it.

Professional Name
Address
City, State Zip

Date

Lydia Cornwallis, D.D.S.
Garner James Medical Center
2208 San Marco Boulevard
Mesa, AZ 85208

Dear Lydia:

My associate, Jack Posner, asked me to relay his apologies for missing your first meeting as President of the Mid-County Dental Society. In a way, it was your fault he ran out of time!

Jack accepted a last-minute 4:30 appointment with Judy Kaminski, a referral of yours. He spent so much time with her—partly because of her need for reassurance and partly because of her profusion of problems—that he was unable to make the meeting.

We both thank you for referring this very interesting patient (we'll have a complete report for you within two weeks), and we're happy to be of assistance for any other surgical needs that may occur. Jack said he'll call you when he returns from Phoenix next week to see what he can do to help you in your new duties.

Cordially,

Darren Greer, D.D.S.

- When the press of events forces a colleague to miss an appointment, be sure to acknowledge regret. The "missing person" should also express regret as soon as possible.

Company Name
Address
City, State Zip

Date

Ms. Madelyn Crowley
Practical Incentives, Inc.
430 Hillside Road/Suite 200
Lawrence, KS 66046

Dear Ms. Crowley:

I'm sorry my oversight put a crimp in your schedule. I made the mistake of relying on memory instead of checking my calendar.

Thank you for being so gracious about my lateness, and for allowing me to to have fifteen minutes of your time. I trust you'll find the samples I left with you of sufficient quality and interest to overcome my faux pas.

I look forward to getting off on the right foot next time!

Cordially,

Grant Donnelly

- It's usually more believable if you admit to a human foible than a contrived one.

- Thank the prospect for letting you "off the hook."

- Reinforce the quality of your products.

Company Name
Address
City, State Zip

Date

Mr. Anthony L. Tam
East Asia Trading Company Pte Ltd.
7301-15 Block #1, Uno Road
Aberdeen 3499, Hong Kong

Dear Tony:

I've solidified our plans. Please confirm that these arrangements are suitable.

1. I'll pick you up at the airport Sunday afternoon, then take you back to my place for a good old American barbecue. I know you're an adventuresome eater, and I'll be interested in your reaction to my wife's homemade barbecue sauce. Then, if your jet lag isn't too terrible, you might want to join us for an evening concert.

2. We'll spend Monday together and review your product lines. I think I have some terrific outlets for them. At five, we'll meet Anne Boynton and Pat Heard to discuss how you might establish an Asian program for them.

3. On Tuesday, we'll drive into New York for a meeting with Forster & Schiff's international division. They seem interested in getting you to market their line. I've assured them your market is booming.

Looking forward to seeing you again. Have a safe trip.

Cordially,

Arnold Schnoll

- With a little bit of effort, you can continue selling your client. Instead of just confirming the itinerary, convey a sense of excitement about the business prospects.

Company Name
Address
City, State Zip

Date

Mr. Calvin Rubin
Keystone Security Systems
702 West Hampton Boulevard
Talladega, AL 35160

Dear Cal:

I've been grinning from ear to ear since I received your letter yesterday. I'm very appreciative that you took the time and effort to let me know how satisfied you were with my consulting services. (The check was nice, too. Thanks for the speedy payment!).

Since you were pleased with what you called my "bailout service," I'd appreciate it if you'd pass my name on to one of your clients: Spartan Financial Advisors. I've heard that they're going through some networking miseries lately, but I can't get anyone in power to talk to me.

Perhaps you can break the logjam. I think you realize that I can be of immense help to them, and when I am, it will reflect well on you, too.

I'll call you next week to see if Spartan was receptive to your recommendation. Thanks a million. It was great working with you.

Cordially,

Phillip Traynor

- People like to help. If you have a good relationship with your client, you can always ask for a non-competitive referral.

- Affirm that the referral will make your prospect look good because of the outstanding job you'll do.

- Advise that you'll follow-up on the request. Good intentions sometimes are forgotten without gentle prodding.

Company Name
Address
City, State Zip

Date

Mr. Avery Rosenbloom
Evergreen Insurance & Casualty
Old Marlton and Conestoga Roads
Lodi, OH 44254

Dear Avery:

I need a favor. I'm in the running to do a domestic feasibility study for a giant bank, and they've asked me to supply a few references.

Since we've had some notable successes together (the reconfiguration of changing loads/requirements and the salvageability of current equipment studies), I hope you'll consent to my submitting your name.

I would really appreciate your help, and I'll call for confirmation.

Regards,

Ken Williston

- People respond well to being asked for help.

- It's useful to remind people of successful ventures. Many of us have short memories.

- Always state that you will call for confirmation.

Company Name
Address
City, State Zip

Date

Mr. Neville Stonefort
Big Money Digest
3838 Little Neck Road
Omaha, NE 68113

Dear Mr. Stonefort:

Your subscribers and our buyers have a lot in common. They share average incomes in the $50,000 range, they're predominantly males, and they're mail order buyers—to name a few similarities.

I propose that we swap mailing lists. By cooperating with each other, (1) no cash has to change hands, and (2) we won't have to pay commissions to list brokers to rent the others' lists. That represents a six figure savings between us.

There are several details we need to work out, and I think they need to be handled in person. I'll give you a few days to review the enclosed demographics of our 2.5 million desk and pocket organizer buyers. Then I'll call to see when you might be free for a meeting.

This is a very significant step forward for both our organizations. I hope you'll take the opportunity to explore it with me.

Cordially,

Sylvan Cohen
Executive Vice President

Enclosure

- Establish similarities to set the tone immediately.

- Demonstrate how the similarities can be used to advantage by both companies (particularly in dollar savings).

- Supply supporting data to reinforce your desire to meet and discuss the possibilities.

Company Name
Address
City, State Zip

Date

Mr. Kyle Washington
Duston, Palmer & Kates
1103 E. Pattison Avenue
Huntington, WV 25713

Dear Kyle:

Before we decided to raise our advertising rates for next year, we randomly surveyed our advertisers. We explained that the cost of 70# coated text was rising again, and we could hold our rates only if we dropped our paper quality.

Much to our surprise (and delight), over 80% of the respondents said they would prefer a "moderate" increase in rates to a decrease in paper quality. "A magazine devoted to the arts," said one, "is dependent on quality reproduction." That was representative of the overall response.

We're holding the increase to an average of 8.7% (only 6% for full pages; a fraction over 10% for the smallest space—see enclosed rate card). But we're giving you an <u>opportunity to reserve space at the old rate</u>. If we receive a contract from you prior to January 1, we'll honor the current rates for the entire new year.

Take advantage of this last chance before the rates go up. Call your regional representative to reserve your high-quality, high-interest advertising space.

Cordially,

Edmund Darlington
Publisher

Enclosure

- Price increases are usually very mechanical, very "corporate." With a little creativity, they can become sales letters, instead of "tombstone" notices.

- You can usually "bump" sales by combining a "last chance to buy at the old rates" appeal with notification of a price increase.

Notification of Price Decrease (7-39)

Company Name
Address
City, State Zip

Date

Ms. Linda Hall
Hall and Coates
1298 E. Stony Brook Street
Poplar, MD 21220

Dear Linda:

Your last excuse for not buying a fax just went out the window.

I just received our price list for next year's models. As I recall, you said
if the model that makes perfect copies of halftones and other fine details
ever went under $1,000, you'd buy it. Guess what?

Isn't mass production wonderful? Faxes are becoming almost as
common as telephones, and the pricing has dropped accordingly. I
can't believe that I was selling a similar model three years ago for over
$2,000.

You know you shouldn't hold out any longer. The prices have
stabilized, and inflation will eat away at any lingering production
economies.

You might as well go ahead and make out your purchase order now. I'll
call to see when you want delivery.

Cordially,

Arthur Silver

- Tell the customer the price went down and explain why.

- Ask for the order.

Company Name
Address
City, State Zip

To: All Shepperd Dealers

From: Jason Brown, Senior VP, Sales

Date:

Subject: Streamlined Product Line

First of all, thank you for delivering our biggest year in history. While we're justifiably proud of the attention and detail that goes into manufacturing our barbecue grills, we know that it's our dealers who make us #1.

We've combined the results of a lengthy product review with many of your comments. The conclusion is that we have too large a line. Of our ten models, six of them represent almost 92% of the sales. Effective immediately, we will stop production of models 1012, 1074, 2109, and 2208.

This streamlining will allow you to display the entire line at once, giving your customers a chance to really review features on a side-by-side basis, and eliminate confusion over models that were too close in style and features.

Thanks for helping us help you. This change will increase sales and help you focus inventory only on productive models. Good selling!

- Always note your distributor's role in your sales success.

- Explain why the reduction in models will help sales and inventory.

Company Name
Address
City, State Zip

Date

Jonas Nystrom, Ph.D.
Information Testing Systems, Inc.
1340 Northwoods Park
Princeton, NJ 08541

Dear Jonas:

I'm particularly proud to announce the newest member of our sales team, Lydia Korman. She brings a special dimension to both of us, because she's been exceptionally successful from both sides of the desk.

Before moving into sales, Lydia managed information services development for Hunter/Rohm. This included financial analysis, purchasing, and telecommunications.

The point, of course, is that she understands user needs and puts that excellent background to work in designing systems that fit your requirements. And you may have some interesting stories to swap since she took her advanced degree (a doctorate in Computer and Information Science) at your alma mater, Dartmouth.

You're going to enjoy working with her, Jonas. She has much to contribute to your organization. Either she or I will call soon to arrange a get-acquainted visit. I'm looking forward to seeing you again and introducing you to our newest asset.

Cordially,

Jerry Rhodes
Vice President, Sales

- Explain why the new person is of value to the customer by listing parts of his/her background that are meaningful.

- Customize the letter to fit the client.

- Tell the client you will personally introduce the new salesperson. Make it an important event.

Company Name
Address
City, State Zip

Date

Ms. Stefanie McCarthy
Prentiss-Pursell Marketing, Inc.
33 Concord Station
Cheyenne, WY 82005

Dear Ms. McCarthy:

If you read last April's issue of <u>Printing Production</u> <u>Magazine</u>, you'll remember it featured Robert Packard on the cover and described him as the "dean" of the graphic arts industry. I've enclosed a reprint in case you missed it.

Since that article appeared, Mr. Packard put together a team of investors and sought to acquire an innovative printing company. Out of the thousands of printers in the country, he chose us because our unique approach to printing—and strong emphasis on customer service—mirrored his own celebrated approach to graphic arts success.

Last week the deal was completed. Mr. Packard is our new CEO, and he's promised to make a good thing better. His promise is that Jordan/Packard Printing will bring you better printing at highly competitive prices because of increased volume and new technology. (In just two months, we'll be able to provide in-line envelopes, micro-encapsulation of fragrances and other printing specializations that have been available in only a few selected world centers.)

I can't wait to tell you what our new pricing, enhanced printing, and faster turnaround time can mean to you. You're going to like working with our new management team!

I'll call you to set up a meeting to discuss all the opportunities.

Sincerely,

Raymond Hughes
Vice President, Sales

- Always sell the idea that new management means success. Some clients get nervous with change.

- Be positive and enthusiastic about new opportunities for your clients and prospects.

Company Name
Address
City, State Zip

Date

Mr. Robert Fulton
Houston Gear Company
23 Green Park
Helena, MT 59623

Dear Bob:

I wanted you to hear the news from me before your read it in the newspaper or received an impersonal form letter from our PR department: We've changed the name of our company. In two weeks, we'll be known as McGraw-Lauder & Associates.

That may not seem like a terribly significant change from McGraw & Associates, but it is. It represents our commitment to provide you and Houston Gear with fresh insights, new business ideas, and innovative EDP operations. By joining forces with Franklin Lauder, we've further energized our high-impact, problem-solving capacity.

I want you to meet Franklin. When you do get together with him, you'll understand immediately what he brings to both our organizations. How's your calendar for next week?

Looking forward to seeing you soon.

Regards,

Murray Baron

- Although you'll want to send a generic announcement to all of your clients, a personal note to special clients will be appreciated. Even a name change can be an excuse to continue selling yourself.

Company Name
Address
City, State Zip

Date

Mr. Owen Meadows
57 Shorewood Street
Baltimore, MD 21299

Dear Mr. Meadows:

Merchandise is easy to replace; your time and faith in us isn't. However, we'll do our best to satisfy you on all counts.

1. We've received complaints from a number of people who purchased the same model Izumi portable television as you did. The TVs were all part of a bad production run from the manufacturer. We've since received a new shipment and checked each one <u>thoroughly</u>. They're exactly what you expected in the first place: high resolution, brilliant color, and stereo sound.

2. We'll waive our fee to deliver your replacement television and pick up the defective one. Just let us know when someone will be home, and we'll try to accommodate your schedule. If you'd rather make the swap at the store, call in advance, and I'll have the new television ready for you. You won't have a moment's delay.

Please call me at 555-8122 to make arrangements. We apologize for your inconvenience.

Sincerely,

Sonia Black
Customer Service Manager

- Acknowledge the customer's complaint and your intention to replace the merchandise.

- Be specific about what the customer needs to do.

- Reassure the customer that you will handle any problem.

Apology for Delay in Shipment (7-45)

Company Name
Address
City, State Zip

Date

Ms. Anne McGauley
137 West Mt. Vernon Street
Lawton, OK 73505

Dear Ms. McGauley:

You have the patience of a saint, and I can't tell you how much I appreciate it. The gold-plated faucets for your remodeled hall bathroom will be delivered within two weeks (by November 18).

I finally have the whole story for you. I apologize for giving you information (sometimes inaccurate) in dribs and drabs. As you know, the factory in North Carolina had a fire. They said they'd be back in business within two weeks, so I told you there would be a three-week delay.

What they didn't tell me was that they couldn't repair the damage until they settled with their insurer. That took nearly a month. But everything has been resolved, and the unit will be in our hands shortly.

Thanks for sticking it out with us. The moment the faucets are installed, the long wait will almost have seemed worth it. They're beautiful, and will add another showcase feature to an already beautiful home.

Thank you for your business.

Cordially,

Jerry Steiner

- Think of long delays you've been involved with. The worst part is not knowing what's going on. By keeping the customer informed, you make him/her part of the process. It's appreciated.

- Reinforce the buying decision to take some of the sting out of the long wait.

Company Name
Address
City, State Zip

Date

Mr. Sven Saltnes
Kraakstad Import Ltd.
3220 Cloverdale Avenue
Cleveland, OH 44188

Dear Sven:

While our insurance will cover the cost of the damaged crystal we shipped from your Stockholm factory to your New York City warehouse, I realize it doesn't begin to cover the inconvenience. Please accept my apology on behalf of the company.

Our inspectors have suggested that the breakage occurred because of the extreme cold, rather than rough handling. Although your boxes meet our basic requirements, they feel strongly that better insulation would avoid a recurrence. Would you mind checking into that? If you have difficulty locating a box manufacturer who can accommodate you, I'd be happy to offer a recommendation.

Thanks for continuing to use National Transport Service. I'll call you soon to be certain the insurance claim was handled to your satisfaction.

Cordially,

Brian Cochran

- Make the apology and assure the client compensation will be forthcoming.

- Make suggestions for avoiding the problem in the future.

- Thank the client for his/her patronage.

Company Name
Address
City, State Zip

Date

Mr. Steven Kauffman
Kauffman Enterprises, Inc.
11 Princeton Street, NW
Washington, DC 20024

Dear Mr. Kauffman:

We boast the Capitol's largest limousine fleet, and yet we couldn't accommodate your business party. I'm proud we're so well thought of that we're constantly booked. But I'm sorry when we have to say no.

I hope you were pleased with our recommendation for a substitution. If you couldn't have our service, I wanted you to have one that would give your party the special treatment it deserves.

Thanks so much for thinking of us. Please keep us in mind for your future events. I want the opportunity to show you why we're considered the best. Good luck with your new business!

Very truly yours,

Elton Clearwater

- You can turn disappointment into a sense of satisfaction that you cared enough to say, "I'm sorry."

- Tell the customer how special his/her business is to you.

- Ask for future business.

Company Name
Address
City, State Zip

Date

Mrs. Paul Lambert
228 Wenonah Drive
Cedar Grove, WV 25039

Dear Mrs. Lambert:

I never knew how many people read our advertisements until the newspaper inadvertently listed our price as $29 instead of $229!

Thanks for understanding that we couldn't possibly honor the typesetter's mistake.   But because you were inconvenienced, we've enclosed a coupon that entitles you to 10% off any merchandise in stock. The coupon is good all year, and is even applicable to discounted items!

We appreciate your patronage and want you to continue to purchase our appliances and service for many years to come.

Cordially,

Sal Borregine
Owner

- State the error.

- Acknowledge that you're aware an inconvenience was caused (even if it wasn't your fault).

- Apologize by offering a special service.

Apology for Out of Stock (7-49)

Company Name
Address
City, State Zip

Date

Mr. James Barker
Century Hardware
450 Latham Ave
Schenectady, NY 12311

Dear Mr. Barker:

Will you help me decide if our tool buyer is a genius...or something considerably less?

During a recent buying trip, he found a new source for the best tool kit we've ever seen. We thought he was a genius, and we pushed our advertising department to the limit to get this product into the flyer which you mailed in your trading area last Friday.

Unfortunately, Century Hardware franchisees all over the country were overwhelmed by the response. Our buyer totally underestimated the tool kit's appeal . More rain checks were given out for this one item than for any other item in the entire history of Century Hardware!

It was a case of "not enough of a good thing." However, the manufacturer has put on an extra shift, and we anticipate a shipment within two weeks. We won't promote this kit again until you honor all your rain checks. You'll receive a notice when the kits come in.

We're very sorry your customers were inconvenienced, but you will have the tool kits soon. And it was our most successful tool promotion ever.

Sincerely,

David Channel
Vice President, Merchandising

- Yes, a simple "we're sorry" would suffice, but something extra helps customers (particularly franchisees) feel that the company cares.

- Be sure to advise that you will ship as soon as the missing merchandise is available.

Company Name
Address
City, State Zip

Date

Mr. George Bayard
79 Northwest Lane
Grand Island, NE 66803

Dear Mr. Bayard:

Our fulfillment people try so hard to please, they sometimes cause themselves problems. Let me explain.

As our mailer indicated, we were lucky enough to purchase the entire inventory of a famous-maker shoe company that went out of business. Unfortunately, the supply—as stated—was limited (first come, first served).

When we received your order for cordovan shoes, size 10E, they were already sold out. You should have been offered a choice of other colors available in that size. Instead, one of our shippers—who knew we were running out of size 10s in every color—decided to "do you a favor" and send you a brown pair, the next closest color.

I apologize for the inconvenience and aggravation we caused. I hope you'll understand that it happened out of a desire to help. If you'd like to keep the brown shoes, they're yours at half-price (only $34.95). If not, please return them at your convenience, freight collect.

Thanks for using our shop-by-mail service. I hope you'll let us serve you for many years to come.

Sincerely,

Patricia Steele
Customer Service

- By putting an unasked-for substitution into human terms, you can neutralize ill feelings.

- Offer an incentive for the customer to keep it.

- Express your desire to continue to do business.

Company Name
Address
City, State Zip

Date

Mr. Hugh Devereaux
Hunsberger & Shore Consultants, PE
534 Pacific Coast Highway
Hilo, HI 96720

Dear Mr. Devereaux:

Thank you for taking the time to complete the guest comment card concerning your recent stay at The Palace (San Francisco). We're sorry our concierge was unable to provide the assistance you required.

Please accept our apologies for the less-than-satisfactory experience. Since you're accustomed to staying at Palaces all over the country, you must know how much we pride ourselves on our service and attention to detail. Please be assured that corrective measures have been taken to prevent such occurrences in the future.

As a gesture of concern over this matter, and in an effort to restore your faith in our hotel, we would appreciate having the opportunity to welcome you back as our guest for one night, at our expense. When it's convenient, please contact me directly so that I may personally look after all arrangements.

We look forward to serving you again soon.

Sincerely yours,

Gilbert Corliss
Manager

- Explain that the poor service was unusual, and that you've taken action to insure against a repeat performance.

- Apologies are nice, but an action backing up the apology is even better. The offer of a free room or meal, for example, will help wash away any ill feelings.

Company Name
Address
City, State Zip

Date

Mr. Craig Moore
Airline Catering Service, Inc.
5280 Babbitt Avenue
Minneapolis, MN 55473

Dear Craig:

It's noon, and I'm still recovering from a morning meeting with our accounting management. I wish you could have joined me (misery loves company), since the directive I received concerns you—and thousands of other customers, as well.

According to the State tax people, the cups, filters, and other supplies we've been providing for your coffee service over the years are taxable. The State computes that we owe a staggering amount in back taxes. They originally told us the merchandise was exempt. The new State Treasurer has taken the attitude that "I'm not liable for past administration errors."

The point is, you'll be getting a revised invoice for this month's shipment that will include State sales tax. While I think the company's being scrupulously fair in not asking you to pay any back taxes, I apologize for this abrupt change in billing. Since this ruling affects every vendor, Craig, you'll find our pricing still reflects the best buy in the industry.

Sorry to be the one to break the news, but I wanted you to hear it from me before our accounting department sends its no-frills explanation. I'll call you in a few days.

Cordially,

Jack Richman

- A warm letter may not ease the burden of the increased cost, but it will avoid making you the butt of the prospect's ire.

Company Name
Address
City, State Zip

Date

Mr. Elmo Comiskey
Consumer's Warehouse Co-op
4909 Blue Grass Road
Louisville, KY 40297

Dear Mr. Comiskey:

First and foremost, we've credited you for the amount of $995.02 covered by invoice 335922-7. Secondly, thanks for letting us know about the error so quickly.

You're right, of course, that we agreed two months ago to put you on quarterly billing. Your next invoice isn't due for sixty days.

I'm sorry for the confusion this caused. Our Accounting Department has been reminded of the arrangement, and I can assure you this won't happen again.

Sincerely,

Richmond Melbourne

- Put the customer at ease immediately by stating that the problem has been taken care of.

- Thank the customer for pointing it out.

- Advise that the error will not occur again.

Company Name
Address
City, State Zip

Date

Mr. Seth Gershman
599 Third Street
Howard, SD 57357

Dear Mr. Gershman:

I don't blame you for being upset with us. If I were in your position, I'd be equally upset.

I've checked our records and, yes, we found that the camping equipment you purchased was returned. Why we've continued to bill you—despite your repeated calls and letters—is not only a puzzle, it's very frustrating. We work hard at minimizing problems like this.

If it's any consolation to you, I've called a meeting of our credit department to try to get to the root of the problem and avoid a recurrence. We value your business, and we'll do whatever it takes to make sure your future dealings with Stargell's Department Store are all pleasant ones.

Please give us the opportunity to continue to serve you.

Sincerely,

Jennifer Carthage
Manager, Customer Service

- Express your understanding of the customer's frustration.

- Tell the customer you are trying to correct the problem.

- Let the customer know you appreciate him/her.

Company Name
Address
City, State Zip

Date

Mr. Matthew Manning
28 Williamstown Road
Winterthur, DE 19735

Dear Mr. Manning:

We apologize for applying the wrong discount to your order, PO # A 3068-49, dated February 16.

An incorrect computer entry applied the discount for 200 units instead of the 2,000 units you actually ordered.

We have made the necessary adjustment in our records, and have sent you a new invoice. We hope you weren't inconvenienced by our error. Your continued satisfaction with our services is most important to us.

Cordially,

Eunice Bradshaw
Customer Relations

- Apologize for the error.

- State the cause of the error and how it has been corrected.

- Express confidence about a continuing relationship.

Company Name
Address
City, State Zip

Date

Mr. Richard Clifton
Cliffside Lumber
4842 East Highway 113
Mechanicsville, NJ 07730

Dear Mr. Clifton:

At this point I honestly don't know what happened to your shipment. I'm just glad you didn't wait longer before calling and checking.

We're air shipping (at our expense) new panelling and decorative edging, so you'll have them in time for your Spring Fix-Up Sale. They will arrive on Thursday, and you'll be able to meet your advertising obligations.

In the meantime, we're working on the missing shipment. We need some answers to be sure we don't put you or anyone else through unnecessary anxiety again. As soon as I know what went wrong, I'll let you know.

Thanks for your help, and for being on the ball. With customers like you, we try even harder.

Cordially,

Sam Wyckoff

- Acknowledge the problem and express appreciation that the customer brought it to your attention before it became a calamity.

- Assure the customer you're taking steps to avoid a recurrence.

Company Name
Address
City, State Zip

Date

Mr. Franklin Dickey
Conductor Division, Lannel-Warner Corporation
16330 Elsinor Street
Albuquerque, NM 87102

Dear Mr. Dickey:

Please accept our apology for the way in which you were treated by our order department. Under no circumstances should a customer of ours be shown anything but the utmost respect.

By way of explanation (not an excuse), we've had a change of personnel in our order department, including the supervisor. Obviously, we haven't done our job in training our new people to give our customers the courtesy and friendliness they have come to expect.

Thank you for bringing this problem to our attention. A more rigorous training program has been instituted to ensure that this behavior will never happen again. Your continued business means a great deal to us.

Sincerely,

Arlene Bernard
Customer Service Manager

- Apologize for the rudeness.

- Accept the blame.

- Tell the customer what corrective action you have taken.

Company Name
Address
City, State Zip

Date

Mr. Mark Montgomery
Palmer Auto Supplies
42 Mason Street
Kingsport, TN 37664

Dear Mr. Montgomery:

At first I had planned on removing Warren Pierce from your account. I know how dissatisfied you've been with the number of late shipments and the apparent misinformation he's given you about delivery times.

While that would be the easy thing to do, it wouldn't be the right thing to do. I checked into the matter and learned that we've had difficulty getting straight answers from our warehouse in Indiana. In addition, our traffic manager compounded that problem by repeatedly telling Warren each shipment would arrive "within 48 hours."

In short, we had a breakdown in communication and allowed it to filter to you through Warren. He is a fine young man who is terribly upset about losing credibility with you. I'd prefer not to penalize him for an error not of his making. (Plus, I believe he has much to offer you.)

I don't want to lose your account. If you would feel more comfortable with a different salesperson, I'll make the switch. But I truly hope you'll allow Warren to stay on as your representative.

Please think about it. Whatever you decide, rest assured that we've corrected our communication problem.

Sincerely,

Cindi Patchin
Vice President

- When a customer is dissatisfied, deal directly with the source of the dissatisfaction.

- Assure the client the problem is solved.

Company Name
Address
City, State Zip

Date

Mr. Gary McLain
President
Lighting Professionals, Inc.
1224 E. Main Street
Ogden, UT 84445

Dear Mr. McLain:

I received your letter questioning the charges for your last ad in Brilliant Ideas—the Lighting Magazine. I believe I can explain why you were charged at the open rate, even though, as you stated, you advertised in our magazine three times.

If you check point #2 of our rate card, you will see that our discounted rate for three insertions applies to ads placed within one calendar year. While your first two ads did appear in last year's issues, your last ad ran in January of this year, making it ineligible for the discounted rate.

We are very careful in preparing our rate cards to ensure that the information is spelled out clearly. Now that you are aware of our policy, you'll be able to take full advantage of our discounts. We value your business and hope you'll continue to advertise in the industry's leading publication.

Very truly yours,

Margaret Stone

- Don't be argumentative, but clearly state your position. Offer documentation.

- Tell the customer you value his/her business and want them to continue dealing with you.

Company Name
Address
City, State Zip

Date

Mr. Scott Lewis
The Exercise Shop
3580 Modesto Place
San Diego, CA 92132

Dear Mr. Lewis:

I don't blame you for "chomping at the bit," waiting for our 190H
FlexiGym single stack home gym to arrive in your showroom. When it's
displayed, you'll be thrilled at the new sales it will generate.

You can avoid delays on future orders by including the name of the
product and the model number on your purchase order. Had you done
that, the unit would have been in your showroom now. We have
eighteen models, and billing can't release shipping instructions without a
number. You didn't return our calls for a few days, so nothing could be
processed.

Also, we ship by truck. We are guaranteed delivery to the West Coast
within 10-14 days. In your case, it took the full 14. All of this means
you'll have the FlexiGym in five weeks instead of four.

We pride ourselves on prompt delivery. Be certain your purchase order
includes the proper information, and you'll never be disappointed.
Thanks for your business. Let me know if you need additional
brochures to give to your customers.

Sincerely,

Peg Simms
Customer Service Representative

- Tell the customer you understand his/her sense of disappointment.

- Explain how the customer can avoid delays in the future.

- Thank the customer for the business.

Company Name
Address
City, State Zip

Date

Mrs. Claire Eidman
882 Winona Lane
Sulphur Springs, TX 75482

Dear Mrs. Eidman:

I love optimistic people. But I think your optimistic nature may have been the source of our misunderstanding.

Our company policy is <u>never</u> to give a specific time for delivery. We'll name the day, but not the hour. (Too many factors are unpredictable for us to try to pinpoint a time.) When you told our dispatcher you wanted your furniture delivered by noon, she told you she'd try. Somehow, you interpreted that as a "yes." We did try, but our truck didn't arrive until 3:00 p.m. You were gone by then, and we had to reschedule.

Delivery problems aside, I hope you get many years of pleasure and pride from your new furniture. Thank you for buying from us. I hope we have the opportunity to serve you again.

Cordially,

Glen Carruthers
Store Manager

- Explain the source of the misunderstanding without pointing a finger too harshly.

- Suggest that you were not at fault.

- Compliment the customer on his/her purchase and ask for future business.

Company Name
Address
City, State Zip

Date

Mr. Justin L. Madison
358 East Allentown Street
Lovelock, NV 89419

Dear Mr. Madison:

I'm truly sorry our actions have upset you. As you're aware, our commitment to our customers is to provide the highest level of service of any bank in Nevada. I appreciate hearing from you when we fall short of that goal.

In researching your account to determine why you were assessed so many late charges, I noticed that your mortgage payment is usually received a day or two after the due date.

Our mortgage policy is quite clear: Payments must be received by the due date. If they're held up in the mail, it is not our responsibility. However, I've seen to it that the five late charges have been removed from our records and your account credited. But we can't continue to be so forgiving with subsequent late payments, and we won't repeat this good faith gesture.

I suggest you mail your payments a few days earlier or bring payment to one of our branch offices to insure prompt credit.

Thanks for using Jackson Financial. If any questions remain, please call me at 702-555-5959.

Sincerely,

Lincoln Wray
Vice President

- Don't alienate a customer just to prove you're right. Express your understanding of the complaint.

- Demonstrate that you're willing to let bygones be bygones, but future discrepancies cannot be tolerated.

- Thank the customer for using your service.

Company Name
Address
City, State Zip

Date

Mr. Liam Flannery
Arroyo Nucleonics
Building 3B
Sedona, AZ 86341

Dear Liam:

After a very thorough inspection and test procedure, I can report that the failures of the trip system breakers you're experiencing are avoidable simply through proper maintenance.

The only thing you need to do is step up the frequency of testing. In fact, we're working with Bob Simon to have the system include testing of the breakers at the end of each day's shifts. We've just completed the first enhanced test with your tech staff on Units 1 and 2.

There may have been some confusion, Liam, about how these breakers function under varying conditions. If you'll check our procedure bulletin E-1058, which your tech department received when we installed the new system, you'll see that they are functioning as specified. By stepping up your inspections to the recommended level, reliability is assured.

Thanks for bringing this question to my attention. I hope every "problem" is so easily resolved.

Regards,

Alan Simpson
VP, Engineering Support

- It's never easy to tell an important client he missed the boat, but it can be done well. State that you were personally involved in the review.

- If there's a specification sheet, advertisement, or any document that supports your position, quote from it.

- Thank the client for communicating.

Company Name
Address
City, State Zip

Date

Mr. Robert Young
142 Kensington Avenue
Richmond, VA 23242

Dear Mr. Young:

I'm sorry you're upset that we are not fixing your eight month old garbage disposal. As you know, we've followed our warranty to the letter—and beyond.

When you purchased our XE-100 model, you declined installation in return for a $25.00 discount. As noted on your warranty, if a factory-authorized serviceman performs the installation, you're covered for parts and labor for one year from the date of purchase. If you don't use an authorized serviceman, you're covered for parts (not labor) for a period of three months.

When you called us for warranty coverage, we gave you the benefit of the doubt. You were already two weeks past your three month cut-off, but we made an allowance because you're a good customer. In other words, Mr. Young, we didn't charge you for parts even though we were well within the spirit and letter of the warranty to do so.

If there are any other questions about the warranty, or other Roberts Company products, please call on my personal line (612) 555-0819.

Sincerely,

Patrick Orso
Customer Service

- State that you have fulfilled your obligations "above and beyond" the call of duty.

- Explain the terms of the warranty in non-technical language.

- Tell the customer you appreciate his/her business, and invite a personal call for more information.

Company Name
Address
City, State Zip

Date

Mr. Edward Lerman
Vice President, Administration
Goodman Motor Freight
6038 E. Airport Road
St. Paul, MN 55101

Dear Ed:

We've insured you and your drivers for almost 22 years in one of the more harmonious relationships in the industry. I don't want it to end because of a misunderstanding with your controller's office.

Your company demands that we pay for an accident involving your driver, Mr. Norris Jones. I'm not sure why Mr. Jones was driving one of your vehicles. Our standard examination (see the attached report) disclosed that Mr. Jones' lack of visual acuity—with or without corrective lenses—made him ineligible to be a heavy vehicle driver.

If your company wanted Mr. Jones to drive, someone should have applied for a medical waiver (section 391.47 of the Federal Motor Carrier Safety Regulations guidelines). Without the waiver, Mr. Jones is not covered by our policy.

This isn't a case of wrapping ourselves in a technicality, Ed. There would be no question about payment had Mr. Jones been physically suited to drive a heavy vehicle. Will you talk to your controller and see if I'm missing something?

Thanks for interceding.

Regards,

Lyle Davis

- Explain your position without emotion.

- Quote applicable rules or regulations without being sanctimonious about it.

Company Name
Address
City, State Zip

Date

Ms. Louise Banner
Vice President, Computer Operations
Xenon Industries
111 Apian Way
Reno, NV 89510

Dear Ms. Banner:

I regret the problems caused by the down time at your computer installation in Reno. Now that the crisis is over, I'm sure you'll feel differently about instituting a lawsuit for loss of services.

I've checked into the matter thoroughly and here's what I've learned. Our field engineers arrived at your site within 24 hours of the problem being reported, and had your computer up and running by 6:00 the following morning. They would have arrived earlier, but heavy fog at O'Hare airport delayed their flight for eight hours. They tried to arrange a charter, but the FAA ordered all aircraft to stay on the ground during the weather emergency.

I'm sure you can see we did everything that was humanly possible to get your X1000 back in service in the shortest possible time. And by patching you into our Denver mainframe while your computer was inoperative, you really lost very little processing time (less than four hours).

I'll be coming to Reno next week and would like to discuss the matter with you then. I'm hopeful you'll decide not to go forward with a lawsuit, given the details of the situation and the excellent service record of our company during the last eight years.

Very truly yours,

John Rodale
Senior Vice President

- Letters dealing with serious problems should come from a top company officer.

- Explain the difficulty and the steps your company took to rectify it.

- Reaffirm your excellent track record.

- Arrange a meeting; in situations of this nature, a face-to-face discussion is almost always called for.

Company Name
Address
City, State Zip

Date

Mr. Stephen Shuler
Hawk/Link, Incorporated
7218 Sandy Ridge Plaza
New Castle, DE 19720   RE: Purchase Order
                             5218A. Ref. No. H1907QS8.

Dear Mr. Shuler:

This is a job that's had so many twists, turns, delays, and sidesteps, we could have used a full-time researcher just to track who said what and when. It's confusing, but fortunately we have all the records to review.

I've enclosed a copy of the historical data in our file, dating back nearly three years. If you'll look at specification 1-5218A on page 7, paragraph VII, section 3, and page 8, paragraph VIII, section 7, you'll find the references that were missing in your file.

The CV Flow Test for the 3" valve was clearly agreed upon (at a cost of $12,812.00). And even though the work was done more than two years later, we maintained the pricing. Now we'd appreciate your lifting the "embargo" you placed on payment.

I'll call you next week to see if any questions remain and to talk to you about future jobs. We enjoy working with Hawk/Link.

Sincerely,

John D. Stockdale

Enclosure

- To ease the sting of proving your client wrong, let him/her know you're aware of the complexity of order records.

- Refer to documentation that supports your position.

- Tell the client you'll follow up. Be sure to affirm that this is a desirable relationship.

Selling Yourself 8

Have you ever had the experience of reading a "help wanted" ad and having bells go off in your head? The job requirements fit you so well, you might have written the ad yourself. You <u>knew</u> you were right for the job, so you dashed off your resume and waited expectantly for the call. And waited. And finally it dawned on you that the job that was perfect for you went to someone else—you never even had a chance.

What made the difference between your resume—which was ignored—and another—which got the applicant the job? The answer is in the impression the resume made (or didn't). Many people don't think of the resume's role of creating a "first impression." They're too busy focusing on the interview or looking even farther into the future. What they don't realize is that unless their resume makes just the right first impression, there won't <u>be</u> any interview.

Job Search. There are two parts to a job application: the cover letter and the resume. Both are important in ensuring you'll make it to the interview phase. The cover letter to the resume is very similar to the cover letter that accompanies a proposal. It focuses on highlights in the attached document that represent major benefits to the buyer (in this case, the prospective employer). It's the key to stirring up interest in the main event that follows (the interview).

Think of how you prepare for an interview. You put on your best clothes. You fuss in front of a mirror. You comb and recomb your hair, polish your shoes, put on your best face. You should do no less with your printed message, your first impression to a prospective employer.

It might help to understand how the cover letter and resume relate to the interview if you think of the job search as an advertising campaign. The cover letter is the "tease," and the resume is the full-page blockbuster. If you don't do a good job with the "tease," your reader may never get to the blockbuster.

Some of the best examples of a "tease" in advertising are the coming attractions for new movies. The snippets that are chosen for the audience previews are designed to show the picture in its best light. That's exactly what a cover letter should do for a resume. Excite the reader about the feature presentation that will follow.

Resumes can take many forms. Select the one that best suits your strengths. It can be chronological, listing each job separately by date of employment, starting with the most recent job and working backwards. This format works best for people who have steadily progressed with each job, and who have spent a number of years at each step along the way.

If you've had many jobs with short tenure in each, you might want to opt for a functional resume, which highlights key responsibilities and achievements rather than focusing on company names and job duration. A senior executive may be best served by a letter resume. And, of course, there are combinations. Just remember: a resume is your advertising literature. It is not a place where you should be modest. You'll want to put the best possible interpretation on your work history.

Selling Your Product. Modesty is not a virtue when you are the focal point of your sell. You need to convince your potential buyer that you are the expert and that your product or service will provide him or her with an edge the prospective buyer is missing. The same principles of selling discussed throughout this book apply here: 1) get the reader's attention, 2) identify a need and tell how you will fill it, 3) convince the reader to buy from you, and 4) ask for the order.

Remember, when selling yourself, market your strengths as effectively as you would sell someone else's product.

Your Name
Address
City, State Zip

Date

Mr. Tyler Mercer
Quality Pleasure Boats
1307 E. 12th Street
Bellevue, WA 98007

Dear Mr. Mercer:

Do you have a salesperson on staff who has designed scaffolding for modifications on a mast?   Is there anyone in sales who has meticulously measured every inch of a drydock floor because there was no room for error?

I'm a Master Shipwright, one of only two on the West Coast who is qualified to work on steel <u>and</u> wood decking. And I've received twelve consecutive years of outstanding performance ratings from the San Diego Naval Shipyard, an achievement that is not easily duplicated.

I want to put my skills to work for you, Mr. Mercer. Not in building ships and boats, but in <u>selling</u> them. I'm confident that I can do a better job of explaining what makes your boats great buys than anyone on your staff.

I'll be in Bellevue the week of July 10, and I'd like to discuss a sales position with you. I'll call next week to see if you're interested in having a master builder on board. It will certainly give you braggin' rights with potential customers.

Cordially,

Kenneth Cavanaugh

- Changing careers requires a strong belief in your abilities. Make the reader sense the depth of these feelings.

- Think about this letter from the reader's perspective—not from your own. What can you do for <u>him</u>?

- Use the letter to showcase the skills that apply to the position. Don't waste time with extraneous information.

Your Name
Address
City, State Zip

Date

Mr. George Durand
Macro Executive Marketing
130 Martin Avenue/Suite 1100
San Rafael, CA 94903

Dear Mr. Durand:

Someone once told me never to approach a headhunter; a headhunter
has to find you. Frankly, I haven't become a success by waiting for
anyone to find me. So let me save you the time and effort of looking:

1. I'm the <u>top</u> salesperson for the polymer division of one of
   the nation's leading chemical companies.

2. I'm earning six figures, and have been for seven years.

3. I want to move into sales management but have no
   immediate opportunity in my company.

I can give you a combination of performance, knowledge, superior time
management and client contact skills, and youth (I'm 37). I'd like to
demonstrate my communication skills during an interview. If you're
pressed for time, perhaps you'd be my guest for lunch.

I'll call on Friday to arrange an interview.

Sincerely,

Rick Zaslow

- Aggressiveness sells salespeople. Demonstrate your selling skills by breaking convention. You have everything to gain by being bold.

- List your key selling points (don't send a resume).

- Be insistent about an interview, and follow up your demand for one.

Your Name
Address
City, State Zip

Date

Mr. Michael Cahn
Personnel Department
Grove Apparel
4804 N. Locust Street
Athens, GA 30613

Dear Mr. Cahn:

Thank you for making my interview so enjoyable. You conveyed a real sense of excitement about the marketing assistant position. I hope I was able to leave you with a similar feeling about my qualifications for the job.

I'm confident that my experience in researching and developing marketing plans for a Fortune 500 company, coupled with my enthusiasm and the ability to "get the job done," make me an ideal candidate.

I appreciate your time and interest. I hope to have the opportunity to contribute to Grove Apparel's continuing growth.

Sincerely,

Karen Adamson

- To demonstrate your serious commitment to the job, always send a follow-up letter.

- Start with a brief "thank you." Reiterate your pertinent history. Ask for the job.

- Keep the letter brief.

Your Name
Address
City, State Zip

Mr. William Bass
Coreander & Sullivan
1256 Worthington Street
Topeka, KS 66666

Dear Bill:

I just returned from a relaxing, productive vacation on the West Coast. I brought back a few extra pounds, a great tan, and a new understanding about what I want to do for a living. The last item is the reason for this letter, and I hope you can give me some valued advice about it.

During my three years as a corporate training director, I've had the opportunity to delegate countless projects to a dynamic, creative staff. Their professional skills have made my job easy—and, recently, somewhat less than rewarding. Managing others who are doing what I want to do has become frustrating and demotivating. I remember nostalgically when their projects used to be mine. The feeling's not new; I've had it for months. But I can't shake it anymore.

My objective, Bill, is to find a hands-on position in a project-oriented organization where I can use my skills in development, design, and program implementation. I believe I have a lot to offer.

I would appreciate any ideas you might have about my decision and how I might pursue my career goals. I think I have the beginning of a great success story—what I need now is a middle, a transition step. Please be in touch. I'll treat for lunch if you're planning to be in town.

Regards,

Scott Forsythe

- One of the best ways to get a new job is to let people in the field know you're seeking one.

- Be specific about what you want or you won't get it!

Sender's Name
Address
City, State Zip
Phone Number

Date

Dear Sir/Madam:

My twelve years of experience as plant manager of a medium-sized petrochemical company makes me well-qualified for the Director of Plant Operations position, advertised in Sunday's <u>Inquirer</u>.

During my tenure, I managed a tough union shop but never experienced a work stoppage. I'm a strong negotiator and communicator. Both management and workers respond well to my style. Incidentally, my plant was rated the most efficient of its type in last year's American Petroleum Institute's annual survey.

May we discuss how my skills can most benefit your company? I can be reached at the above phone number after 6 pm.

Sincerely,

Harlan Thomas

- Quickly establish the connection between the advertisement and your background.

- Pinpoint one or two key accomplishments to illustrate your grasp of the position.

- Ask for an appointment.

Your Name
Address
City, State Zip

Date

Mr. Cleveland Brinker
METRO Cellular Systems
1052 N. Courtyard Road
Houston, TX 77081

Dear Mr. Brinker:

I'd just purchased a METRO cellular phone when I read your Help Wanted ad in the Chronicle. I was so impressed with your phone, I decided to apply for the job.

I did a lot of comparative research before purchasing the XL50 model, and its performance has justified my findings. It's the best in the business, and I'd like to be part of the team that tries to put one in every car in the country.

My resume (enclosed) will tell you that I fit your basic requirements: I have five years in sales, I own a late-model four-door car, and I have a successful record of selling tangibles and intangibles. A meeting will demonstrate my knowledge of this marketplace, and my desire to put that knowledge to work on your sales force.

I can help you move cellular systems.

Sincerely,

Richard Leyva

- Try to show some form of affinity with the product or company to which you're responding (I own one).

- Briefly explain that you match up well with the requirements listed in the ad.

- Ask for a meeting to sell yourself. Let your enthusiasm shine through.

Your Name
Address
City, State Zip

Date

Mr. Claude Milton
Bello Textiles
Old Waverly Road
Albuquerque, NM 87156

Dear Mr. Milton:

I was extremely pleased to receive your offer for the Sales Manager
position at Bello Textiles. I'm confident that my ten years of experience
in a number of sales capacities in the textile industry have prepared me
for the challenges at your fine company.

I have one point to discuss, however, before I can accept the position.
At all the other companies for which I've worked, expenses were
reimbursed on a weekly basis. Your letter indicated that
reimbursements would be made monthly. Since I anticipate incurring
significant expenses for trips to both the East and West Coast plants
twice a month, it will be important to have expenses reimbursed weekly.
If this is not possible, I will require a cash advance to cover those
expenses.

I'll call you early next week to discuss this with you. Since this is the
only open issue, I'm sure we can resolve the matter and clear the way
for me to start at Bello on the 19th as you suggested.

I'm raring to go!

Sincerely,

Merrill Chase

- If there is a job offer-related issue, deal with it <u>before</u> you take the job.

- Be specific about your concerns, suggest a solution and, ideally, an alternative as well.

- Reiterate your strengths and your desire to take the position.

Company Name
Address
City, State Zip

Date

Mr. Peter Collins
Kahn & Nugent
4002 Woodward Avenue
Allentown, PA 18195

Dear Peter:

As you may have guessed, our entire sales force has been given notice. Such is the fate of those on the wrong side of a merger.

Bloodied but unbowed, I've started a job search (with the blessing of my company; they've given us a generous six month phase-out). I'd like to include a letter of recommendation from you with my resume. It's pretty impressive for a potential employer to see ex-clients "selling" a salesman.

Will you do it? I think we've had the kind of relationship that lends itself to mutual support...and I could use yours right now.

Thanks for everything. I'll talk to you in a week or so.

Cordially,

Brian Wooster

- When the ax falls (as it does increasingly in an age of mergers and acquisitions), seek help from every direction.

- Don't bad-mouth your current company. It makes you look bad.

- State what you want and how you'll use it.

Your Name
Address
City, State Zip

Date

Mr. Jonathan Rosen
Rider Marketing Corp.
1390 Endicott Street
Shreveport, LA 71109

Dear Mr. Rosen:

After only ten months with National Business Systems, I find that I am the casualty of a major corporate cutback.

I'm now the proud possessor of superb selling skills, a letter of regret from NBS, an apartment with a two-year lease in a new city, and no immediate place to put my skills to work. With your knowledge of the local marketplace, I'm hopeful that you can help me.

The enclosed resume outlines my successful sales experiences in insurance and retail marketing. With your perspective, you may be able to suggest some key people to whom I should speak.

I appreciate your time and thoughts very much. I'll call you in a few days to see what you can suggest. Thank you.

Cordially,

Linda Smith

- Instead of asking for a job directly, you may get more assistance by asking for help. It puts no pressure on a prospective employer, who may make recommendations or may interview you himself/herself.

- Enclose a resume.

- Let the prospect know you will call.

Your Name
Address
City, State Zip

Date

Ms. Sally Gardner
Personnel Director
OGI, Inc.
4204 Valley Lane Corporate Center
Great Valley, IA 36363

Dear Ms. Gardener:

I have yet to see a resume that can <u>really</u> tell a story of what's behind an individual, particularly when that individual is short on work experience but long on drive and desire. Please allow me to "fill in between the lines":

1. I averaged 17 credits a semester, more than most students. I wanted to take advantage of as many different courses as possible and still graduate in four years.

2. Despite my heavy credit load, I was associate editor of the school paper, working until one in the morning, two days a week, throughout my junior and senior years.

3. I held part-time jobs, including stints with AT&T (soliciting new installations) and West Coast Video (retail sales). I also held full-time jobs every summer, waiting on tables and caddying.

4. With it all, I maintained a B+ average and received strong recommendations (enclosed) from many professors.

I'm bright, and I work hard. I'd like to put those attributes to work in your management trainee program. I'll call you next week to set up an appointment.

Sincerely,

Timothy Ryan

- Paint a picture of confidence.

- Demonstrate your ability to do lots of things well, no matter how non-job-related they may seem.

- Be sure to establish a follow-up.

Your Name
Address
City, State Zip
Phone Number

Education
1987-1990 University of Iowa, Ames, Iowa
           BA in English (Double Minor: Economics, Film)
           Elected to National Golden Key Honors Society for academic
           excellence.

Writing Experience
1987-1989 The Daily Iowan (University of Iowa's award-winning newspaper)
           Film Critic/Film Editor
           Wrote numerous reviews and film-related articles. Promoted to editor,
           with responsibility for editing all entertainment articles.

1987-1990 Sun Publishers, Inc., Boone, IA
           Editorial Assistant (Summer)
           Proofread and edited scripts and workbooks for children's books and
           videos, including <u>The Watch Children</u> and <u>How Many Stripes Does A
           Zebra Have?</u>

1988   Video Outlook Magazine, Des Moines, IA
           Assistant Editor (Summer)
           Wrote and edited articles, columns and stories dealing with the
           development of video retailing.

Other Experience
1989-1990 University of Iowa Credit Union, Ames, IA
           Assistant to Credit Manager
           General office help, investment research.

1989   GT&T, Ames, IA
           Salesperson (Fall)
           Fall solicitation program to sell products, services, and new installations.

- When primary experience is in part-time and summer work, lead off with education.

- Group any jobs—no matter the chronology—that demonstrate competencies you want the prospective employer to focus on.

Your Name
Address
City, State Zip

Date

Ms. Mary Hurst
Trinity Sales Corp.
577 W. Eagle Street
Englewood, CO 80110

Dear Ms. Hurst:

Without any formal sales training, I quickly found a niche at Walden Ironworks. In my first year, I negotiated more than one million dollars in contracts to builders and architects. With increased responsibilities in my second year, I negotiated new discounts with key suppliers, increasing gross profits by nearly 5%.

I know I have bright prospects at Walden; I've been told that a Regional Sales Manager job is just around the corner. But I want to live in Colorado, and I'd like to work for a company that's considered "the best in its field." If you have an opening for someone who has a knack for selling hard-to-crack companies, I'd like to have the opportunity to show you why I've come so far, so fast.

I think we have a lot to offer each other. I'll call in a few days to set up an appointment.

Cordially,

Ken Kragen

• Demonstrate that you're someone "on the way up." Highlight your key accomplishments.

• Tell the prospective employer you'll follow up.

Your Name
Address
City, State Zip
Phone Number

OBJECTIVE
Sales position with growth potential.

QUALIFICATIONS
A short, but dynamic record of outstanding sales achievement. The ability to learn quickly, work hard, and become a top producer in an outstanding sales organization.

PROFESSIONAL EXPERIENCE
1988 to   Walden Ironworks, Kansas City, Kansas
present   Sales Representative/Consultant

             Walden is a distributor of doors and hardware to commercial and residential construction companies and architects. With virtually no sales experience, I took a weak territory and built it into seven figures in the first 12 months. I assumed vendor negotiation responsibility in my second year and developed new purchasing standards.

1985-1988   Little Opera House Dinner Theater, Denver, Colorado
             Technical Director

             Management of technical program including, set, light, and sound design.

EDUCATION
1981-1985   University of Colorado, Denver, Colorado
             B.A., Communications

INTERESTS
             Creative writing, public speaking.

REFERENCES ON REQUEST

- Offer qualifications that reflect your experience and ambition.

- Highlight your current sales experience.

- If your interests relate to your career path, even indirectly, show them.

Your Name
Address
City, State Zip
Phone Number

OBJECTIVE
Sales management position.

EXPERIENCE

1988
to present
Regional Sales Director, Instructional Material
McBurney, Low, and Associates, Baltimore, MD

Developed a previously closed market in five states. Responsible for recruitment, training, and direction of six salespeople; Won Top Sales Region two consecutive years. The company has merged with Littleton Publishers.

1986-1988
Special Education Sales
McNabb Hall Company, New York City

Doubled sales in one year and was rated second in profitability in the entire United States for 1987.
Left for a better position.

1984-1986
Eastern Regional Sales Manager, Audiovisual Sales
Domino Book Company, Chicago, IL

Upon being named Top Salesman of the year in 1985, was promoted to management position. Was responsible for recruitment, training and direction of three salespeople.
Domino discontinued regional sales directors.

1983-1984   Salesman
             Open Forum Readers, Chicago, IL

             Sold and serviced school accounts in two states and trained two
             consultants to implement program application.
             Because of a change of management, sought another position.

1981-1983   Assistant Director, Trade Sales
             Protect Finishes, Grand Rapids, MI

             Began as a trade salesman, and promoted to Assistant Director
             position after one year.
             The retail division was discontinued.

PERSONAL INFORMATION
Married with two children.
Active in church and community affairs, acting as rehabilitation advisor for high
school "problem" students. Recently involved in teaching literacy to inner-city drop-
outs and training others in the community to do the same.

EDUCATION

1977-1981   University of Michigan, Ann Arbor, Michigan
             BA in Business Administration with major in Labor Relations
             MBA with major in Marketing

- Resumes of people who have held a number of jobs should include reasons for leaving.

- Focus on key points. Otherwise your resume can take on book-like proportions.

Your Name
Address
City, State Zip
Phone Number

Date

Mr. H. Cabot Sutter
President
Troy Agricultural Products
1722 W. Alameda Street
Sioux City, IA 51112

Dear Mr. Sutter:

We're entering an era that many economists are predicting will be "challenging." Early evidence, according to leading business journals, shows that the economists are correct.

It's more important than ever that your sales and marketing efforts be led by someone with a comprehensive business overview, particularly in agribusiness. I'm a senior executive who would like to play a role in steering Troy through what one economist called "the thickening fog bank."

Think about how a person with these accomplishments might best fit into your organization:

- o Created strategic and tactical marketing plans for Fortune 500 company

- o Directed national sales forces for three Fortune 500 giants

- o Established national dealer network for leased sales

I'd like to put my 25 years of sales and marketing success to work for Troy. May we meet at your earliest convenience? I'll call you next week to set up an appointment.

Sincerely,

Charles Ingram

- Senior executives should not send resumes. Strong letters, listing key accomplishments are recommended. Letters should be directed to the president or chairman.

Your Name
Address
City, State Zip

Date

Mr. William Parrish
Station Manager
WGBK
3118 Walker Square
Hollywood, FL 33022

Dear Mr. Parrish:

Do you have a place for a salesperson who, in less than a year, generated a 40% sales increase and then was promoted to Assistant Sales Manager?

I'd like the opportunity to tell you about the role I played in helping my station achieve top three status in Miami...and how I think I can put my skills to work for you and WGBK.

Thanks for your interest. I'll call to see when we can get together.

Sincerely,

Edward Stein

- Although the resume accompanying this letter may not be tailored to a specific audience, your cover letter should be. A change of a word here and there, and you will have a customized cover letter that demonstrates keen interest to the prospective employer.

- If you don't want to be called at your office, suggest that you will phone for the appointment.

Your Name
Address
City, State Zip
Phone Number

OBJECTIVE   To put my sales, marketing, and management skills to work for an aggressive, results-oriented firm.

BACKGROUND   Eleven years of successful sales and management
SUMMARY   experience. I'm a strong closer who has achieved success via prospecting, telemarketing, direct sales, and constant follow-up. I've sold purchasing agents and presidents, and I've created marketing plans that have opened new avenues of business.

PROFESSIONAL
ACCOMPLISHMENTS

Sales Management   Increased territory sales from $200,000 to $280,000 in just nine months (didn't get a chance to do more because I was promoted to Assistant Sales Manager).

Restructured sales force and increased national sales by 22%.

Created a telemarketing squad that quickly achieved profitable status, jumping from zero to more than $350,000 in a year.

Marketing   Developed a marketing strategy that helped turn around a troubled company, tripling sales in the first year, then doubling them in the second.

Developed a media presence through press releases and public seminars.

PROFESSIONAL EXPERIENCE

1987-present	Salesperson/Assistant Sales Manager Radio Station WSHH, Miami, Florida
1985-1987	Salesperson National Life Insurance, Ft. Lauderdale, Florida
1982-1985	Salesperson Atlas Business Schools, West Palm Beach, Florida
1979-1982	Salesperson Office Automation, Inc., Miami, Florida

EDUCATION

1975-1979	University of Texas, Austin, Texas Graduated with Honors, Business Administration
1990	Seminar: Building Relationships with People
1989	Seminar: 25 Biggest Mistakes in Selling (and how to avoid them)

- With a solid record of sales success, focus on your achievements rather than on specific jobs.

- Include related educational programs, including self-study, seminars and workshops. It shows a commitment.

Your Name
Address
City, State Zip

Date

Mr. William Stillwell
Sales Manager
General American, Inc.
32 Peach Blossom Avenue
Peoria, IL 61645

Dear Bill:

I hope you're as pleased as I am that I decided to work for you and
General American. Can you believe a year has gone by so quickly?
And what a year! According to the annual report, sales are up, profits
are up, and the future holds considerable promise.

I think you'll agree that I've made major contributions to our success. I
exceeded my first year's goal by nearly 40%, and I'm projecting another
major increase for this new year.

So I'm sure you'll understand why I think a raise in my base pay is in
order. I've earned it. Last year I added more clients than any other
salesperson, and more will follow.

When I was hired, you said if my performance was "what it should be,"
you'd make an adjustment in my base. I believe it's been even better
than you expected.

Please let me know when it would be convenient for us to meet and
review compensation. Thanks!

Cordially,

Sandy Rawlins

- Treat this as you would any other sales effort. Point out the features and benefits you
  provide, and ask for a meeting to close the sale.

- Base your pay raise request on <u>your</u> performance.

Company Name
Address
City, State Zip

To: L.C. "Bud" Fields

From: Barry Gordon

Date:

Subject: Leave of Absence

I love my job.

As one of your inside sales coordinators, I have the chance to be an entrepreneur, manager, consultant, telephone marketer, promoter, and researcher. I probably omitted a few dozen other jobs, but you get the idea.

Yet I have a nagging feeling I can do a better job. I'm two full-time semesters away from having the knowledge that will give me an additional edge. I need eight uninterrupted months to finish my MBA and start applying it to our sales and marketing goals.

Those eight months would translate into two more years of night school. I really want to complete the degree as soon as possible...but I don't want to leave the company. Will you grant me an eight-month leave of absence, without pay, from September 1 to May 1?

The payoff will be big for both of us, Bud. I'll bring marketing expertise to the department that's not available to us now...and staying late won't be a problem once I'm finished with school!

I'd like to meet and discuss the concept with you. I know this has never been done here before (I checked with Personnel), but I think there are some compelling reasons to do it now.

I'll call you to reserve a time. And thanks in advance for your consideration.

- State your reasons for wanting the leave, along with any possible benefits to the company.

- Ask for a meeting to discuss the issue.

Company Name
Address
City, State Zip

To: Warren Evans

From: Leon Crowder

Date:

Subject: Transfer to Mid-West Region

I've heard that Hunter Stoddard has resigned as mid-West Regional Sales Manager. I know that's not official yet, but assuming that I'm correct, I'd like you to move me into that slot.

This will have a positive snowball effect for the company:

1. You put your best regional sales manager (me) in an area that, by your own admission, needs strengthening.

2. You give my job to Laurie Schutter. Laurie's been increasingly frustrated at having "nowhere to go in the company" (her words), and this will keep her with us. She has the fire, determination, and respect needed to succeed as a regional manager.

3. You reward Ray Brothers for his great performance in a small territory by giving him Laurie's territory.

Everybody's happy (including my wife who very much wants to be closer to her elderly parents) with this arrangement, and that means the company benefits in a big way.

The logic appears irrefutable, Warren. What do you say?

- This somewhat informal approach is appropriate for people who are familiar and comfortable with each other. It's easily adaptable, however, to a more formal style.

- List the reasons for the desired change. Make it easy for the reader to follow your logic.

- Ask for the "order."

Company Name
Address
City, State Zip

Date

Mr. Edward Weiss
Carteret Chemicals
4111 DuPont Way
Oklahoma City, OK 73173

Dear Mr. Weiss:

Does this sound familiar?

The finance department works with a Burroughs system (pre-UNISYS); Research and Development is strictly IBM; Sales uses Western Union Electronic Mail and, of course, no one can access anyone else's information no matter the urgency!

> Q. How does this happen?
> A. Everyone is so busy, no one takes an overview.

> Q. What's the impact on the company?
> A. Nothing goes smoothly because no one knows what's going on.

> Q. How do you "fix" it?
> A. Choose one:
> _ Spend about $250,000 to bring in new hardware.
> _ Bring in the "connectivity" expert who can make
> your computers talk to each other...with no
> disruption in the workplace.

That's really not much of a choice, is it? Will you give me about 30 minutes to explain how I perform corporate "connectivity?" Think about your internal computing problems and we'll talk about them when I call you next week.

Sincerely,

Sylvan Greenblatt, Ph.D.

- Selling yourself is just like selling any service—stress the benefits to the prospect.

- Don't be afraid to be original in your presentation (question/answer format).

- Suggest that the prospect prepare him/herself for your call. Then you'll both be ready to talk business.

Company Name
Address
City, State Zip

<u>If you can't answer all of these questions,
chances are you'll *never* reach the boardroom.</u>

Dear Non-Financial Executive:

Do you know how your company compares to industry averages in liquidity, leverage, activity, and profitability? No? I'll bet the 24-year old guy with the MBA does. He was trained to know that kind of information and how to use it.

Does the price-earnings ratio of your company's stock reflect your assessment? You say you don't even understand the question? You can bet that the CFO does...and in today's business clirᵃate that puts him at least a rung or two above you on the corporate ladder.

Do you know the mix of financing used by your company? Do you know how this mix reflects the business characteristics of your company and the industry?

If you don't know the answer to these and dozens of other financial questions, you might as well forget those dreams of moving up, up and away...unless you sign up for my three day survival course on jungle economics!

Give me just three days, and I'll give you the financial background you never even knew you needed. I'll teach you the lingo that the financial guys use to exclude you. And I'll show you how to use your new information to get where you want to be...where you <u>deserve</u> to be.

Make a decision that will earn you thousands of dollars of additional income each year, and add prestige to your life. Mail the enclosed postpaid card <u>now</u>, and take the step that will move your career to a new plateau.

Bill Reilly
Financial Street Fighter

P.S. I'll take 10% off the seminar price if you mail your reservation before February 20!

- The success of a mailing like this is dependent on targeting the audience. It's written to appeal to a middle-aged executive's dreams of success and fear of failure.

- Use questions to involve the reader.

- Demand a decision.

- Use a strong P.S. to get the order.

Company Name
Address
City, State Zip

Date

Mr. Norbert Paul
Albert Paul Developers, Inc.
200 North Pennsylvania Boulevard
Scranton, PA 18589

Dear Mr. Paul:

When the PANTEL Group purchased a huge tract of land in rural New Jersey about ten years ago, most developers scratched their heads, shrugged their shoulders, and snickered that "the old man" was losing his touch.

That area, of course, is no longer rural. In fact, it's the most important high-tech strip outside of Silicon Valley in California. It's now called Greenwood Hills, and it may be the biggest boomtown in America.

But PANTEL wasn't the only developer to be out in front of the pack. Lincoln/Turner in Colorado, Canterbury in Arizona, and CarTech in Missouri are just a few of the developers who stay on top by using the <u>Population Econocast</u> monthly research report.

Our patented computer model has tracked shifting trends across the U.S., providing invaluable demographic and real estate information that is worth, conservatively, millions of dollars.

If you plan to be a leader in the field, you need access to accurate research reports. Mail the enclosed card—or call 312-555-7567—to reserve your subscription to Population Econocast Report.

Sincerely,

Clay Shore

P.S. Subscriptions received before April 1 will receive, <u>absolutely free</u>, our booklet "The 10 Largest Growth Markets for the Nineties."

- If you can convey that sense of "I know something you don't," you'll hook your audience, especially if big money is involved.

- List major subscribers for credibility.

- Use a strong P.S. to increase response (free premium, time limit, etc.)

Company Name
Address
City, State Zip

Date

Mr. Christian Paulsen
Prescott Manufacturing Company
660 Highway 33
Marked Tree, AR 72365

Dear Mr. Paulsen:

As a senior marketing executive, you've probably admired the marketing strategies that propelled Panadyne's folding machines, collators, and shredders into prominence less than a year after their decision to compete in the U.S.

Perhaps you read in the <u>Wall Street Times</u> about the successful repositioning of the Langenfeld product line after its acquisition by Japan's Itabashi Corporation. Or heard about the less publicized—but equally effective—marketing triumphs for Woodlands National Bank, Espresso Italian Foods, and Greenmount Farms.

I'd like to meet you and show you how these corporate strategies can be put to work for Prescott. I have several ideas that can make an immediate sales impact, and a few more that promise long-range prosperity.

Can you clear about an hour of your time? I'll call next week to work out a date for our meeting. I'm looking forward to meeting you.

Sincerely yours,

Robert Hunt
President

- This is an example of the old advertising adage, "Sell the sizzle, not the steak." There are many implied benefits in this letter, but nothing specific. If you're too specific, you may miss the target and preclude a potential meeting.

Company Name
Address
City, State Zip

Date

Mr. Arthur Cremens
Books by Mail
642 Weston Avenue
Carlsbad, CA 92008

Dear Mr. Cremens:

You can be at the forefront of a publicity wave that will sweep the country. It's focused on the commissioning and unveiling, in Washington, D.C., of a special memorial to our fallen law enforcement heroes. Here's how you can benefit from it:

1. Many of the nation's police organizations are prepared to promote the sale of my proposed pictorial essay about local police across the country. As publisher, you'd reap these substantial sales.

2. This commemorative book should have special appeal to your large list of book buyers, particularly since a royalty from every sale will be paid to the memorial fund.

3. I've taken nearly 1,000 photographs of police forces throughout the U.S., many of which show police in action, on the job, as they've never been shown before.

To sum up, I have a distribution network (police organizations across the country) that can't miss; the photography already exists; and you have a ready-made market with your traditional buyers. Let's talk about a contract!

Would a meeting on the 29th or 30th of this month fit your schedule? I'll call to confirm.

Enthusiastically,

Lindsay Hoover

- When you're trying to sell an idea, book, service, or anything else, you must look at it from the potential buyer's point of view.

- Be specific about what the buyer will gain.

Selling with the Fax 9

You can't ignore a fax. Phone calls may go unanswered, letters may go unopened, advertisements may go unread. But the fax? A fax is delivered immediately and read at once. A facsimile transmission says, "I'm important, I'm timely. Read me!"

The immediacy of the fax presents many opportunities. But because it's so convenient and accessible, many people forget that it's relatively expensive to use compared to a letter. Trivializing it marks you as a poor businessperson. Save your fax transmissions for occasions that are worth the cost and deserve the attention. And by not overusing it, you'll keep the fax as a tool for making the greatest impact.

A fax shows immediate interest in doing business. It can spell out the details of a last-minute quote and avoid bad feelings that may occur when numbers are misinterpreted during a phone call. It will take the abstraction out of discussions about visual matters and put a conversation into concrete terms.

A fax is at its best when it's prepared with the same thought and care you put into a letter. Because the fax machine is so easy to use, some people feel justified in sending sloppy, grammatically incorrect, hand-written notes. Remember, you're trying to persuade someone to your point of view. Would you rush into that person's office at the last minute with your shirttails flapping, your hair plastered to your forehead, out of breath and uncollected? Then don't do it with your faxes.

Send a fax when plans, delivery dates, or specifications must be changed at the last moment. When deadlines loom, a fax can you can save you embarrassment and earn you appreciation.

When selling overseas, <u>nothing</u> comes close to the advantages of a fax. A courier service can cost up to $35 for a letter to the Orient, while a fax will get that letter there immediately for about 1/10th the cost. It's also helpful in getting around time zone problems.

With a fax, you can reach several locations at virtually the same time. You can confirm a conversation. You can approve contracts, advertisements, strategic plans with no delay. Or you can get the attention of difficult-to-reach people. You can react to emergencies. And there's a major advantage of a fax over a phone call. There's an accountability, a written record. Misunderstandings over what was said or heard are avoided.

One final suggestion: Keep your fax messages brief. The longer they run, the less the sense of urgency. Some people even resort to telegram language—leaving out nonessential words—to heighten the sense of urgency.

Whatever style you use, remember that faxes should be given the same thought and attention you give to all your sales letters.

Company Name
Address
City, State Zip
Fax Number

FACSIMILE TRANSMISSION
Page 1 of 1

Date

Mr. Graeme Fornel   Phone: 011-3-5551234
Computer Centres Ltd.
542 Chapel Street
Melbourne 3000, Australia

Dear Graeme:

I've reviewed the highlights of our phone conversations with my Vice President. We're extremely enthusiastic about doing business with your company.

Acknowledging the "tyranny of distance," I'd appreciate your faxing the following at your earliest so that we can put together a proposal:

    o Your estimated annual requirements of our F386 computers, and
       the anticipated order flow of those units.

    o Will you want the full line of peripherals? Please specify the items
       and approximate annual requirements for each.

    o Will you want software, or will you be purchasing locally?

We've been looking for an Australian distributor for a while because we believe our line of computer equipment will be very well received in your country. We want to present a proposal to you as quickly, as possible so would appreciate your quick response.

Kindest regards,

Robert Espinosa

- The fax provides a sense of urgency. In this case, the overseas recipient knows immediately that the American company is truly interested. That may forestall his approaching other manufacturers.

- State the desire to move quickly.

Company Name
Address
City, State Zip
Fax Number

FACSIMILE TRANSMISSION
Page 1 of 2

To: Bob Workman   Phone: 555-6892

From: Virginia Porcelli

Date:

Subject: Time Is Running Out

We're selling our older stock at a much faster rate than anticipated. If we don't have your order by the end of the week, you will have missed the opportunity to purchase at the old rate. The minute we start fulfilling from our new inventory, the price goes up.

I know you wanted to take advantage of the old rates, Bob, but I can't stop other customers from buying. As a reminder of what's in store for you if you miss the Friday deadline, I've enclosed the complete new price list (on average, the increase is 12%).

Please place your order by <u>Friday</u>; we won't be able to honor the old price on our new inventory.

- The fax can help budge a slow-to-move customer. Plus, you have a written record that he/she was notified.

- Advise the customer of the high cost of waiting.

- Give a final deadline date.

Company Name
Address
City, State Zip
Fax Number

FACSIMILE TRANSMISSION
Page 1 of 3

To: Jack Ireland, Esq.   Phone: (606) 555-5692

From: Carter Hazelton

Date:

Subject: Need Immediate Approval!

I have a meeting scheduled with my client, Vivian Hopemont, at 2 p.m.
I had assured Vivian I would have the final contract ready for her to sign
when she arrived, but I neglected to send you the final draft for review
on behalf of your client.

Would you please read the following agreement immediately.

Thanks for your prompt attention. If there's any problem, please call me
at 617-555-4848, and we'll resolve it. If you're satisfied that everything
is as agreed, please sign both pages, and fax them to me. A final draft
will be waiting for your client.

- The fax is perfect for last-minute emergencies. Get right to the point and clearly state problems/options/solutions.

- Do not rely on the telephone when you can transmit the words. Ask for a signature as a record of the transaction taking place.

- For an emergency, follow-up with a phone call to be sure the fax was received and understood.

Company Name
Address
City, State Zip
Fax Number

FACSIMILE TRANSMISSION
Page 1 of 1

To: Mary Ellen Boothe   Phone: (333) 555-1234

From: Sam Rodriguez

Date:

Subject: Video Pricing Confirmation

I just spoke with the publisher of <u>How To Communicate and Win</u>, and he confirms that you will be granted a 60% discount off the retail selling price.

Since you now have time to place the product in your Fall catalog, I'll assume it will be inserted as planned. I'm glad we could work this out. I believe your audience will buy video self-improvement courses in large numbers.

Let me know how many units you want, and when you want them.

- Use your fax message to confirm specific, pressing details.

- Keep the message brief (it adds to the urgency).

- Ask for a commitment.

Company Name
Address
City, State Zip
Fax Number

FACSIMILE TRANSMISSION
Page 1 of 1

To: Al King (HOTEL GUEST, ROOM 1308)

From: Ed Chaffee

Date:

Subject: Territory Reassignment

I know you're flying in tomorrow, but I wanted you to think about this before I meet with you and the rest of the staff.

I'm ready to give you Texas and Oklahoma in addition to your regular territory. That's going to put a tremendous travel burden on you if you say yes. On the other hand, you'll "travel" into six-figure income just by combining territories...and we both know you'll build it to the number 1 sales region it can be.

Will you call Arlene tonight and discuss the pros and cons with her? When you come in tomorrow, I'd like a yea or nay so I can decide how we're going to proceed. Sorry about the short notice, but things are moving at a hectic pace. Incidentally, if you want to talk to me tonight, my home number is 214-555-9431.

You know you're being groomed for a regional manager's job within 2 or 3 years at most. So we're not talking about a lifetime commitment. If you get the idea I want you to take the additional territory, you're right. You can do a great job with it and make a great income. But it's your call.

See you tomorrow.

• Last-minute changes or ideas can be accommodated via the fax. Explain the decision you're seeking.

Company Name
Address
City, State Zip
Fax Number

FACSIMILE TRANSMISSION
Page 1 of 5

To: Julia Harris   Phone: (312) 555-8990

From: David Nichols

Date:

Subject: Request Approval of Tractor Insert Layout

We've redesigned your four-page insert to put emphasis on the photos rather than on copy. I agree with you; it makes a stronger statement.

Speaking of strong statements, the printer has made one of his own. If we don't get the mechanicals to him by Thursday morning, we're going to miss the deadline for delivering printed inserts to the magazine's bindery.

Please call me when you receive this. I have two artists waiting to do the final boards, but I need your approval first. Pressure aside, I think you're going to generate a ton of new dealer business with this insert. It's a great new approach to a traditional farm product.

I'm waiting by the telephone.

- State the purpose of the fax to set the tone for the reader.

- Create a sense of urgency by quoting a deadline.

- Reassure the client that the approval will help generate business.

Company Name
Address
City, State Zip
Fax Number

FACSIMILE TRANSMISSION
Page 1 of 7

To: Susan Henderson   Phone: (404) 555-1234

From: Paul Rose

Date:

Subject: Advertising Deadline

Susan, we need to communicate. Your phone has been on electronic answering, and I can't wait any longer for you to respond. I've enclosed another set of copies of the new ad pages you requested, but I can't transmit them to the various magazines without authorization from you. If I don't have your authorization by tomorrow, we're going to miss the insertion deadlines for at least three of them.

You don't have to call. Just initial each of the following six ads and fax them back to me at 555-4526, which will allow us to make our increasingly threatening deadline.

I'll be waiting by the fax...

- A supportable sense of urgency (missed deadline, lost profits) will usually force a recalcitrant client to respond.

- Advise that there is no need to respond other than by fax.

- Convey that you are counting on an immediate answer.

Company Name
Address
City, State Zip
Fax Number

FACSIMILE TRANSMISSION
Page 1 of 1

To: Winston Claybourn   Phone: (506) 555-1212

From: Raymond Buckley

Date:

Subject: Summary of 10:45 a.m. Phone Conversation

After every important phone call, I summarize my notes, first as a reminder of what was said, and second to be sure I heard it right. The major points were:

1. You will issue a Purchase Requisition for us to install a PMC and PDU to provide raw and filtered electrical power to your computer labs.

2. The units will be installed as soon as you've completed the specially-prepared air-conditioned room that is necessary for peak performance (by April 12).

3. We will perform all maintenance to your satisfaction over the 15 year lease/purchase period or replace the unit(s) at no cost to you.

If your understanding is different from this, please get back to me by next Monday, July 12. If I don't hear from you by then, I'll start making preparations from our end.

Thanks for the business.

- If experience tells you your negotiating counterpart is notoriously forgetful, sending an immediate fax will reinforce the phone conversation and put it on record.

- Put the onus on the prospect to get back to you if there's any problem or disagreement.

Company Name
Address
City, State Zip
Fax Number

FACSIMILE TRANSMISSION
Page 1 of 1

To: Meyers Office Equipment Catalog Recipients

From: Liz Almeda, Catalog Manager

Date:

Subject: C A T A L O G   M I S P R I N T ! ! !

We pride ourselves on our low pricing, but not even we can sell a $485
steel four-drawer security cabinet (item #3R452, page 13) for $4.85.
Please staple this fax to the catalog page, or make the change by hand.

The only good that comes out of this typo is that it highlights one of the
best values in a value-packed catalog. Comparable four-drawer
cabinets cost as much as $110 more. Maybe the fates wanted to be
sure you saw this handsome, yet durable, product.

Thanks for your understanding.

- This sort of fax can be sent to your best customers. A similar notice should be mailed to all recipients.

- Remember: any correspondence with a customer is a chance to sell. (You may have given the wrong price, but the product is still very much a bargain!)

Company Name
Address
City, State Zip
Fax Number

FACSIMILE TRANSMISSION
Page 1 of 4

To: Richardson Sweet, Esq.   Phone: 555-7142

From: Paula Duggan

Date:

Subject: Errors in Kauffman Contract

Thanks for sending the final draft for review. I've looked at all three pages. Unfortunately, there are a number of typos and grammatical errors. I've marked all the problem spots for your review.

Please fax a revised copy for final approval, which I will check for corrections.

- State the problem immediately to be sure the message isn't lost.

- Request a revised copy (let the attorney know you'll be checking it carefully).

Selling by Direct Mail **10**

One thing direct mail experts agree upon is that the best promotion in the world won't work if you don't send it to the right list.

For example, one retail chain dramatically increased its men's shirt sales by redirecting its mailings to women instead of men. A survey had indicated that women were the primary buyers of shirts for their sons, boyfriends, husbands, and relatives.

The message is to go beyond the creative content of the mailing and to look carefully at who the potential buyer is. For example, if you're planning to sell a porcelain figurine of a Great Dane, don't send your letter to dog owners. Get a list of Great Dane owners.

You need to think about your audience: What does it want/need? How will your product or service fill that want/need? This is called "positioning." For example, do you sell a Great Dane figurine as an "investment" or as "art?" Which is more important to the dog owner? Do you sell a business travel book as "a guide to discounts" or "a guide to luxuries?" Do you sell the fear of death to a potential buyer of life insurance...or do you sell peace of mind? Match the appeal to the audience. Different segments of a market may respond to different positionings. Proper positioning can increase response by 50% to 100%.

Another critical factor in your direct mail solicitations is the degree to which you get the reader involved. You've seen the elaborate sweepstakes promotions which force you to hunt for stamps and tokens. This sort of involvement device increases response substantially. Of course, its cost can offset an increase in response, so be judicious in its use. With letter solicitations like the ones in this chapter, you can incorporate less expensive involvement devices such as tests, surveys, question & answer formats, coupons, and certificates. All can be helpful in getting the reader into the message.

Successful direct mail frequently forces action by offering an incentive to order quickly. A first-come, first-served limited edition ("while supply lasts!"). A special discount for "early-bird" ordering. "Guaranteed delivery for the holidays if you order by November 15."

Many direct mail experts agree that a good letter is far more important than a spectacular color brochure. The letter speaks to the individual; the brochure is considered an advertisement.

Take a look at a recent direct mail piece that has compelled you to order. Chances are, it included the four major elements of any successful sales letter:

1) Get the reader's attention.
2) Identify the reader's needs and show how you can fill them.
3) Persuade the prospect to buy from you.
4) Get the reader to act.

Selling Products. Questions make excellent "openers." Used skillfully, they get the reader involved, the greatest challenge of any letter. Present the prospect with features and benefits of the product that respond to his or her needs. Make an offer the reader will be hard-pressed to refuse (discount, free trial, money-back guarantee, two-for-one). Ask for the order with a postage-paid reply envelope or card or an 800 phone number. "Bill me" offers traditionally out-pull "payment-with-order" offers by margins of 2 to 1 or more.

Selling Services. You need to make the potential customer understand immediately <u>what</u> the service is. Then follow-up with the benefits to be derived from buying the service. As in selling products, define your offer clearly and give your customer simple instructions on how to order. Always keep in mind the "What's In It For Me?" thinking of the potential buyer. If you can demonstrate the value of the service convincingly, you'll get the sale.

Company Name
Address
City, State Zip

Date

Mr. David Ledbetter
Carlisle Steel, Inc.
2200 Alloy Way
Pittsburgh, PA 12256

Dear Mr. Ledbetter:

Can you imagine popping a disk into your personal computer and, within the first hour, actually improving your own personal productivity as well as your employees'?

That might be a bit difficult to believe, but it's true...and we'd like you to take a no-risk look for yourself! We want you to examine a remarkable new software program that puts into practice Bill Loehmann and Ken Harris' renowned Management By PC concepts.

The Management By PC book series captured the imagination of the nation's business managers. Now, instead of just reading about the process, this software package actually guides you through the steps: no guesswork, no wasted time, no missteps. In just one hour, you'll see how to set specific, measurable, manageable goals...and in one week you'll be getting action plans and commitments from your employees.

Just send in the enclosed order form, and we'll send you the Management By PC software for a FREE 30-DAY TRIAL! If for any reason you decide not to master the skills, simply return the software to us in the condition you received it and tear up the invoice.

Take advantage of this introductory offer and send the order form today.

Sincerely,

John D. Calhoun
Vice President, Management Software

P.S. Remember, there's no risk with our free 30-day trial, so order today!

- P.S.'s usually get read first, so use them for important information that will help close the sale.

- Use an introductory question to involve the prospect.

- Urge the prospect to act quickly.

Company Name
Address
City, State Zip

ALL NEW! The where-to-stay
and where-to-go guide, now available
in the U.S., written
by Europeans for Europeans
who are visiting the U.S. on business.

Dear American Business Traveler:

How would you like to know which American hotels are frequented by
cosmopolitan Europeans? Which restaurants capture their fancy.
Which clubs are recommended. And which shops cater to their tastes.

You'll learn some of the best-kept secrets in the U.S., secrets that will
make your own business trips in this country more unique and
enjoyable. In fact, you may even learn about regional customs that can
help you get the sale that's been evading you.

The official European Business Traveller may be the most detailed book
of its kind. You'll not only find new accommodations and dining rooms
that cater to the businessperson; you'll learn where to go for secretarial
services, thank you gifts, medical help, and more.

Send the enclosed card for a no-risk preview of business America, as
seen by our European counterparts. Gain a new perspective on your
own country.

Cordially,

Nigel Hawkins

P.S. Purchasers receive periodic updates of special rates and discounts
not advertised in America! This book will earn you big savings.

- The word "new" is a magic word in mail order. If the product is less than six months old, it is legal to use it.

- Highlight any discounts or special incentives.

- The P.S. is one of the most likely things to be read in a sales letter. Make it say something that will help close the sale.

Company Name
Address
City, State Zip

Dear Great Dane Owner:

We've joined forces with the Great Dane Society of America to offer you an original work of art, titled The Gentle Giant.

This handsome, hand-crafted and hand-painted original figurine was developed under the guidance of Linette Starkins, often referred to as the Grand Dame of championship judging, and Hollister Matthews, Executive Director of the Great Dane Society.

The Gentle Giant depicts the ideal form of this popular breed. It is accurate to the most exacting detail, portraying the Great Dane in a championship pose that highlights his exquisitely muscled body. Each figurine is crafted in the finest bisque porcelain and is mounted on a black marble base. The engraved number and title of The Gentle Giant is etched in 24 karat gold.

We invite you to acquire this elegant art work. Please read the accompanying brochure for full details. Then mail the enclosed reservation card (or call TOLL FREE 1-800-555-DANE). The Gentle Giant will not be sold in stores.

Sincerely,

Ralph Meadows

- Establish your credentials to the target audience (Great Dane Society to a Great Dane owner list).

- Describe the materials used for the collectible.

- To generate maximum response, make it clear this is a mail-order only offer.

Company Name
Address
City, State Zip

Are you tired of ho-hum meals?
Does your family crave something different?
Do you want the excitement that a whole new world of cooking offers?

Dear Family Chef:

If your meals have lost that old sparkle and spice, it's time to discover wok cooking.

Put an end to tedium and boredom with our beautiful stainless steel electric wok. Cook in it, serve from it. It works wonders with Chinese meals, and puts life into stews and deep-fried foods such as potatoes and even donuts!

Wok cooking is fun, it's quick, and it's healthful. It requires less oil than other frying methods (because of its shape), and it works wonders with vegetables. Stir-fry them in a wok, and they'll retain their color, vitamins, and snap.

And there's more. With your purchase of our Haberware wok, you'll receive a bonus gift...

> the new bestselling cookbook, Chinese Cooking and Beyond, a
> $19.95 value...YOURS FREE! It's chock full of great wok recipes,
> from h'ors d'oeuvres to full course family and holiday meals.

Don't miss this chance to put new zip into your family's meals. Order today. Just mail the enclosed postpaid card.

Yours for more interesting cooking,

Elliott Jackson

P.S. This free bonus offer is good only while supplies last, so order today!

- Questions arouse reader curiosity. Use them to lead into a response.

- Show the special features and benefits.

- Graphically offset the special bonus to reinforce the offer.

- Use the P.S. to close the sale.

Company Name
Address
City, State Zip

If your idea of a great day of shopping
is having a salesperson slobber all over you
and charge you full retail for fine men's clothing,
do yourself a favor...shop somewhere else.

Dear Clothes Hound:

At Ernie's you're probably going to have to wait for a salesperson
(believe it or not, you'll have to take a number). We always have more
customers than we can handle.

So what's the attraction at Ernie's? It sure isn't the bare walls or the
location. But it is the $45 Oxford shirts that sell for $14. And the Tim
Papilos 100% silk ties that are just $7. It's the designer suits selling for
up to $600 in the fancy shops that we sell for under $200. It's the
famous-maker coats and shoes and accessories that are 60% off retail.

If you're willing to put up with the inconvenience, I promise you the
buys of a lifetime. I have to. Why would anyone put up with this lack of
service for any other reason?

Visit Ernie's from 8:00 a.m. to 9:00 p.m. every day (except Sunday,
noon to 5:00). Do I have a deal for you!

Ernie Moskowitz

- The character of a company, store, or institution is reflected in the correspondence it sends. In this case, the bargain-basement image is not only intentional, it is the rationale for its existence.

- With imagination, things that are often considered negatives can be turned into positives. People will put up with a lot to get great prices.

Company Name
Address
City, State Zip

Date

Mr. Edward McAuliffe
Rolling Hill Hospital
1000 Commerce Way
Atlanta, GA 30326

Dear Mr. McAuliffe:

If you agree with these statements, we need to talk as soon as possible:

1. Cash flow is probably the single most important element in your business today.
2. Slow paying accounts cost you money.
3. The expense of recovering money through collection agencies or attorneys virtually negates any gain.

There is a solution to your collection problem—a comprehensive collection system that enhances your cash flow with none of the the high costs associated with cash recovery.

You control all elements of the intensive (two letters, three phone calls) 30-day collection drive. You receive all work cards for your records. All inquiries, correspondence, and collections go directly to you. And perhaps most remarkable of all, your all-inclusive charge for this concentrated 30-day service is only $10.00 per account.

Take a moment to complete and return the enclosed reply card and we'll send you the complete plan to examine—and explain how we can charge you so little for so much.

Sincerely,

William R. Bennett
Vice President, Sales

- A problem/solution opening puts the prospect in a receptive frame of mind.

- Use a reply card to solicit inquiries.

Company Name
Address
City, State Zip

Date

Ms. Ellen Stevens
VP, Administration
Proteus Industries
33 Allen Parkway
Port Chester, NY 10573

Dear Ms. Stevens:

When Port Chester area businesses need temporary office help, more than half turn to Carlyle Temporaries.*

Our company has been helping businesses like yours for more than twenty years! But our longevity and our impressive client list are not why you should use our services. They're simply the reason customers keep coming back to us. We not only provide the best-trained office personnel, but we back up every worker with the Carlyle guarantee. If you don't feel a Carlyle temp has provided the level of service and productivity you expected, simply tell us and you will not be charged.

Send for our free booklet "10 Steps to Efficient Use of Temporary Secretarial Help." It explains when to call in temporary help, how to get the most from the help, and a number of other extremely helpful hints our customers have asked us for over the years.

We look forward to providing office assistance to you for your next project. In the meanwhile, if you have any questions, please call us at 555-6753.

Sincerely,

Barbara Coit
Vice President

* Source: "Industry Area Statistics" survey, conducted by A.M. Bigelow, Inc.

- Start with a sentence that gets attention.

- Give the reader plenty of reasons to use your service.

- The offer of a free booklet about your industry will impress the prospect, and give you a list of <u>serious</u> prospects to contact by phone or in person.

Company Name
Address
City, State Zip

DELIVERY ALERT!

It's 4:00 p.m. and your proposal
has to be across town by 5:00 p.m.
How do you get it there?

Dear Overburdened Businessperson:

You worked up to the last minute to get everything just right. And to be absolutely certain your proposal (or report, contract, gift, etc...) was received on time, you hopped in your car and delivered it yourself. Or you sent your trusted secretary while you manned the phones for the rest of the day.

You probably don't even want to think about what that trip cost you in time, let alone jangled nerves, parking, etc. But you might want to think about giving yourself some breathing space by using Snappy Courier Services for those critical have-to-be-there times.

If you're in Center City Philadelphia, we can get your package to Cherry Hill for under $20.00...and in less than one hour. We can get it to Bucks County for about $30.00. Wilmington for under $40.00. And while we're delivering, you can be developing new business. And be assured, all of our drivers are bonded and insured, guaranteeing you safe delivery of all your packages.

Please keep the enclosed rate sheet and our name and number handy, because when you need us, you need us in a hurry!

Sincerely,

Gene Westphal
Manager

- Use situations that fit the audience. People will buy what they can identify with.

- Contrast the cost of your service with the cost and inconvenience of the prospect performing the same service.

Company Name
Address
City, State Zip

<u>Can you guess why National Tele-Call</u>
<u>handles all 800# inbound calls for</u>
<u>SportsCall, Monroe Gifts, The Morgan Fund,</u>
<u>TV Dial Magazine, and other key clients?</u>

Dear Marketing Manager:

I don't have to tell you how important telephone service is to the success of your advertisement. If you don't have the right telemarketing service to answer your calls, you may as well throw your advertising dollars out the window: the impact would be the same.

We're the biggest because we deserve to be. We're staffed 24 hours a day, 365 days a year. We currently handle 22.5 million calls a year through 325 telemarketing stations. And we have an ongoing verification program that eliminates errors before they become disasters.

With our sophisticated computer system, we can collect caller data and deliver it to a client within 24 hours for speedy fulfillment. (We can also handle fulfillment services when and if required.)

Call 1-800-555-0001 for a free brochure describing our services and hear how our professionals process your inquiry.

Sincerely,

Jack McDonald
Vice President, Marketing

- Use your client list to sell your service.

- Project the confidence that comes with being the best.

Please take a moment
to complete this survey

	Yes	No
I enjoy live theater.	_____	_____
I enjoy live concerts.	_____	_____
I enjoy dance.	_____	_____
I enjoy virtuoso performances.	_____	_____

Based on what we already know about you, you answered YES—enthusiastically—to all four questions. The question is: why don't we have your subscription to the Phoenix Ballet?

There's great drama and light comedy...modern and classical dance...Prokofiev, Ravel, Copland, Stravinsky, and Tchaikovsky...lavish sets and imaginative art...exotic costumes...breathless excitement...and joy.

Our Spring program will take your breath away. Look at the enclosed brochure, then mail the reply card, or call 1-800-555-0201 and get the most for your entertainment dollar. The Phoenix Ballet. An event. A must.

Giselle Courtland
General Manager

P.S. Order by May 31 to be assured of the best seats.

- Focus your energy on the cover letter of a direct mail solicitation. A good one can produce more orders than a fancy four-color brochure.

- This letter attempts to show the most exciting aspects of the musical presentations, appealing primarily to the non-ballet subscriber.

- Ask for the order.

Company Name
Address
City, State Zip

Date

Mr. William Fry
Home Manufacturing Corporation
490 West Mt. Pleasant Avenue
Rochester, NY 14530

Dear Mr. Fry:

Are you prepared for the new wave of importation the Japanese government will allow next year? Are you aware of the impact this new policy can have on your business?

We're the marketing company that guided Linton Industries into Japan, opened a sales office there for Bethel Products, and selected the advertising agency for Carter & Sperling. We can help <u>you</u> get a piece of the Japanese pie, too.

If you're interested in reaching one of the world's leading marketplaces, just make one toll-free, no-obligation call to learn what you need to do to get there. Call me at <u>1-800-555-8765</u> for answers to questions such as:

  o What is the cost of office space in Tokyo? What is the availability?

  o Will the U.S. government be of assistance? What roadblocks should I watch out for?

  o Which banks will be most responsive to my needs?

  o Is there a legal firm that can represent our interests well?

You may not know all the questions to ask or where to get the answers you need...but we do! Call and I'll explain how Home Manufacturing can tap into a lucrative new territory.

Sincerely,

Yasahiro Nakamura
President

- Offer sample questions that will lead to your services.

- Help the prospect feel comfortable about calling.

Company Name
Address
City, State Zip

<u>Chances are you've thought
about joining a health club...</u>

but no one made it easy enough to entice you. And, frankly, you're not sure it would be worth your investment—or if you'd stick it out long enough for it to pay off.

You're not alone. <u>A lot</u> of people feel that way. So I called a staff meeting and asked everyone to contribute ideas for getting people like you to try us. And here's what they came up with:

- o FREE membership for <u>you</u> for ten days.
  No pitches. No pressure. No restrictions.
- o FREE membership for a <u>friend</u> for ten days.
  We know you'd be a lot more comfortable with a friend along during the trial.
- o Unlimited use of our squash and racquetball courts.
- o Unlimited use of our indoor and outdoor pools.
- o Unlimited use of our exercise and weight rooms.
- o Unlimited access to our aerobics and martial arts classes.

Honestly, if you can't make yourself attend regularly during your FREE 10-DAY TRIAL PERIOD, you'll know you shouldn't waste your money on membership. But my bet is you'll fall in love with what many members call "the pleasure dome."

Bring this letter with you to get your 10-day FREE membership card. I'll be waiting to greet you personally.

Healthfully yours,

Rita Eldridge
Director

- By confronting people's concerns, you'll gain their confidence.

- Spell out the details of the offer (try to avoid the nasty little small print so many companies use: "certain restrictions may apply.")

Company Name
Address
City, State Zip

If you've been holding out
because you were waiting for us
to make a better deal...
you're a pretty sharp customer!

Dear Cable Subscriber:

You win. You can end your long holdout. You've made us understand what it's going to take to get you to subscribe to SHOWCASE, the number one movie and entertainment channel.

We know this means total surrender to your demands, but it's more important to get this entertainment stoppage over and done with than to win negotiating points. Our concessions:

1. FREE hook-up ($29.95 savings)
2. First three months FREE ($42.00 savings)
3. Exclusive movies not seen on other channels
4. Exclusive sporting events (such as next month's Dugan-Vargas championship fight)
5. Exclusive comedy specials, including Arby Tucker's hilarious look at the American family
6. Automatic entry into our GRAND BAHAMAS SWEEPSTAKES (prizes worth over $150,000—see enclosed brochure)

We've even paid the postage on the enclosed reply card. Or you can call, TOLL-FREE, 1-800-555-1111. You drive a hard bargain, but you're worth it! Just end the holdout!

Sincerely,

Ted Wilhelm

P.S. We can leave this "surrender" offer on the table until June 30. The deal is in your hands.

• This is a new twist on a classic direct mail letter. What makes it unique, is the "total surrender" approach. Without it, it would be just another limited time offer.

• List your "concessions."

• Put a time limit on your offer to force action.

Company Name
Address
City, State Zip

Dear Business Manager:

We design <u>custom</u> auto, truck, and business equipment leasing to suit your particular needs. Here are just a few of the options we can offer you:

    o   No Money Down

    o   Off Balance Sheet Accounting

    o   Purchase Options

    o   No Financial Statement for up to $35,000 on Equipment

    o   Reduced Payments for First Three Months

We offer advantages by the bucketful! Call Barbara Schaeffer for a NO OBLIGATION QUOTE. 1-800-555-0100.

- Postcards are inexpensive vehicles for getting easy-to-interpret messages to target audiences.

- Clearly state what you're selling. Don't overcrowd copy on a postcard.

May I send you

a $10 book (suggested retail price)

ABSOLUTELY FREE?*

Looking Good On Computer, written by computer whiz Boris Solnikov, will show you how to make every document you produce look better and be more readable!

To obtain your FREE COPY, complete all information, and drop this card in the mail! You'll receive this valuable book in about four weeks.

Name _____

Title _____

Company _____

Address _____

City _____ State _____ Zip _____

Type of Computer You Use _____

Type of Laser Printer You Use _____

*Offer good for laser owners only

- Card decks are great for generating names.

- Qualify the names ("type of laser printer you use"). You don't want to give a premium away to someone who can't purchase the product you plan to sell.

Communicating with the Sales Force 11

At a national sales meeting, the Number One Salesperson was complaining to anyone within earshot about how bad the company was. Finally, a newcomer said to Number One, "You make more money than anyone in this room. What would it take to make you happy?" The salesperson pointed across the room to the president of the company and said, "Just a pat on the back."

Within a month, Number One had left the company and put his considerable skills to work for a competitor.

We all work for much more than just money. We work for respect, recognition, and satisfaction. We never tire of being appreciated. Sales Managers who assume that paychecks are the only motivator are cheating themselves of top employee performance.

Don't leave your persuasive skills at home when communicating with the sales force. Think of them as customers needing care and attention if they are to meet your objectives. Particularly in large companies, where salespeople are spread all over the country, letters and memos will reinforce your appreciation of the sales staff's work and your commitment to its success. Use the same tone and degree of informality that you would if you were conversing with your staff in person.

Sales Management. Every letter or memo offers an opportunity for you to make a positive statement. If, for example, there's to be a change in a long-standing corporate travel policy, explain why, emphasizing the positive aspects ("more for us instead of the rental agency").

How do you deal with the resignation of a top salesperson? Do you ignore it? Blow it off with a one-line announcement? Instead, use the written word to communicate a message that explains the departure while expressing confidence and optimism about the future.

Take that extra moment to treat your salespeople as clients, by listing the benefits of an action. Don't assume that they'll figure it out on their own. Sell them on policy and administrative procedures, don't just jam it down their throats. The result will be a more cohesive, happier team that concentrates on the job at hand.

Employee Motivation. If a long-time client had just received a special award, hit a milestone birthday or anniversary, or was appointed to a key civic committee, you'd write a letter praising his or her contributions. Pay that kind of attention to your salespeople. Special accomplishments always should be singled out for recognition. When you do, you'll build camaraderie and pride. There's magic to seeing one's name in print. Make the employee in question feel good about you, the company, and himself or herself.

Do you remember what it was like to start at a new company? A hearty welcoming letter helps bypass the awkward stage and gets the new person into the flow from Day One. How about cutbacks? Everyone is nervous when they start to occur. Use the cutbacks as motivators for the survivors. Emphasize the positive aspects that others may not see, and build a committed, motivated sales force that looks ahead and not over its shoulders.

Don't just use your selling skill in the outside world. By praising key achievements, recognizing opportunities, and creating challenges, you will communicate the message that yours is a company that cares about its employees and recognizes achievement.

Company Name
Address
City, State Zip

To: All Salespeople

From: Jerome Wright

Date:

Subject: New Pricing

We're releasing our new pricing to all customers (see attached list). On average, it reflects an increase of just over 11%.

First of all, we're allowing a 60 day "window" for your current customers to stock up at current prices. Use these next two months to boost "last chance" sales aggressively.

Secondly, do <u>not</u> apologize for the increases. They're overdue. We've held pricing longer than we should have, and your customers are a lot more aware of market realities than you may think.

- On American products, we've had a substantial bump in costs due to new minimum wage standards.
- On imported products, we're still suffering the effects of a weak U.S. dollar.
- Raw material costs have risen dramatically over the past two years.

We represent top quality, top service, and fair pricing. Sell our advantages.

- Salespeople often shy away from price increases. Boost their confidence about the need for the increases.

- The better the reasons you give for the increases, the better your salespeople will be able to explain it to their customers.

Company Name
Address
City, State Zip

To: All Store Managers

From: Curtis DiSoto

Date:

Subject: Special Pricing for Back-to-School Promotion

An old retailer once told me his key to success. "It's not what you sell it for," he said, "it's what you buy it for."

Our boys sweater and knit buyer, Don Greenburg, must have taken a page from the old retailer's book. He's made a buy that guarantees every sweater and knit shirt will be less expensive this year than last year. What a way to kick off your August Back-to-School Promotion!

Our advertising will refer to "an old-fashioned price roll-back" which, we anticipate, will mean at least a 20% pick-up in traffic in the boys department. This unusual price decrease also gives you an opportunity to exercise your selling skills. Coordinate your shirts and slacks with these wonderful bargain sweaters and knits!

Please review the enclosed product and pricing sheet. At your next staff meeting, get the entire sales staff excited about Don's great buy. We're going to bring in the traffic; it's up to your people to deliver the sales!

- Tell your staff why the price will decrease.

- Explain the impact the price decrease will have on your customers.

- Tell the salespeople they have an opportunity to increase their sales as a result.

Company Name
Address
City, State Zip

To: All Salespeople

From: Mike Beech

Date:

Subject: Territory Reassignments

Casey Stengel once said, "The secret of managing...is to keep the five guys who hate you away from the five who are undecided."

Since I'm not sure which is which, I thought I'd send you these new assignments, instead of bringing you into the home office. Actually, I think you'll find these changes exciting, because they offer each of you a chance to grow... and prosper.

The company's cautious expansion plan is working. We remain well-capitalized even as we're expanding our reach deeper into the Northeast and Southeast. This expansion means you'll each have some new start-up territories—and that means a bit more travel during the next few months.

Read the enclosed territory reassignment plan, and meet with me at the designated time. If you have a problem with your expanded territory, I'd like to know about it <u>now</u>. I've worked with you over the last three months preparing for this eventuality. But if you still see a problem, let me know and I'll try to correct it.

This is a period of growth and adjustment for all of us. If things work as planned, we're about six months away from bringing in reinforcements to help. <u>Let's make it happen</u>!

- The first two paragraphs may seem superfluous to some managers, very important for setting a tone to others. If you're comfortable with humor, it's a nice way to introduce some subjects. If you're not, don't even think about it.

- State the reasons for the changes. (In this case, the sales manager has already explained the reasons.)

- It's important to discuss territory changes directly with each salesperson, preferably face-to-face.

Company Name
Address
City, State Zip

To: Sarah Lees

From: Carl Bachman

Date:

Subject: Territory Reassignment

You've been doing a great job...and I'm going to help you do it better. Instead of forcing you to fight tunnel traffic every day (losing valuable selling time), it makes sense to let you concentrate on Manhattan. I'll hire someone to cover Northern New Jersey.

This change of territory will mean you can schedule more calls (no wasted time driving to suburban locations), concentrate more on developing the giant Manhattan market (there are still 1,082 firms you haven't contacted yet!), and make <u>more money</u>.

I'd like to effect this change in about 90 days. Frankly, I'll be lucky to find someone of your caliber...but I have to try. It's best for you and best for the company. Please call me by Friday to set a meeting date to discuss the territory change.

Looking forward to hearing from you. Keep selling!

- Even if you prefer to discuss this sort of topic in person, it's important to put it on paper to give it a sense of weight and finality.

- No one wants to give up a piece of a lucrative territory, so it's important to state positive aspects.

- Commend the salesperson for the job being done. Explain that this move is in his/her best interests.

Explanation of Changes in Commission Plan (11-05)

Company Name
Address
City, State Zip

To: All Printing Salespersons

From: Peter Reagan

Date:

Subject: Changes in Commission Structure

The cost of paper has risen so dramatically, it's taken us a few months to really understand what's going on in the marketplace...and to focus on our own economic position.

After many hours of reviewing various compensation plans, we've come up with a new commission formula. It offers you the opportunity to earn more than ever before, while taking into account the new realities of paper costs.

Effective <u>immediately</u>, commission on any printing job will be paid on the <u>non-paper portion</u> of the job. Frankly, with paper running over 50% of most jobs—and as much as 70%—we were flirting with fiscal suicide by paying commissions on gross sales.

To compensate for the change in structure, starting commission will be 10% (instead of the old 5%). It will go to 12.5% after $100,000 in net sales (sales less paper costs) and 15% after $250,000 in net sales. Page 2 details a number of different scenarios to show exactly how the new commission structure will affect you.

As you'll see, once you get near the $500,000 net sale figure, you'll actually earn <u>more</u> than you did on $1,000,000 in gross sales. This program <u>rewards motivated salespeople</u>.

I'll review everything with you during our monthly meeting.

- Anything affecting a salesperson's income will be scrutinized <u>very</u> closely. Explain <u>why</u> the change was made, and you'll get people on your side. Keep them guessing, and you'll have discontent.

- Give examples of how the new program works.

Company Name
Address
City, State Zip

To: All Sales Personnel

From: Dick Maneri

Date:

Subject: Getting the Most for Our Car Rental Dollar

I'm tempted to give our controller the "Salesperson of the Month" award because he's just made a major contribution to our profitability. And, as you all know, the more profitable we are, the bigger our bonuses!

Stu negotiated a deal with Apex Auto Rentals, an aggressive new company that's been growing rapidly. We've never contracted with a rental agency before, but Apex opened our eyes. Based on our car rentals last year, we'd have spent $14,678 less if we had rented exclusively with them.

In addition, we now have blanket coverage for rental insurance, so please <u>decline</u> any other coverage. That will save us another $2,200. And we urge you to <u>refuel your cars</u> before returning them to the agency. That's another $1,400 in our collective pocket.

That's over $18,000 in pure profit—equivalent to the profit from a $124,000 sale! You'll receive complete details from Stu's office on our rental agreement. Please read them carefully. If there are any questions, go directly to Stu.

Stu's gotten our year off to a great start. Now let's see how much we can build on it!

- Too many policy change notices sound cold and bureaucratic. Warm them up by looking at the positive aspects. Tell <u>why</u> the change is helpful.

- The Sales Manager sets the tone. If he/she is enthusiastic and supportive, the staff will follow suit.

Company Name
Address
City, State Zip

To: All Salespeople

From: Frank Rauch

Date:

Subject: Selecting the Right Computers and Software for You

We've been telling top management for three years that, given the right tools, we can boost sales by 30%. We're about to get everything we asked for!

On October 22, here at HQ, there will be a one-day forum with our own EDP people and a team of outside consultants (NOTE: check with your regional managers about travel schedules). We're going to review (hands-on):

- two different hard disk laptops
- two floppy disk laptops
- four integrated software packages
- three near-letter-quality dot matrix printers

You'll work with all the laptops and software programs; understand the tradeoffs between various hardware (for example, capacity vs. weight) and software (menu bars vs. power); learn how to dial the all-new Sales Force Inquiry Menu; and select specific hardware and software that most appeals to you.

The company has spared no expense to give us what we asked for. Now it's up to us to deliver on our part of the agreement!

- Many salespeople are scared off by technology. It's important that it be presented as a plus to their sales efforts.

- Be specific about the purpose of the meeting and what will occur.

- Reinforce that management is going all-out for them.

Company Name
Address
City, State Zip

To: All Sales Staff

From: Eli Kress

Date:

Subject: Meet John Patterson

On Monday morning, John Patterson will be joining us in the new capacity of <u>Special Sales Coordinator</u>...a position that will mean <u>more commissions for you</u>!

We've asked you to devote 100% of your time to retail sales because there's so much business in that market—and that hasn't changed. We don't want to miss other opportunities, however, so we've hired John to follow-up every non-retail sales possibility. If he converts one of your leads, you earn a 3% override! (You say you like him already?)

John is uniquely suited for this new position. He was Director of Special Sales for Lawton's Seasonings where he broke all sorts of sales records for non-traditional sales. (His "season's" greetings promotion is an industry legend.) Prior to his productive stay at Lawton's, John was part of the special sales team at Fenton & Coles, a publisher of software.

John is past President of the Massachusetts chapter of the National Sales Executive Club. He's married with three children (ages 6, 9, and 12). And most important, he's a six handicap golfer!

Plan to meet John in the President's office on Monday at 9:00 a.m. sharp (coffee and breakfast rolls will be served). We'll explain the override program and how it will help you build income.

- The arrival of a new employee—whether it be a secretary or sales manager—is an opportunity to be cheerful, positive, and enthusiastic about the future. A carefully worded advance memo will help the new person be accepted by your present personnel.

Company Name
Address
City, State Zip

To: All Employees

From: Al Shearer

Date:

Subject: Addition to New Benefits Package

Although many of you had originally expressed reservations about our acquisition by Alliance Insurance, I think you've been quite pleased with the outstanding benefits package that was announced last week. I've worked for major-league organizations all my life, and I've never seen one quite so generous.

<u>But there's more!</u>

Alliance rewards educational excellence with <u>college scholarships</u>. Their way of encouraging our children to aspire to great achievements is to offer grants based on grades, extra-curricular participation, and community involvement. If you have a high school student in the family, I urge you to review the attached eligibility requirements <u>now</u>.

Incidentally, I think our new company has gone out of its way to make all of us feel part of the team. Let's repay their confidence with a commitment to going 20% over goal! We'll talk about that during our next meeting. In the meantime, sit your kids down and tell them to start hitting the books.

- Periodic updates about employee benefits are good policy. They're reminders of company commitment.

- Tell the employees that they're appreciated and that productivity is the way to repay a caring management.

Company Name
Address
City, State Zip

To: All Salespeople

From: Carson Peddie, Jr.

Date:

Subject: Robert Franklin's Resignation

The unhappy news is that after 12 remarkably productive years, Bob Franklin will be leaving us to assume a sales management position with a New York City-based firm. The good news is that he's moving into a field that's not competitive with ours! I've always said I'd hate to sell against him.

I'm very happy that Bob is getting the opportunity, as he put it, "to take a shot at management." He's a dedicated, hard-working, creative guy who will succeed at everything he tries. At the same time, I'm not very happy to lose someone who's been our top salesperson for 9 of his 12 years here, including the last four in a row.

Bob has agreed to give us 60 days notice, which gives me time to search for a replacement. If any of you wants to take on the challenge, I'm willing to consider a change of territory. I'd rather transfer this very lucrative business to an experienced insider than to a newcomer.

Please be sure to give Bob a hearty send-off. And let me know by the end of the week if you want to talk about changing territory.

- Never ignore a key resignation. As much as it may hurt to lose the individual, acknowledge it with dignity.

- Comment on the individual's achievements.

- If possible, turn the loss into a challenge for existing salespeople to take over the territory, etc.

Company Name
Address
City, State Zip

To: All Sales/Marketing Staff

From: Nick Green

Date:

Subject: Jim Schiller's Retirement

I have very mixed emotions about Jim's imminent departure. I'm happy he'll be doing the things he's rarely had time for: reading, painting, and traveling without deadlines. But I'm going to miss him very much. You don't replace an original, particularly one who has been a part of our sales team for 27 years.

Jim asked me not to make this announcement read like a eulogy, and I agreed. We'll save that for his retirement dinner, which is the reason for this memo. You're invited to attend a dinner in Jim's honor:

> Saturday, May 22, 7:00 p.m.
> Mazzano Romano Ristorante (12th and Market Streets)
> Black tie optional (hey, Jim doesn't retire every day!)

Spouses are invited. Will you call my secretary, Rachel, by the 14th to let her know if you can attend? Let's show Jim how much we appreciate everything he's done for the company—and for each of us personally.

- Retirement parties are an opportunity for team-building. Set a positive tone that shows how much the company appreciates loyalty and service.

- Be specific about the details of any company event (date, place, time, R.S.V.P., etc.)

Company Name
Address
City, State Zip

To: The Sales and Marketing Team

From: Lynn Weiss

Date:

Subject: Don Anderson's 10th Anniversary

Do you know the old Henny Youngman joke? "I've been married five great years. Five out of ten isn't bad, is it?"

Don Anderson's been with us for ten years, and all ten have been great ones. Don has been a member of the million dollar club eight times, and he's cracked the celebrated two million dollar club three times. If we had a Hall of Fame, Don would be a shoo-in.

We're having a reception for Don at 4:00 p.m. this Friday, January 14, in my office. Please join me for a toast to Don's last ten years—and to the next ten as well.

- Recognition is an important motivator, not just to the recipient of the praise, but to his/her colleagues, as well.

- If there is some sort of "event" to commemorate a service anniversary, be sure to issue the notice well in advance to give people time to plan to attend.

Company Name
Address
City, State Zip

To: All Employees

From: Art Fuller

Date:

Subject: Meet Our New Salesperson!

When you arrive Monday morning, there will be a new face in the sales department.

Mary Ellen North—our production coordinator—has been promoted to the advertising sales team. Mary Ellen has been an extension of the sales force for so long, she's been considered an honorary member. We're just making it official.

Who could be better suited for this job than Mary Ellen? She's probably worked with our clients more than the salespeople have, prodding them to get their negatives in before deadline, rushing last-minute ads into the magazine, mediating miscommunications, and making our clients feel good about us.

We're proud of Mary Ellen's past performance, and we're excited about her future. We're particularly delighted that we could fill the position from within.

Good luck, Mary Ellen, and good selling!

- A company that promotes from within tends to maintain a better esprit de corps because the message received is that everyone has a chance to move up.

- List some accomplishments that helped earn the promotion.

Company Name
Address
City, State Zip

Date

Ms. Marti Fuller
1428 West Washington Square
Greenwich, CT 06831

Dear Marti:

I want you to know how much I appreciate your contribution to the company. You didn't just break a sales record, you rendered it obsolete!

I don't mind telling you that you've taken us to a new plateau of thinking. What you accomplished with the Army contract should not be an isolated phenomenon. We now have it within our power to become a force in the military market.

Your drive, aggressiveness, and belief in yourself have sent a message to everyone in the company. We can accomplish anything we put our hearts and minds to.

I hope you don't mind if I expound this message during our company luncheon in two weeks. And I'll drive it home by presenting your bonus check for a remarkable contribution to our business.

Thank you.

Very truly yours,

Nicholas T. Seaford
President

- A personal note from a company officer can be a real motivator for the salesperson.

- Tell the salesperson how important the accomplishment was to the company.

- If a bonus is involved, refer to it.

Company Name
Address
City, State Zip

To: All Employees

From: Charles Zucker

Date:

Subject: Honors for the Phelan family

If our office seems brighter today, it's probably because of Donna Phelan's 500 megawatt smile. Her daughter, Rochelle, just graduated Magna Cum Laude from George Washington University. She's planning a career in the foreign service.

To those of you who had the opportunity to meet Rochelle (she worked in our warehouse during the last two summers), it's no surprise she's done so well. She has her mom's charm, ambition, and intelligence. We were hoping she might join us, but we'll have to be content with just one Phelan for now. (We still have a shot at Jack, who's a senior in high school.)

When you see Donna today, take a moment to share her happiness. Congratulations to the Phelan family!

- Announcing "family" events and milestones helps foster a warm feeling among employees.

- Encourage others to acknowledge special events.

Company Name
Address
City, State Zip

To: All Employees

From: Barbara Fullwood

Date:

Subject: Community Service Award for Robert Avila

Since Bob is a low-key person (except when it comes to sales), most of you may not be aware that he's the Chairperson of the Crestview Board of Education.

During last week's board meeting—which was packed because of the discussion about new taxes—the boiler exploded, creating a situation that was ripe for disaster. According to Dr. Leonard Livingston, Cresthaven's Superintendent of Schools, Bob was a hero.

> "Bob had the presence of mind to direct people through different exits, avoiding a panic stampede. He immediately mobilized a group of parents to aid the injured until help arrived, and he managed to get the school maintenance staff in to work through the evening to minimize water damage. His quick action may have saved lives and tens of thousands of dollars. Bob Avila is not just a community leader, he's a community hero."

Last month, Bob saved the department with a $400,000 government contract. This month, he did something far more important: he saved lives and set an example for all of us.

Congratulations, Bob. We're very proud of you.

- One person's accomplishment is a source of pride to everyone. Make it a point to dramatize employees' actions outside the workplace.

Company Name
Address
City, State Zip

To: The Staff

From: Art Reynolds

Date:

Subject: Thomas Keenan, M.B.A.

On Thursday morning you may not recognize Tom. He won't have bags under his eyes, and may not even need six cups of coffee to "kick-start" his engine.

For the first time in four years, Tom will have gone to sleep at a normal hour. After long years of pushing himself to the limit—at work and at Missouri State night school—Tom will be granted the degree of Master of Business Administration on Wednesday, May 12.

An MBA is tough enough to get under normal circumstances. Obtaining one under the pressure of a full-time job (and demanding boss!), a family of three youngsters, and a no-nonsense night school schedule, is a remarkable achievement. We've come to expect great things of Tom, and now we know why. He has the determination and the will to succeed that drive him to greatness.

Tom, we're all proud of you and admire your accomplishment. Congratulations!

• Recognition is, in many ways, a more powerful motivator than money. Underline the employee's persistence in the face of tough odds...that's what selling is all about!

Company name
Address
City, State Zip

To: All Sales Personnel

From: Jayne Maples

Date:

Subject: Company Picnic—The Campgrounds
June 24, 10:00 a.m. - 4:00 p.m.

It's official! We're starting a great new tradition...which isn't easy with a company our size. The county has granted our request to "occupy" the Campgrounds for a day, and it's going to be special.

We've arranged for a hillbilly band, food beyond belief, games and rides for the kids, and, most important, a round-robin softball tournament between departments! You'll get a complete schedule of events with your pay envelopes, but a word about the softball tournament:

> Since we're considered the Aggressive Arm of the company with everything that title implies, let's prove everyone right. Let's win the tournament! We'll start practicing tomorrow night. Bill's the manager, and he's getting the practice field for us. Let's show the rest of the company what we're made of at the picnic!

Mark the 24th on your <u>home</u> calendar, and start getting your spouses and children ready for this big event! It's about time we all got together as a group. Incidentally, if any of your sons or daughters are really good players, bring them to practice!

- A company event is an excellent time to "rally the troops."

- Display your enthusiasm, and it will filter down.

Company Name
Address
City, State Zip

To: The Sales Team

From: Burt Greis

Date:

Subject: Personnel Cutbacks in Other Departments

Management has made a real show of confidence in our sales team. Manufacturing, engineering, and operations staffs have been trimmed by nearly 10%, while we've stayed intact.

The reason? Management understands that we're the lifeblood of the company. Many shortsighted firms cut sales personnel when times are tough. Ours is smart and aggressive enough to understand that breaking out of a slump requires a fully-staffed sales force, not a reduced one.

Let's thank management for its continuing vote of confidence in the best possible way: BRING IN MORE SALES! Please join me at 9:00 a.m. Thursday in my office to talk about how we can arouse a slumbering marketplace!

- It's tough to keep spirits up when colleagues are being laid off. So it's particularly important to motivate staff during this time.

- Motivational memos are fine, but they should be backed up with an action plan.

Company Name
Address
City, State Zip

To: All Sales Personnel

From: Roy Albemarle

Date:

Subject: The Cavalry's on the Way!

We've just completed our fifth straight losing quarter, but help is just over the horizon.

First of all, the rate of loss has been braked. We're out of the free-fall and leveling. We're now in a position to project break-even or better for the next quarter, and substantial recovery in the following quarters. Here's why:

- o You've done a terrific job introducing the new Jiffy adhesive roller cleaners to the retail and premium marketplace. We project over one million pieces for this quarter, and almost three million the next.

- o We've had a marketing breakthrough! The American Basketball League has given us reproduction rights to their team logos, and our Taiwanese manufacturing plant is already at work producing imprinted plastic visors and duffel bags. More about this at our weekly meeting tomorrow.

You've done a courageous job in keeping us afloat during perilous financial times. Even though our old lines became tired, you helped stretch them until we were able to come up with replacements.

From Bill Wiggins, the executive staff, and me, thank you. The future looks promising, and we're delighted that you all rode out the storm.

- Be honest and open about the financials. It always beats rumor and innuendo.

- Be specific about why you feel the future holds promise.

- Commend the salespeople for the job they did during the bad times.

Company Name
Address
City, State Zip

To: Jonathan Rosa

From: Artemis Johnson

Date:

Subject: New Offices for Telemarketing Squad

We're paying substantial dollars—as we should—to our telemarketers. These are the people who bring in the sales for us. But we lower our return on investment by putting them in a very public fishbowl where they cannot, by any stretch of the imagination, do their best work. Here are some of the problems:

1. They're adjacent to the warehouse/fulfillment operation that is a noisy beehive of activity. Truckers, mail personnel, heavy equipment and normal chatter are all disruptive to the sales operation. Interruptions mean lost ideas and dramatically decreased sales.

2. Because they're in a relatively open area, there is heavy employee traffic past their offices. This set-up invites comments and clowning.

The best way to curb the problem is the simplest: Put the telemarketers in a more suitable environment. After reviewing locations in the building and deciding what would be the least disruptive move (and least expensive), I think putting them in the west wing next to Accounting makes the most sense. We can move accounting's "dead files" into the vacated area, giving us the required space.

Simply initial this memo, Jonathan, and I'll have the entire move completed over the weekend. Thanks for your prompt attention.

- Get to the point immediately. Don't make a busy manager guess what you want.

- Present the problem and the solution.

- Make it easy for the manager to say yes ("simply initial this memo").

Company Name
Address
City, State Zip

To: All Employees

From: Lewis Trout

Date:

Subject: False Acquisition Rumors

There have been hints in the trade and general press, as well as whisperings in our own hallways, that we're about to be sold to either Osage Industries or Wheeler Combustion. But the absolute truth is:

1. We're not for sale.
2. We have spoken to <u>no one</u> about an acquisition or merger.
3. We're profitable, we're growing, and we're committed to remaining a privately-held company.

I don't know how these rumors were started, but we need to put a lid on them. Many of us have received calls from customers, some of whom have withheld orders because of the rumors. I'd like you to get in touch with them directly and put a stop to this unfounded and unproductive gossip.

We have the best sales team in the business. Let's get back to doing what we do best!

- Rumors are time-consuming and often demoralizing. By dealing with them forthrightly and quickly, you'll avoid major disruptions.

- List your key points in a way they cannot be missed.

- If the rumor has spread outside the organization, insist that your salespeople respond to it.

Office of the President
Company Name
Address
City, State Zip

To: The Worldwide Sales Team

From: Luther Bridges

Date:

HAVE A GREAT HOLIDAY

This is the time of year that lends itself to reflection. The holiday season is special to all of us...and each and every one of you is very special to me.

I've never felt better about our sales team. As a group, you combine knowledge, enthusiasm, and a healthy competitiveness that has never stepped over the line into rivalry. I've seen you work together at trade shows, openings, sales meetings, and special events. It's obvious you like each other, and I'm convinced that's one of the keys to our success.

As we break for the holidays, please accept my gratitude for everything you've brought to this company. Please extend my best to your families; may we continue to grow and prosper together.

- Although it may be asking a bit much—particularly in large companies—for the president to write individual notes, it is worth the time to customize departmental memos. The middle paragraph, with minor modifications, can be rewritten to make each department feel a sense of recognition from the president.

Promotional Announcements 12

The young copywriter rushed in to show his boss a special Christmas promotion for nationwide newspaper circulation. The seasoned advertising veteran looked at the full-page ad before him and asked the copywriter where the holly wreaths were. He looked again and asked why he didn't see Santa in the ad. And where was the box that said "Only 15 shopping days left 'til Christmas?"

"Son," said the adman, "If you get nothing else out of working for me, get this: "Don't mess with Christmas."

Some things work so well that their basic structure should never be changed. And promotional announcements—be they in the form of letters, advertisements, fliers, handouts, inserts, or stuffers fall into this category

There are key words and phrases that are as fail-safe as anything can be in advertising. "Free" is the single strongest word you can use. "Grand Opening" instantly tells a potential customer that there will be get-acquainted specials that may not be repeated. "Breakthrough" connotes something dramatic, revolutionary (which is a key word itself), and of value. "Guaranteed," "Unique," "Limited Edition," are examples of other words and phrases that stir people to action. Build them into your announcements.

Letter Announcements. Whether they're personalized or not, announcement letters need to grab the reader's attention immediately. A catchy headline, a particularly bold statement or provocative question are all ways to catch the reader's eye. If you use a salutation (not a necessity), establish your relationship to the reader ("Dear Valued Customer"). Ask questions that involve the customer.

Use relevant openings to establish your relationship and the reason for the announcement. In other words, use the same principles that you would follow in any good sales letter.

Mailers. These must be eye-catching because they're fighting clutter in the mailbox. Use indents, bold faced type, and other graphic devices that will draw attention to the message. Promotional announcements work best when you limit them to one strong message.

If you're having a preview party, for example, don't confuse the issue by talking about a new catalog or last year's sales records. Where's the party? When is it? Who's invited? Why should the reader attend? (Special discounts, food, unveiling of new model, etc.)

Provide the details succinctly. A promotional announcement is just that: an announcement. Be brief and to the point; get the reader's attention quickly, and focus on one message only.

One final reminder: Every communication you release gives you an opportunity to persuade someone to think a certain way about you. Even informational announcements should stress customer benefits. So, for example, if you're merging with another company, tell your customer how the merger will benefit him ("help move your freight faster," or "give you more personalized service)." A line or two of benefit copy will make the announcement pay off for you.

Company Name
Address
City, State Zip

GRAND OPENING exTRAVELganza!

Here's your chance to get to know us...
and our chance to offer you
extra money-saving specials
during our GRAND OPENING exTRAVELganza

Dear Traveler:

We're happy to announce that Customized Travel is coming to Hillsdale, bringing money-saving travel assistance to the business and pleasure travelers in this area.

Our staff of well traveled professionals wants you to be every bit as pleased with your travel arrangements as the thousands of customers we've helped throughout the tri-state area over the past 10 years.

We know you are just as concerned about your pocketbook as you are about the comfort and convenience of your travel accommodations. That's why we always book the best trips at the lowest possible prices.

During the month of March, we are offering an extra 10% off any travel you book with us, as our way of introducing our services to you. Simply bring this letter with you when you stop by our convenient Main Street location, and we'll show you what Customized Travel can do for you.

Helen Urdang
Travel Specialist

P.S. Coffee and donuts await you, even if you only stop by to pick up some of our complimentary brochures.

- If you have other locations, state that. It gives the prospect confidence in your company.

- Appeal to the prospect's interest in service and value.

- Offer an enticement of value that brings people into the location.

Company Name
Address
City, State Zip

Is your home or office closing in on you?
Are your files, furnishings, and collectibles
taking up valuable space and creating an eyesore?
Has your garage, bedroom, reception area
or basement been overcome by clutter?

You need storage space...and we have it!

We've just opened a brand new, individualized storage facility on Route 23, south of Oxford Avenue, that provides the solution to your space dilemma.

Do you need to store furniture for a month? We have the space. Do you want a spot for your old files—the ones you can't throw away because once in a blue moon you need something from them? Take a one year lease. Do you want to keep toys and bicycles for your grandchildren's visits but don't have space for them? Use ours.

STORAGE-FOR-YOU rentals answer all your space needs. You get 24-hour access, convenient location, discounted leases (as little as one month, as much as two years) based on length of rental, and if you act now...

Your first month's rent for only 99 cents!

Reclaim your home or office by using our public rental facilities. But hurry: the 99 cent first month special only lasts until July 31...and it's subject to availability.

Call (601) 555-5859 for complete details!

- Aim for people who have a specific problem <u>now</u>. Don't try to sell future needs.

- Offer specific examples that will appeal to a broad-based audience.

- Create a sense of urgency with a firm deadline.

Company Name
Address
City, State Zip

Valued Customer Preview Night!

An after hours spectacular
to introduce you to
our brand-new line of Spring Furniture

Won't you join us for a preview party? We're celebrating the best buys in the history of Aaronson's fine furniture, and we want you to preview our amazing new collection prior to its announcement to the general public.

FRIDAY EVENING, FEBRUARY 25
6:00 P.M. - 10:00 P.M.
AT AARONSON'S ON LONG BRANCH PIKE

As an invited guest, you'll have first choice of our new selection, plus you'll receive a Valued Customer Bonus:

10% OFF ALL FURNITURE!

At the preview, you'll get a taste of Spring and substantial savings! Enjoy our preview party with the Aaronson's staff and other Select Customers. This is an invitation-only event, not open to the general public.

SUPERB BUFFET DINNER

And don't eat before you come over, because we're putting together a fantastic buffet dinner with all the trimmings!

This invitation is your ticket to join us
for a party, preview, and savings!

- Acknowledge the customer as a buyer.

- Make it clear the customer is part of a special group that is invited.

- Highlight the key features.

The Flower Stall Announces a Unique New Service
to Our Business Customers—
The Forget-Me-Not Program

Many area companies have thoughtfully delighted their employees by sending our unique fresh floral arrangements to commemorate birthdays, service anniversaries, and other special events. The good will created by our computer-generated reminder system carries into the workplace.

Here's how easily it works:

1. Give us the list of special occasions you wish to celebrate.

2. Specify the arrangement you want, from the photographs in the enclosed brochure (or give us a price range and we'll select the arrangement for you).

3. We'll send you a notice one week before each recorded date arises, and you contact us only if you don't want the flowers sent.

4. You can also include any special message (pre-arranged or last-minute).

Show your employees you care. Mail the enclosed form to start your own "Forget-Me-Not" program.

Sincerely,

April Bergman
Manager

- Explain the new service clearly, particularly if it is a bit different from what is familiar to the customers.

- Make it simple to use the service.

Company Name
Address
City, State Zip

Hair Today...
Gone Tomorrow.
We Guarantee It!

If you've agonized over unwanted hair, you've probably tweezed 'til you cried...suffered through abrasive waxing...burned yourself with depilatories...sliced yourself shaving (and left ugly, rough stubble behind).

People have been arrested
for doing less damage to others!

Don't do it to yourself ever again. Use the only permanent method, the only safe method, the do-it-once-and-forget-about-it method: ELECTROLYSIS. Use the sensible solution to unwanted hair. Once the hair is gone, it's gone <u>forever</u>. And that's a <u>guarantee</u>!

OUR GUARANTEE:

We will remove unwanted hair
from anywhere on your body
or continue treatment at our own expense.

Come in and visit for a no-obligation discussion and quote that will give you peace of mind. GUARANTEED.

- Use problem/solution when appropriate. In this case, recurring pain vs. a one-time cure.

- Tell the prospect your service is guaranteed.

- Explain the guarantee.

SALON CHIC

brings European flair to you

with Gina Broni, from Milan, Italy.

The newest member of our

award-winning group of stylists

is famed for her "sgargiante" cuts.

Join us for a wine and cheese party

and meet Gina Broni

7:00 p.m., Friday, June 11,

714 Maiden Lane, Larchmont
555-4568

Salud!

- In many businesses, individual employees can command a large following. Spotlight interior decorators, chefs, beauticians, and other service positions.

JUST CAKE

is now called

NOT JUST CAKE

...and I bet you can guess why!

We're still the best bakery in town,

but we've taken the building next door

and turned it into a gourmet deli.

That means you can have NOT JUST CAKE

when you visit our expanded sit-down location at

220-222 West Crossville Street in Marion.

Fax ahead for instant take out service: 555-5374

For more information, call: 555-6769

P.S. Bring this announcement with you and
we'll take 10% off any luncheon item.

- An announcement format can be used for a newspaper ad, hand-out (with menu or price list printed on reverse side), or flyer.

- Offer an incentive as part of your promotional announcement.

Company Name
Address
City, State Zip

<u>Where would Laurel be without Hardy?</u>
<u>Gilbert without Sullivan? Adam without Eve?</u>

Dear Valued Customer:

We hope you'll soon think of us in the same way: You won't be able to think of Mirabelle's without thinking of Added Attractions. We've joined forces to bring you everything under one roof.

Now when you come to Mirabelle's, you'll not only find the outfits of your dreams, you'll be able to accessorize while you're there. Added Attractions has the complementary shoes and bags to offset your new clothing.

Think of us as <u>Mirabelle's Added Attractions</u>...and think of a showcase for sensational ladieswear. A terrific partnership created to serve your fashion needs.

At 300 Landmark Center in Charleston (555-6328).
Come see our newly decorated store.

- Focus on the strengths of each enterprise.

- Explain how those strengths complement each other, making the combination stronger than the two individual stores/businesses.

Company Name
Address
City, State Zip

Date

To Our Customers:

In these days of forced acquisitions and hostile takeovers, I'm proud to announce an old-fashioned merger; one that makes sense for the companies, their employees and—most of all—for their customers.

Lewis Trucking and Collins Freight Forwarders have joined forces to become <u>Lewis-Collins Trucking Services, Inc</u>. This union will bring you faster deliveries and, in many cases, lower shipping costs. And by combining networks, we'll tighten our routes and give you better service. As a combined company, we'll have offices in more than 300 key cities throughout the U.S.

Legally, we start in less than three months. Practically speaking, we're already redefining the routes and schedules that will get your goods where you want them in less time, and often at less cost than ever before.

You'll be hearing from your regional sales representative shortly with all the details. Thanks for your continued patronage. We're going to make you <u>very</u> happy with our merger.

Cordially,

Bob Masten
President

- Let your customers know the merger is a good idea.

- Explain the beneficial impact on the customer.

- State that a representative will follow up with more details.

Company Name
Address
City, State Zip

Dear Long-Time Customer:

My dad started the <u>Corner Store</u> catalog many years ago, and he pounded the secret of success into my head as I grew up in the business. "Give customers what they need," he said with a smile, "and you'll have a winning catalog."

My dad is now semi-retired, and I was thinking about how different his needs are now than when he was running the business. And then an idea hit me, which I shared with him. Create a catalog for you—our long-time customer—who has many of the same special needs as my dad.

The enclosed catalog is the result. It combines items from 22 countries that can play an important role in improving the quality of your life.

You'll find magnifying glasses that make reading fun again. Safety rails that fasten onto tub walls. Clothing with large, easy-to-use snaps (instead of buttons) to ease the strain on arthritic fingers. Walking sticks that open into seats.

Look through the 64 pages of items selected with you in mind. And then take advantage of my dad's special 10% discount. He says the second rule of business is to reward your long-time customers.

Enjoy our new catalog. And if you don't see what you want, will you call me directly? My number is 203-555-4567.

Sincerely,

Jason Parker

- Explain the reason behind the catalog (customers who have been buying for 30+ years).

- Offer a discount as a "thank you" for patronage.

Company Name
Address
City, State Zip

How Would You Like to Win a Rolls Royce?

Okay, so it's a 5-pound chocolate Rolls Royce. It's still quite a conversation piece...and a delicious treat for your next party or event. To win this spectacular confection, all you have to do is come to our downtown Ellenville Nut'n'Candy store, take your best guess of the number of mocha beans in our giant champagne glass, and complete the contest form.

If you win, it's yours. And while you're here, reacquaint yourself with our white and dark liqueur-filled chocolates. Sample our new Italian chocolate from Milan. Have a ball (chocolate or otherwise!). And if you don't see what you want, we'll make it for you.

If you come on a weekend, bring the kids. They'll love watching chocolate and fudge being made.

(In the event of a tie, there will be a random drawing for the winner.)

- A contest is a terrific traffic-builder.

- In a handout or flier, use attention-grabbing headlines and minimal copy.

- Help your customers anticipate what awaits them in the store, and you'll have pre-sold customers.

Company Name
Address
City, State Zip

<u>Here's your opportunity to join</u>
<u>2,000 vocational automotive instructors</u>
<u>at our annual summer workshops.</u>

Last summer, automotive instructors throughout the U.S. learned the newest and best ways to service cars. This summer we want <u>you</u> to be part of these innovative summer workshops.

<u>Place</u>: In our regional service schools, or centrally located public school shops.

<u>Time</u>: One full week, from 8:00 a.m. to 5:00 p.m. each day.

<u>Subjects</u>: Tune-up/emission controls, electrical systems.

<u>Cost</u>: No charge for the workshop. You or your school district are responsible for travel, lodging, and meals.

<u>Enrollment</u>: Complete and return the enclosed form. Be sure to indicate the week you prefer and an alternative week. You should receive notification of dates and location within two weeks of receipt of your request.

This program has become so popular that requests always outnumber the spaces available. Since participants are assigned on a first-come, first-served basis, we urge you to act quickly. No application will be accepted after April 1.

If you want more information, stop in at the Burns Auto Parts and Service shop in your area. We hope to see you this summer.

Cordially,

Mike Avanzare
Director, Training and Education

- Free workshops present an excellent method of promoting a business. But be sure you are targeting groups that buy or can influence those who do.

- Use a graphic device (underlines, bold face type, color) to focus on key points.

- Create a sense of urgency. Specify that enrollment is limited and a cut-off date must be met.

Company Name
Address
City, State Zip

****
SPRING LAWN CARE BONANZA
****

Dear Retailer:

Within a few weeks, homeowners in your area will receive the enclosed brochure offering an introductory special: FREE GARDEN TOOLS with the purchase of <u>Groomall Lawn Mowers!</u>

FREE rakes, spades, weeders, and other lawn tools are the keys to bringing you heavy traffic for the annual Spring spruce-up period. We expect the response from area homeowners to be sensational. And we urge you to be ready for them by stocking up on Groomall Lawn Mowers <u>now</u>. Your customers can't get their FREE tools unless they have the proof of purchase stamps found only on our specially-marked mowers.

We like to think of you as our business partner. We'll entice customers into your store; be sure you have the merchandise to satisfy them!

Our operators are waiting for your last-minute inventory stock-up call. Just dial 1-800-555-2121 and watch your sales grow.

Sincerely,

Wayne Hopkins
VP, Sales

- Manufacturers who sell through retailers need to send constant reminders to their retailers about upcoming promotions.

- Remind the retailers that they will have unhappy customers if the merchandise with the special offer isn't available.

- If you want customers to call, be sure your phone number is prominently highlighted.

Letters from Professionals 13

A professional writes sales letters for much the same reason as anyone else does: to convince others to take a particular action. While the style may vary somewhat from the traditional sales letter, to reflect a professional image, the principles of writing an effective sales letter, discussed throughout this book, should be followed.

In addition, as a professional you should be aware of three aspects of the impression you make:

1) Your trustworthiness
2) Your knowledge and experience
3) Your ingenuity in solving problems capably

Your first job—whether in direct personal contact or through writing—is to sell yourself. <u>You</u> are your product.

Whether you are writing to other professionals or are writing to nonprofessionals, your appearance must be impeccable. Just as you'd want to look the part in a personal interchange, your letters must be without flaw. A faultless communication sells you; a flawed communication can eliminate future business.

Make the letter look attractive. That means short paragraphs, good letter form, accurate spelling, correct grammar, and attractive stationery are all absolutely essential.

How you say things is critical. Sound too folksy and you're judged flippant and unprofessional; use the jargon of your profession to a nonprofessional and you're considered stuffy. If you explain your profession's terminology to someone who already knows it, you insult the reader and may turn him against you. When you aren't sure of the reader's background, an "as you know" often eases you into an explanation you consider vital for your message.

Each communication, no matter how brief, is another opportunity to sell yourself. The reader is interested in your new services, new address, and satisfied clients. But support that interest by mentioning your enjoyment in working with them. Appreciation is never out of style.

Make it as easy as you can for your readers to know who you are, why you're writing, what's in it for them, and where the ball is—in your court or theirs. Hit the mark between too-casual and too-ponderous. Maintain exactly the impression you want the world to have of you—and of your worthy profession.

Company Name
Address
City, State Zip

Date

Mr. Gregory Rogers, Jr.
Bayou Services, Inc.
1250 Threeforks Street
Alexandria, LA 71315

Dear Mr. Rogers:

Paul Weber said you'd enjoy hearing how I the won a big case with the Georgia tax office. He indicated you've had your share of battles with them in the past few years.

As Paul may have told you, the state's official position on his vending machine business was that since his warehouses were located in Georgia, he would have to pay tax on all sales—even though those sales were made solely in Louisiana. Paul's accountants argued unsuccessfully that he had no tax liability in Georgia, since he sold only to Louisiana residents. The short version of the story is, Paul brought me in to speak to the Georgia officials. We negotiated an agreement that reduced his exposure to one tenth of what it would have been!

If you're interested in talking to someone who's scored a major success or two with state tax offices, I'd be delighted to meet with you. In fact, Paul suggested that the three of us get together. I'll call you soon.

Sincerely,

James Farley
Tax Consultant

- Mention the referral immediately.

- A success story that relates to a prospective client's needs can provide a powerful inducement to use your services.

Company Name
Address
City, State Zip

Date

Mr. Joseph McNamara
Vice President, Finance
Food Services, Inc.
2538 Spruce Street
Boston, MA 02264

Dear Mr. McNamara:

May I help you avoid making a potentially serious mistake?

I noticed an article in yesterday's <u>Globe</u> that mentioned you were submitting a proposal to be named concessionaire for all Greenwood Corporation's hospitals in the U.S. As a financial consultant specializing in health care services, I'm more aware of the financial problems of Greenwood—and other hospitals—than members of your staff.

One of the problems you're likely to encounter is reading a hospital financial statement. They're considerably different from what you're used to. You may think a hospital is cash-rich, for example, if it lists unrestricted funds. But those unrestricted funds may also be "board-designated" and only applicable for a specific purpose.

The point is, the hospital market can be profitable if you know your way around it (did you know, for example, that Greenwood owes its current concessionaire over $200,000?).

I can help you avoid the pitfalls that can turn a hospital food operation into a financial abyss. I'll need about 30 minutes of your time to help you decide if I can be of value. I'll give you a call and work around your schedule.

Sincerely,

Victor Holliston
Financial Consultant

- Questions are wonderful involvement devices for bringing a reader right into your message.

- Demonstrate your skill at identifying specific problems that will help the prospect avoid trouble.

Hospital Name
Department
Address
City, State Zip

Date

Sharon K. Weisner, M.D.
1750 Harris Avenue, NW
Brooklyn Heights, OH 44131

Dear Dr. Weisner:

I invite you to utilize the nationally-acclaimed anxiety and depression treatment programs of the Psychopharmacology Research Unit of the Garfield Heights Hospital.

You may have read the recent article in <u>Psychiatric Update</u> that detailed our role in consistently advancing research medications for more than 20 years (see attached reprint). Or you may have seen our unit featured on the recent public broadcasting review of breakthroughs in treating patients with persistent anxiety, panic attacks, or depression.

If you have patients exhibiting these symptoms or who have become dependent on tranquilizers, please consider referring them to us. Our programs are free (supported by grants from the state and federal governments and a number of major pharmaceutical firms). Upon completion of our 8-10 week program, we'll provide you with complete evaluations and treatment recommendations or offer referrals to private psychiatrists or therapists.

This is a wonderful opportunity for your patients to get needed treatment at no cost. Please review the enclosed brochure for admittance procedures. Thank you.

Sincerely,

Elias Mansfield, M.D., Ph.D.
Director

Enclosure

- Establish credentials with reviews.

- Help the reader understand how to use the service and how he/she will be kept informed.

Company Name
Address
City, State Zip

Date

Ms. Toni Miles
Miles Financial Consulting
2922 Montpelier Avenue
College Station, TX 77844

Dear Ms. Miles:

While I'm sorry we couldn't forge an acceptable agreement for you with Investor's Hotline Service, you're better off taking your considerable talents elsewhere.

My opinion is that any company that insists on so many no-payment clauses does so because they're looking for excuses not to pay you. Under their uncompromising language, they could have refused payment for almost any reason. They also could have used your material even though they refused to pay for it.

I know how disappointed you are, but I assure you that this disappointment pales in comparison to what would have happened had you signed under their terms.

I hope we have the opportunity to represent you again.

Very truly yours,

Edward Buchanan, Esq.

- Even when a hoped-for outcome doesn't occur, it's possible to find a positive slant. Explain why the client's interests were well-served.

- Ask for an opportunity to represent the client again.

Company Name
Address
City, State Zip

Date

Ms. Nancy Edwards
Floral Enterprises, Inc.
1102 E. Highway 48
Waterloo, IA 50707

Dear Ms. Edwards:

As you can now attest, negotiating with the IRS can be as frustrating as eating soup with a fork. It requires a lot of patience.

Patience (and preparation), of course, has paid off. I was pleased that you received what amounted to only a long lecture and a negligible penalty. As we discussed, you could have avoided a lot of aggravation, however, and a substantial portion of our fees, if you had paid more attention to record-keeping (particularly with cash sales).

You may want to hire a part-time bookkeeper. That would relieve you of a great deal of data collection and reconciliation (which you said you dislike doing anyway). We'd be happy to provide this service for you. The cost would be largely offset by a reduction in our auditing fees, since organized ledgers will reduce our auditing hours.

If that appeals to you, please call, and we can discuss the details. I'm confident this step will help you reduce stress and help avoid encounters with the IRS.

Very truly yours,

Arlin Gruning
CPA

- You can afford to be modest about your contribution if you "won" the case. The client knows you did a great job.

- Offer future services that can offset similar problems.

Company Name
Address
City, State Zip

Date

Mr. Tucker Stewart
Tobin School Supplies
Old Lincoln Highway
Providence, RI 02920

Dear Tucker:

As you suggested, I followed up with Kyle Fairfield, and he expressed interest in using our auditing services. Now that his company has passed the "magic" $10MM mark, he really needs expanded services.

I'm not sure if Kyle was more impressed by my credentials or the invitation to join me for a round of golf at Tavistock. He's never been there, and he wants to take a crack at it. Will you join us? We have a tentative date for May 19.

Thanks for the referral, Tucker. Maybe I'll let you beat me as your reward!

Regards,

Mike Barrows

- Always acknowledge a referral (even if it doesn't work out).

- Relate general details about the meeting/discussion so the person referring feels a part of the process.

- Try to reciprocate in some way.

Professional Name
Address
City, State Zip

Date

Dennis Humboldt, D.D.S.
New Castle Dental Associates
333 Kenton Street
New Castle, DE 19720

Dear Dennis:

I wonder if it was a periodontist who said "You can lead a horse to water but you can't make him drink?"

I've tried to make your patient, Ronald Steinman, understand that he has suffered a fair amount of bone loss, with more to follow unless he accepts pocket elimination flap surgery for the four posterior sextants (see enclosed report). He refuses to go along with it, but I don't have enough background information to know why.

I appreciate the referral, but I'm frustrated that I haven't been able to convince Mr. Steinman that he has a very unhappy periodontal future ahead of him. Perhaps you can reassure him that the surgery is mandated by his condition, not by my whim.

Thanks again, Dennis. I appreciate your referrals.

Sincerely,

Dom DiStefano, D.D.S.

Enclosure

- Express your conviction that you tried to make it work.

- Thank the associate for his/her part.

ORTHOPEDIC ASSOCIATES

is now affiliated with

DORSET PHYSICAL THERAPY CENTER

To better serve the needs of our active, health-conscious community, we've joined forces to provide complete surgical and non-surgical treatment and rehabilitation exercises for orthopedic injuries. Our doctors are on the premises to monitor your progress with the physical therapy staff.

Please feel free to visit our new facility at:

96 South Main Street, Dorset, VT

Or call 555-3303 for a descriptive brochure.

- Headline the affiliation

- Explain why the affiliation was created and what it will do for the prospective customer.

- Invite prospects to contact you.

Professional Name
Address
City, State Zip

Dear Neighbor:

We're putting our best foot forward so we can treat yours better.

Main Street Podiatry has moved...about 20 feet to the left. We've taken larger quarters in the Main Street Professional Complex to better serve your foot care needs. We're now in Suite 12 instead of Suite 8.

With more offices and updated equipment, we've been able to add two more <u>Board Certified podiatrists</u> who are at the top of their profession.

We now have more doctors (a total of four Board Certified podiatrists), more examination rooms, more treatment options, and less delay for an appointment. Take a positive step forward and visit our expanded facility.

Sincerely,

Thomas R. Laughlin, D.P.M., F.A.C.F.S.
Diplomate American Board of Podiatric Surgery

- Notify your patients (and prospects) of an address change.

- Explain that the move permits better treatment, more comfortable facilities, etc.

Company Name
Address
City, State Zip

Date

Mr. George Bill
Vice President, Finance
Cavalier Hotel
4310 Jamestown Ave.
Fort Wayne, IN 46815

Dear Mr. Bill:

It looks like we're going to have to spend more time than anticipated to complete your audit.

As we discussed, your banquet department did not retain some of the invoices from their catering activities. In our original engagement letter, we had indicated a need to review these documents. Since they don't exist, however, we'll have to reconstruct them from various sources. Unfortunately, this will be considerably more time-consuming than examining source documents.

For the additional time, we'll bill you at our regular rate of $70 per hour (added to our $8,000 audit fee). I've discussed the problem with your sales manager, and she has agreed to hold original documents in the future for a period of three years.

On the plus side, your people have been unusually cooperative and knowledgeable. I can see that you spent a lot of time getting them ready for us. Thank you.

Very truly yours,

Kenneth Albrecht
CPA

- This sort of problem occurs often. That's why it's always important to spell out billing details in the original proposal. It saves arguments and avoids hard feelings.

- If possible, balance the negative with a positive.

Professional Name
Address
City, State Zip

Date

Mr. Roger St. Clerc
282 West Morrison Street
Santa Fe, NM 87501

Dear Mr. St. Clerc:

It may have slipped your mind that you had an appointment scheduled for Tuesday, January 16, at 10:00 a.m.

I know how difficult it is to maintain a busy schedule, and I understand that cancellations are unavoidable. But in the future it would be greatly appreciated if you notified the office—in advance—if a change is necessary. That way a patient in need of treatment can be scheduled in your place.

I look forward to seeing you during your next visit. Please call and reschedule your appointment for a convenient time.

Sincerely,

Dr. Marilyn Girard

- Everyone makes mistakes, so resist the urge to vent your frustration (unless the problem is chronic).

- Tell the patient that a missed appointment takes an appointment away from another patient.

- Reassure the patient you will be happy to see him/her again.

Selling Investments, Real Estate, Insurance, and Banking Services 14

How would you feel if you inquired about establishing a college trust fund for your children, and received the following letter in response (this letter is reprinted <u>exactly</u> as it was received from a major bank—typos and all):

> It is my pleasure to be able to serve you in your banking needs As per your request, enclosed are two sets of signature cards if they are for custodian for your children, please fill in the white cards front and back. If they are in trust for them, fill out the yellow cards In either case, the children do not sign the cards, just the trustee. Enclosed are copies of rates that you requested, our penaly clause is six months loss of interest. Please feel free to call if you have any questions Again, it is my pleasure to serve you.

While this may be an extreme case of writing that can kill a sale, it demonstrates the need for effective letter writing in the industries represented in this chapter.

In the four fields covered in this chapter, the more you personalize, the better your response. Mass mailings to "Resident" or "Dear Executive" are often viewed with suspicion and assigned a low value by the recipient. It may be more expensive to obtain a "by name" mailing list, but it will pay off in added response.

If you're willing to take the time to consider what's important to your prospects, and pay attention to the overall presentation of your correspondence, you can greatly improve the quality of leads and conversions.

Selling Investments. While there are many legal restrictions that must be adhered to in selling investments, there is no reason why creativity should be tossed out the window. When asked why they write a certain way, many people in legally-restricted fields say the lawyers tell them what to say. But when you ask the lawyers, they say that isn't so. They simply tell their clients what they <u>can't</u> say.

Think of the questions people most often ask and weave the answers into your letter. And put your personality on paper. Be creative, and you'll increase your sales.

Selling Real Estate. The best thing you can do for your relationship with your clients is to give them a feeling of confidence in you and your firm. Be sure residential prospects know about your successes in selling similar homes. Give your corporate prospects a sense of your "can-do" approach to finding the right location and making the right deal.

When you offer a client a proposal, don't just list numbers; tell the client how great a deal it is. Use your selling ability to sell on paper and you'll reap the rewards.

Selling Insurance. Personalize your message to the group to which you're mailing. Small businesses have very different needs from larger ones. Executives have different requirements from lower salaried personnel. Your letters should reflect those differences. Don't send the same letter to all categories on your mailing list.

Insurance is often an emotional sell. Be sure to make your letters benefits-laden.

Selling Banking Services. Bankers may face the greatest challenge in keeping their letters from sounding cold-hearted and stodgy. The banking profession is working hard to change this image. Millions of dollars are being spent to advertise friendly service and personally concerned loan officers... all of which can be erased with an icy, ill-conceived letter. Letters from bankers should reflect the warmth of a human-to-human relationship.

Company Name
Address
City, State Zip

Dear IRA Investor:

The Everest Group of Funds has grown by 112% in just the last year. We attribute that growth to special advantages that Everest investors enjoy. For example:

1. There's no load. That means we have no charges whatsoever for buying or selling shares for you. Ask your current fund representative if that's the case with his/her investment group.

2. There are no extra charges. No opening or closing fees, no service charges. While you're asking your fund rep about item #1, ask him/her about this one, too.

3. You can put in as little as $250 to start, and add as much or as little as you want anytime during the year.

Read about the special benefits of the Everest Group of Funds in the enclosed prospectus and information kit. Then complete and send in the enclosed application form or call me directly at 1-800-555-0880. Find out for yourself how we can help you attain deferred tax savings while building your wealth and retirement fund.

Sincerely,

Francis Steinmetz
President

- Establish the reason for writing within the salutation.

- Emphasize key differences between you and your competitors. In the competitive IRA field, a little difference can go a long way.

- An invitation to call the president will often draw extra response.

Company Name
Address
City, State Zip

Date

Mr. Alvin Beckworth
38 Calpurnia Drive
Anaheim, CA 92877

Dear Mr. Beckworth:

After speaking with you, it's obvious that you're thinking about using a so-called discount broker—and, yes, they do charge smaller commissions. But there are some things in life that are worth paying a bit more for.

For example, when you visit your doctor, do <u>you</u> tell <u>him</u> what's wrong with you, what to do about it, and what prescription to write? Or do you rely on his knowledge, background, training, and expertise?

Think about what you <u>really</u> want in a stockbroker. Do you want a full-service firm with a complete range of investments and services; one that provides detailed research reports; experts who make recommendations on industries and individual firms; a professional organization that provides registered representatives who will discuss investment strategies and trades?

Can you afford to work with an order taker who is not paid to steer you away from bad investments or toward good ones? Can you afford <u>not</u> to get the best research? Are you willing to risk your financial health by eliminating professional advice?

You get what you pay for, Mr. Beckworth. I hope you'll reconsider. I'll call you next week to see what you've decided.

Sincerely,

Troy Ashworth

- Analogies are good devices for defining your position. They can be helpful in illustrating a difficult-to-grasp point.

- If your service is more expensive, don't deny it. Explain why you're worth it and what value the client receives for it.

Company Name
Address
City, State Zip

AN INTERVIEW WITH A BISMARK FUND INVESTOR
#6 in a series (Mark Thomas, Marion, IA)

Q. Of all the investment options available to you, Mr. Thomas, why did you select the Bismark Fund?

A. I felt very comfortable knowing the investment was managed by the professionals at Bismark. They have had an excellent track record over the last fifteen years. I don't like taking big chances with my money.

Q. Suppose you need money in a hurry. How difficult is it to get to your funds?

A. About as tough as writing a check. Bismark includes a free check writing option with instant access to my money. I can write a check for whatever amount I want ($500 minimum), whenever I want it.

Q. Bismark is a big, busy fund. How do you get help if you need it?

A. I just dial Bismark's toll free number (1-800-555-5252) and talk to one of their always pleasant, eager-to-help staff.

Q. What would you say to anyone who is considering investing his money?

A. I'd suggest he seriously look into the Bismark Fund. I couldn't be any more satisfied with any fund than I am with Bismark.

Thank you, Mr. Thomas. Good advice.

Read the enclosed Bismark Fund Prospectus that provides detailed information about various investment opportunities. Then complete the enclosed application form and mail it today with your initial investment.

P.S. To learn the current Fund yields and Net Asset Values, call the toll-free number now!

- Investment opportunities are rarely personalized. This interview approach is a more interesting version of the typical lead generator investment letter. Despite the stringent legalities involved with investment letters, there are creative opportunities available.

Company Name
Address
City, State Zip

Date

Mr. Vernon Magee
11 Sunflower Lane
Tupelo, MS 38803

Dear Vernon:

You've worked hard for your money, and I think we're making your money work hard for you. I know how much you're depending on your investments to fund a comfortable retirement income.

That's why I feel so strongly that you're about to make a serious error. There is nothing that supports an investment in Alberta Industries. The president has no track record, the company has not produced anything of value and is, in fact, <u>highly</u> speculative. You're on target for a wonderful retirement, and your proposed route could cause you a serious setback.

Please rethink your position. Naturally, I'll abide by your decision.

Yours truly,

James Patrick

- Offer your professional judgment and whatever reasons support your reluctance to pursue the course of action.

- Assure the client that you will do as he/she requests.

Company Name
Address
City, State Zip

Are you prepared
to throw your money away?

Dear Graduate:

This is probably the only letter you'll receive that offers straight talk about the investing pitfalls that could seriously impair your new life. Here's the lowdown for new investors.

1. If you can't afford to lose it, don't risk it!
   Don't take the chance of starting your new life in a deep hole. Any stock, bond, or option carries a risk.

2. Don't play favorites with an industry!
   If you go into the market, diversify as you build. If you have all financial stocks and there's a collapse, you have nothing left to cushion the blow.

3. Don't get bored!
   There are thousands of stories about people who became "tired of success." They wanted more action. So they jumped from their steady investments into disaster.

Let us help you build financial security. Send the enclosed card to receive our booklet, Straight Talk for the New Graduate. Or call me for a no-obligation review of your current investment potential and opportunity.

Good luck with your new career.

Sincerely,

Karl Dougherty
Account Executive

- Try a twist on your standard approach to induce readership. The headline in this letter is a variation on the more traditional—and trite—"Invest wisely and build a successful future."

- Useful tips, rather than platitudes, help a prospect decide to make contact.

Company Name
Address
City, State Zip

Dear Candlewyck Homeowner:

Did you notice our "For Sale" sign posted at 231 Nathaniel Drive last week? It's now a "Sold" sign. How about the one at 124 Downing Street? That house sold within three weeks.

We've earned a reputation for moving homes faster than any other realtor in the area. And equally impressive, we almost always get you the price you want. When you're ready to sell your home—or even if you just want to determine the kind of price your home would bring—call me for a no-obligation appraisal.

I'm here at your convenience. If I'm not in the office (555-4200), I'll get back to you. And please feel free to call whenever it's convenient for you (from 8:00 a.m. to 9:00 p.m. Monday through Saturday). I'll work around your schedule.

Give me a call. I'll give you the "inside" story about where home prices are heading, and what's happening in the real estate market in general.

Cordially,

Stella Kaufman

- List your successes in the neighborhood.

- Send letters every month; they have a cumulative effect.

- Make the prospect comfortable about calling at his/her convenience.

- Everyone likes "inside" information. But if you offer it, be sure you can deliver.

Company Name
Address
City, State Zip

Date

Mr. Jack Littlepage
GSI Industries
1288 Airport Industry Road
Lester, PA 19113

Dear Jack:

Here's the ammunition you need to convince your management that you should move your plant to our new facility in Pt. Jiguero, Puerto Rico.

1. You need to move since you've outgrown your current facility.

2. You can lease our brand-new air conditioned 13,500 square foot building for ten.years for only $42,100 per year, or just $3.12 per square foot per year!

3. This new building is close to your Aguadilla facility, meaning you would share transportation costs.

4. You'd have access to a large, English-speaking labor pool.

5. There is a 15-year Puerto Rican tax exemption available.

You can have your accountant verify my numbers, but I believe you'll wind up with a tax savings of nearly 50% in the first four years, and just under 40% for the next three.

The Puerto Rican market is hot. Although the rates will always be more favorable than in the continental U.S., they won't stay at this level for long.

Call me if you need more specifics.

Cordially,

Albert Kinney

- Reinforce that you're an ally of the prospect, helping him to give management what's good for them.

- List key points for clarity.

- If true, advise that rates may rise soon (try to force an action).

Company Name
Address
City, State Zip

Date

Mr. Jerome Hersch
Jansen Medical Supplies
4100 Iron River Drive
Rehobeth Beach, DE 19971

Dear Mr. Hersch:

I think you're going to be <u>very</u> pleased with the offer I've put together for you. The landlord wants you as a tenant, and he's really pulled out all the stops to deliver the best pricing and incentives.

By taking a three year lease on the remaining 1,899 square feet on the second floor, you'll receive:

1. 10 months' FREE rent.
2. Addition of 54' of new interior walls.
3. Construction of glass-enclosed conference room.
4. Upgraded carpeting; paint or wallpaper; wood trim around existing doors.
5. Double glass doors at suite entrance.

This is prime office space, right on Route 13 in Milford. It's easy to get to from anywhere in the northeast, and it's within a half-hour of Newark's commuter airport. Your rental rate is a guaranteed $14.65 triple net per year (no escalator clause over the three years) and it includes <u>all</u> utilities.

What a combination: prestige office space, low rental, customized renovations, and 10 FREE months! When shall I send an agreement?

Sincerely,

Clark Sands
Plymouth Realty Group

- Don't assume the customer understands what a good deal you've obtained for him. Be enthusiastic about the opportunity, and list <u>all</u> the key selling points.

Company Name
Address
City, State Zip

Date

Mr. Lester Coyle
Coyle & Coe, Inc.
490 East Bellevue Street
Royalton, VT 05068

Dear Mr. Coyle:

Picture yourself in this setting: the third floor of a modern corporate office center, overlooking the scenic beauty of tree-lined Crystal Lake. (The enclosed brochure shows several interiors as well as the dramatic view from the office windows.)

If you're thinking about new office space in the Royalton area, you have to think of The Tannery Corporate Center. But you'll have to think fast. Of 400,000 square feet, only 39,860 square feet remain. Aside from the view, here's what makes the last 10% of space so special:

> o We'll subdivide the space into any of ten different floor plans (see enclosed), containing as little as 2,800 square feet, all of which may be modified to suit your needs.

> o The low monthly rental of only $15.00 per square foot includes heat, electricity, daily janitorial service, and all repairs. You have a choice of carpet, paint color, ceiling tiles, and overhead fixtures.

Let me show you why The Tannery has achieved 90% occupancy in just six months...and why the final 10% won't last much longer. I'll call to schedule your visit.

Sincerely,

Alan Raymond

Enclosure

- This is a personalized cold call letter. Instead of just listing the features of office space, it asks the prospect to consider himself/herself in the space.

- List the key features (including price if it's an asset).

Company Name
Address
City, State Zip

Dear Small Business Executive:

You know what it's like to be out on your own. There are so many decisions to be made. But now there's one less tough decision to make: your company's medical coverage.

The Coglin Agency can provide you and your employees with the same group benefits that only large companies have been able to offer.

- Choice of more than 1,600 physicians state-wide.

- Unlimited hospital coverage.

- No waiting periods for pre-existing conditions.

It doesn't matter if you're a three, ten, or twenty person business. <u>Call 1-800-555-0909 or return the enclosed postage-paid reply card today for more information and rates!</u> The Coglin Agency has you covered!

Sincerely,

David Coglin
President

- Create a sense of understanding of the prospect's position as a small businessperson.

- Don't try to put too much in the letter. Highlights can draw you solid, qualified leads.

- Toll-free numbers and/or business reply cards will give you the highest lead count and deliver the best return on your advertising investment.

Company Name
Address
City, State Zip

Date

Mr. Carl Williams
Vice President, Manufacturing
Buckeye Copper Tubing
Center Point Industrial Park
Baltimore, MD 21219

Dear Carl:

We have one major objective: to help you reduce the number of employee accident and injury claims and the subsequent dollar loss in service time and productivity.

That's why we place so much emphasis on employee training. If we were your insurer, we would send a team of specialists to your various locations twice a year to conduct loss control programs for your regional and site managers.

You may be surprised to learn that the companies using this service lose 32% fewer man-hours than companies that do not. Prevention programs pay off. And the good news is that you don't pay anything for this valuable training service.

Please read the enclosed statistical analysis for verification. Then think what it could be worth to you to save at least $10,000 in premiums and tens of thousands of dollars more in man-hours. I'll be in touch.

Cordially,

Graham Johnson

Enclosure

- Free services impress clients—particularly when the services save money.

- Highlight what you can do to make a difference (training).

- Discuss dollar savings—if they're significant.

Company Name
Address
City, State Zip

FOR NON-SMOKERS ONLY!!!

How would you like to have as much as <u>triple</u>
your current life insurance coverage
for <u>less</u> than you're currently paying?

Dear Health-Conscious Executive:

You're about to reap the benefits of taking good care of your health.

If you...

     (1) are willing to take a physical exam (at our expense)
     (2) have not smoked for at least 12 months

...you're eligible for the life insurance policy that is the talk of every executive suite.

If you're 35 years old, you can have a $500,000 executive protector policy for under $500 a year. (Comparably low rates are available for older applicants.) Can you imagine paying such a low premium for this kind of protection? That's as little as <u>one-third</u> of many life insurance premiums.

Mail the enclosed card for details, or call 302-555-8989. You'll receive a complete rate schedule and information on how to set up your physical exam (at your home or office).

Congratulations on earning another great benefit of good health—lower health insurance premiums!

Sincerely,

Len Jorgensen

- If you're looking for a specific market segment (non-smokers), make the appeal prominent.

- Give examples of savings.

- Make it easy to respond.

Company Name
Address
City, State Zip

"Jury Awards $850,000 for Dog Bite."

"Woman Falls on Sidewalk; $1,200,000 Judgment."

"Housekeeper Sues Family for Radon Poisoning."

Dear Homeowner:

These are a few of today's headlines. Do they give you cause for concern? With the courts constantly broadening the concept of legal liability, it's possible for you to be liable today or tomorrow for something that was unthinkable just yesterday.

Ask yourself what would happen to you and your family if you were <u>sued for a million dollars</u>. Could you survive that kind of judgment? Could you survive a $100,000 or $50,000 judgment? Can you afford not to look into extended personal liability protection?

Because tomorrow is so uncertain, I urge you to review the enclosed brochure. Think about the implications, and then call me at 201-555-8642 to discuss a policy tailor-made for your needs.

Sincerely,

Clayton Jefferson

- Actual headlines (rather than abstractions) provide the required jolt to make this kind of letter work.

- Ask questions that will make the prospect think about his/her situation.

- Ask for an immediate action.

Company Name
Address
City, State Zip

Date

Mr. and Mrs. Theodore Bouljerian
434 Mimosa Drive
Belle Fourche, SD 57742

Dear Mr. and Mrs. Bouljerian:

Why do you think so many parents are buying life insurance for their children? Here are just a few of the compelling reasons you should consider joining them:

1. You start to build cash value for your child at a very early age. When the child needs cash (for college, an emergency, or to start a family), it's there.

2. By starting while your child is young, he or she will have protection that might not be available later because of illness or injury.

3. A substantial policy costs <u>very little</u>; and the sooner you start, the smaller the premium.

Please review the enclosed sample plan that shows how easy it is to insure the dreams you have for your child. I'll answer all your questions when I call next week.

Cordially,

Gina Marino

- Starting with a question involves the reader.

- List the answers to your question.

- Prepare the prospects for your follow-up call.

Company Name
Address
City, State Zip

Date

Ms. Constance Clayton
77 Squire Lane
Little Rock, AR 72207

Dear Ms. Clayton:

We appreciate your opening a checking and money market account with us. We also want you to know that we're prepared to help you in a number of other ways.

Our business is to lay the cornerstone for your financial security. We maintain a team of planners and strategists that includes professionals in real estate, finance, insurance, accounting, investments, trusts, and personal and corporate planning.

We're specialists at creating personal and professional financial successes. Put our experience to work for you. We will help you pinpoint your goals and devise methods for achieving them. And we will help you manage your assets to produce and preserve your wealth.

We invite you to build your financial foundation with First State Bank of Arkansas. Please come in and let me show you how we can help accomplish this.

Very truly yours,

Ralph Higgins
Vice President

- Express appreciation soon after a new account is opened.

- Outline the services that are available. Many people think of a bank as only a place to cash a check.

- Ask for a specific action ("come in and let me show you how...").

Company Name
Address
City, State Zip

Date

Mrs. Alton Corley
2819 Knights Road
Spirit Lake, IA 51360

Dear Mrs. Corley:

We need your approval to help your assets grow faster.

Our Trust Investment Committee has reviewed your portfolio and recommends that your assets on the attached list be sold and reinvested in a $17,000 Short Term Corporate Bond. This will yield 9-1/2%, an increase of 1% over your current investments.

If you'd like to take advantage of this opportunity, please sign, date, and return the enclosed copy of this letter in the envelope we've provided for your convenience.

If you have any questions, please give me a call.

We appreciate your continued patronage.

Cordially,

Richard Huxley

Enclosure

- Be sure the prospect knows immediately that there's a benefit to be gained by reading this letter.

- State the advantage of following your advice.

- Make it easy for the prospect to say "yes" by explaining what needs to be done.

Company Name
Address
City, State Zip

Date

Mr. Adam Bengston
Bengston Enterprises, Inc.
84 W. Lehigh Avenue
Chatanooga, TN 37456

Dear Mr. Bengston:

Good news. We have favorably reviewed and evaluated the supporting data for your building project. We have also identified and evaluated the potential underwriters, investors, and lenders.

Now we invite you and your associates to meet with us at our headquarters in Memphis. We'll outline our offer to secure the financing that will meet your capital requirements. Some of the key terms that will be presented to you include:

1.	Loan Amount	$ 5.5 million
2.	Fee	$7,500(upon delivery of underwriting agreement)
3.	Term	20 years
4.	Interest Rate	9.5% composite
5.	Equity	to be negotiated
6.	Underwriting Fee	$39,000 (approximately)
7.	Extensions	yes

I think the speed with which we were able to present our proposal demonstrates how highly we regard you and your project. I'll call you in a few days to set a meeting date.

Yours truly,

Thomas C. DiStasio
Vice President

- Don't make the prospect hunt for good news.

- List the key terms to avoid confusion.

- Reaffirm your willingness to make a deal, and ask for a meeting.

Company Name
Address
City, State Zip

Date

Mr. Robert McGinnis
528 Winchester Road
Burbank, CA 91520

Dear Mr. McGinnis:

We've found another way to make your money work for you at Burbank Federal S&L. We've established a working relationship with Redi-Fund that allows us to invest short-term cash in your account (in multiples of $1,000) on a daily basis.

Redi-Fund is a daily open-ended fund that invests all its assets in short-term tax-exempt obligations such as Bond Notes, Bond Anticipation Notes, Revenue Anticipation Notes, Tax Anticipation Notes, and Tax-free Bonds with short maturities. We anticipate the net asset value per share will remain constant. Dividends are earned daily at varying rates and paid monthly.

When you have a moment, read the enclosed Redi-Fund prospectus. We cannot, of course, take responsibility for the accuracy or completeness of this prospectus. If, after reading the prospectus, you decide that this fund makes sense for your cash investments, please sign the attached authorization form and return it to us.

We'll keep you advised of other opportunities. We continue to search for ways to make your money grow.

Sincerely,

Willard Griffith
Senior Vice President

- Even though there are legal restrictions placed on what you can say in certain types of financial correspondence, there is no reason to clutter a letter with heavy "whereases" and "heretofores."

Company Name
Address
City, State Zip

Date

Mr. and Mrs. Arthur Zucker
13 Hempstead Road
Concord, NH 03301

Dear Mr. and Mrs. Zucker:

You have the power to secure the financial future that will protect you and your family.

It doesn't matter how troubled the times, it doesn't matter if you make $20,000 or $200,000. What does matter is that you (1) obtain reliable information, (2) know how to plan carefully, and (3) learn the right strategy for you.

You'll have the chance to do all three by attending a FREE money management seminar conducted by Old Concord National Bank. Don Kingsley, Executive Vice President of Old Concord, will show you how to put your dollars to work earning the financial independence you deserve.

This is a special seminar for <u>customers only</u>. Space is limited in our community room, so let us know if you will attend. Please mail the coupon below and check the date that's convenient for you.

Learn the ins and outs of retirement planning, preserving your estate, and risk management.

Sincerely,

Glen Portland
President

- A customers-only seminar reinforces the value of working with your institution. It offers a sense of belonging.

- Help the customers feel comfortable about attending, no matter what their income.

- Ask for a commitment (coupon, phone call).

Bank Name
Address
City, State Zip

Date

Mr. Leon Murtaugh
1322 W. Bayard Street
Columbus, MS 39703

Dear Mr. Murtaugh:

I just stamped your file "pre-approved."

That means you can take an automobile loan for up to $20,000. No meetings. No lengthy credit reviews. No explanations. You're pre-approved. Period. (I've attached a description of our 3, 4, and 5-year payment schedules.)

Go to your favorite automobile dealer and select the car of your dreams. Then take this letter to any Columbus Bank & Trust office and receive your pre-approved loan. You don't have to wait any longer to purchase that new car (or truck) you've wanted so much.

One more thing: we have the lowest auto loan rates in town! You not only have up to $20,000 waiting for you, the interest rate is so low that your car shopping will be a real joy.

Happy shopping,

Frank Marner

Enclosure

- Personalize the letter.

- Sell and re-sell "no strings attached."

- Throw in additional inducement (lowest rates).

Credit and Collections 15

The key to writing successful credit and collection letters is remembering that you are focusing on very sensitive issues. These letters don't deal solely with money matters—but with people's pride and self-image.

The job of these letters is to recognize your customers' feelings while you're dealing effectively with the credit and collections processes.

Granting and Refusing Credit. Turn an approval of credit into an event. Praise the customer for his or her good standing. Mention how pleased you are to be doing business with the company and the individual. Take advantage of every opportunity to make the customer feel good about doing business with you.

There are many reasons why credit may not be extended. Because someone is not creditworthy at the present time, however, is not to say he or she won't be creditworthy at some point in the future. Show concern and caring for the person or company's position and don't permanently poison the relationship. Explain the reason for the decision and offer concessions that will allow the customer to save face and feel valued.

Collection Letters. Many collection letters are awful. Not because they're poorly written (although many are), but because they're offensive.

Think about when you've missed a payment on a bill. You may have been ill, on vacation, or away on a business trip. Your payment may have been lost in the mail, you may have forgotten to pay or, frankly, you might have been momentarily short of funds.

Now think about the collection letter you received. Probably made you a little angry, didn't it? You'd paid your bills faithfully to that company for months or years, and then you received a nasty little note with a dire threat if your $21.00 payment wasn't made within five days.

Attempting to intimidate or bully the customer into paying usually results in the delinquent payer becoming angry. Instead of fostering a sense of cooperation and mutual trust, the typical collection letter fosters a strong dislike for the company responsible for sending it. And all too often, even though the bill may be paid, the ill will generated loses a customer who might never again be involved in a no-pay problem.

Collection letters often violate the key precept of a good sales letter. They don't take the reader into account; they're written only from a self-serving point of view ("You owe us money. Now pay it, or else!"). Think of the collection letters you send as an advertising campaign. In this case you want to sell the customer on paying the bill. Each letter should feed off the previous one; there should be a sense of continuity. You may want to have increasingly "important" signatures on each letter (for example, from Customer Service Representative to Credit Manager) to add a sense of growing concern to the sequence.

There will always be deadbeats. But never lose sight of the fact that the vast majority of people you write to are decent, honorable human beings. Treat them as you would like to be treated.

In the words of Dale Carnegie, a man whose name is synonymous with getting the most out of people, "If you want to gather honey, don't kick over the beehive."

Treat credit and collections—and the people on the receiving end—with the same professionalism you put into selling your product, service, and image. It will pay off for you with increased collections—and appreciative customers.

Company Name
Address
City, State Zip

Date

Mr. Henry Patchell
Director of Food Service
St. Cloud University
Stillwater Hall
Stony Point, NY 10980

Dear Henry:

I know what a crunch you folks are in financially. I've done my best to put off the inevitable, but the University has been unresponsive to working out any sort of payment program for the $220,000 it owes.

You've done a great job in trying to hold things together, but we're going to have to withdraw any additional credit. We'll take St. Cloud through the last four months of the school year, but my management says it will have to be:

1. On a cash basis, in advance. Each week you'll have to deliver a check to cover the next week's service.

2. With a systematic pay-down schedule to get your account current within six months.

This is done with great regret, Henry. We're trying not to cut you off cold, but the University is going to have to sit down with us to avoid a complete shut-down of food service. Can you arrange a meeting next week? Let's fight to save our relationship and a potentially embarrassing situation.

Please call me by the 15th to set a date.

Sincerely,

Virginia Bridges
Sales Manager

- Acknowledge the difficulty of the situation, without apologizing for your company's stance.

- State clearly that the credit will be withdrawn and what terms for continuance will be offered.

- Be sure to direct any negatives at the institution rather than at individuals.

Company Name
Address
City, State Zip

Date

Ms. Leona Appleton
673 West Gate Avenue
Fredericksburg, VA 22402

Dear Ms. Appleton:

The sooner you complete the enclosed application form, the sooner you'll be able to enjoy the special benefits and sales our card holders boast about!

When we receive credit approval, we'll send you an official letter of welcome. Save it because it will include several new cardholder specials! When your credit card arrives (about two weeks later) you can redeem your special offers.

Thanks for choosing The Midway for your shopping needs. If you have any questions about the application form, please call 703-555-3434. If you hurry, you'll have your card in time for Christmas shopping!

Cordially,

Mattie Wingate
Credit Manager

- Every correspondence is a chance to make the customer feel good about you and your service. Be enthusiastic about his/ her decision to take your credit card.

- Give the customer a time frame.

- Give a telephone number in case the customer requires assistance.

Company Name
Address
City, State Zip

Date

Mrs. Ethel Stein
SleepRite
11 Willowdale Shopping Plaza
Wells, MI 49689

Dear Mrs. Stein:

I missed the boat. I was concentrating so much on the selection for your initial order, I never gave you the enclosed financial disclosure form to complete. Without it, my company can't extend it's normal credit terms.

I'll see to it that you receive speedy credit approval because I don't want to hold up your order. I know how important the merchandise is to your Spring Sale. Just return the form to me immediately (be sure to give us three current credit references), and I'll personally take it to our credit manager.

Thanks again for selecting us as a new supplier. I'm sure this is the start of a profitable, long-term relationship.

Cordially,

Ian Fortune

- Advise the new customer that you will rush the application through channels.

- Specify anything of particular importance (to avoid delays).

- Thank the customer for the business.

Company Name
Address
City, State Zip

Date

Mr. Welles Hasse
Credit Manager
National Tire Company
3200 West Park Drive
Kent, WA 98042

Dear Mr. Hasse:

Mr. David Ennis, of Lincoln Auto Parts and Accessories, has offered your company as a credit reference. Since Mr. Ennis has given us a sizeable purchase order (and a fairly urgent deadline), I'd appreciate a quick response.

Specifically, how long has Lincoln been a client? Is their average order over $5,000? What is their average payable period?

Thanks for your help. If we can ever reciprocate, please ask.

Sincerely,

Kirk Leland
Credit Manager

- Identify the prospective client, and specify exactly what information you seek.

- If you need the information quickly, say so.

Company Name
Address
City, State Zip

Date

Mr. Jerry Hurd
Owner
Jerry's Haberdashery
42 Olive Street
Eureka, CA 09090

Dear Mr. Hurd:

I was pleased to receive another order from you this morning for twelve dozen assorted men's dress shirts. Obviously, you've found our Mohawk brand to be a welcome addition to your store. Our national advertising delivers high visibility and increased traffic.

I'm also pleased to inform you that you've passed our credit approval process with flying colors. You don't have to send a check with your order—in fact, you have preferred customer status, with an open line of $15,000.

Welcome to the Mohawk team, and thanks for selecting us as a new supplier. We appreciate your business and look forward to working with you for many years.

Cordially,

Colleen Smith
Credit Manager

- Even credit approval letters can continue to sell your company and its products. Don't miss the opportunity to make the client feel good about having you as a vendor.

- Thank the client for his continued business.

Company Name
Address
City, State Zip

Date

Mr. Charles H. Thomason
Allied Farm Insurance
525 Shelton Avenue
Omaha, NE 68114

Dear Mr. Thomason:

It's no surprise to either of us that your company passed our credit review process in record time.

As a way of saying we want your business, we've established a $100,000 open-to-buy credit line (the largest we've ever issued), against which you may order at any time. Simply call me, my assistant, Jan Lyon, or our production director, Carla Leaming, for fast action.

You'll be receiving an official notification and welcome from our Vice President of Finance, Joe Vincente. He'll outline payment terms and procedures (which are exactly as we discussed).

Thank you for selecting us as your forms manufacturer. We'll see to it that your 425 U.S. locations are well supplied and current. I'll be in touch.

Very truly yours,

Matthew Ryan
VP, Sales

- Compliment the client on the speedy approval, indicating that his/her company is particularly desirable.

- If appropriate, give the names of contacts who can provide assistance.

Company Name
Address
City, State Zip

Date

Mr. Curtis Patrick
Grand Cuisine
481 S. Elm Street
Twin Falls, ID 83301

Dear Curtis:

I have a "half-a-loaf-is-better-than-none" solution for getting our superb copper-ware into your lovely shop.

Although our finance department won't bend its no-credit stance for new retailers (at the 12-month mark, they'll reexamine your application), they have authorized me to extend an olive branch.

Since you have to pay cash with order, they're willing to give you a 5% discount on all goods, reflecting cost of money. Secondly, they're willing to waive our minimum order requirements to make it easier for you to start experiencing the profits that come with our beautiful line.

Our products enjoy a fast turnover. You won't have to worry about your money being tied up in inventory for long. According to a retailer survey we just completed, the average shelf life of our copper bowls and decorative molds, for example, is just 14 days.

That may not be the whole loaf you were hoping for, but it's certainly a workable compromise (maybe three-quarters of a loaf!). I'll call to get your starter order.

Cordially,

Richard Bonner

- Credit rejection can sour a prospect forever. If you're willing to offer face-saving opportunities, you may salvage the prospect.

- State that the company wants the business even though it won't deviate from the standard policy.

Company Name
Address
City, State Zip

Date

Mr. Miller Weston
Ranier Manufacturing Company
401 Alloy Creek Road
Redmond, WA 98073

Dear Mr. Weston:

We want to do business with you, but we're going to have to be "creative" about credit sales...at least for a while.

As you're well aware, we discount our chemicals rather heavily. Because we work on such tight margins, we can't afford to be extended for as long a period as a number of your current suppliers indicate is your norm.

We can offer you a 2% discount for cash with order. That means you'll get our industry-best pricing, plus a cash-incentive discount. When your payable schedule improves with other vendors, we'll be happy to put you in a credit position.

We're looking forward to working with you. You should experience a rather dramatic drop in your product cost when you start using Tyler Chemicals.

Sincerely,

Wendy Imperiale

- Acknowledge the difficulty without being negative. Be positive about the cash discount.

- Offer a ray of hope and the desire to do business now.

- Explain that it's to the prospect's advantage to purchase on any terms.

Collection Letter, Warning of Credit Suspension (15-09)

Company Name
Address
City, State Zip

Date

Mr. Leopold Almandinger
922 Maple Street
Fort Collins, CO 80553

Dear Mr. Almandinger:

We don't enjoy dealing this way with our customers, but we're just ten days away from having to suspend your credit privileges.

Won't you help us avoid this action? If we receive your payment of $129.98 by May 12, your account will remain intact and your credit standing will remain unblemished.

We've enclosed a postage-paid reply envelope for your convenience. Please use it promptly. Thanks for your cooperation.

Sincerely yours,

Penny Yamaguchi
Credit Department

- Make it clear that you don't <u>want</u> to take any punitive action.

- Make it equally clear what will happen if payment (state the amount) isn't received by the deadline (state the date).

Company Name
Address
City, State Zip

Date

Mrs. Evelyn Garland
369 Frontier Street
Casper, WY 82601

Dear Mrs. Garland:

I've always said I could set my watch by your monthly payment; it was always on time. I'm not sure what happened this month, but I'm concerned.

Is there a reason we didn't receive this month's payment? If there's a problem of any sort, please call (555-5929) and let me know. Your credit record with us has been excellent, and I wouldn't want you to spoil it.

Thanks for your prompt attention. And thanks for being such a good customer.

Sincerely yours,

Kevin Brewin
Customer Service Representative

- A constant peeve of good customers is getting the same nasty letter "deadbeats" get. Try to match your collection letters to the "crime."

- Offer to help if there's a problem.

- Tell the customer you appreciate his/her business

Company Name
Address
City, State Zip

Date

Mrs. Evelyn Garland
369 Frontier Street
Casper, WY 82601

Dear Mrs. Garland:

This is our second notice regarding your final payment on the deluxe
Kool-Flo refrigerator/freezer you purchased from us nearly eight months
ago.

We know that sometimes things happen to delay payment. Layoffs,
illness, and accidents are all part of life. If you've had a problem that
has forced you to postpone payment, we'll try to work something out to
accommodate you.

But we can't operate in a vacuum. We don't know why you're 90 days
overdue on your final $285.22 payment. We're sure you wouldn't want
to do anything to hurt your credit position. Yet we haven't heard from
you.

Your account has moved into the seriously overdue category. Please
send your payment in the enclosed postage-paid reply envelope, or call
me at 555-1111. I want to help you settle this matter.

Thanks for your prompt attention.

Sincerely,

George Newbury
Credit Representative

- Adding a human touch to collection letters will help you with many debtors. People <u>do</u> respond to a non-threatening, yet firm, letter that offers understanding.

- Tell the customer how much is owed and how long overdue.

- Ask for the money, but offer to help if assistance is needed.

Company Name
Address
City, State Zip

Date

Mrs. Evelyn Garland
369 Frontier Street
Caper, WY 82601

Dear Mrs. Garland:

We're in the appliance business, not the collections business...but that should be obvious to you because we've been unsuccessful in having you pay your bill (which is now 120 days overdue).

Since we're not terribly good at collections, we have no choice but to turn your account over to someone who is good at it. Unfortunately, that will (1) put a blot on your credit record and (2) make us feel bad that we were forced to take this action.

You can solve both problems by sending us your payment of $285.22 within seven days of receipt of this letter. If you choose not to, your account will be transferred to our collection agency.

We've enclosed a reply envelope for your convenience. Please use it; your credit standing depends on it.

Sincerely,

Sharon Newcastle
Credit Manager

- Don't lose the "human" touch, even with the final letter in a collection sequence.

- State your resolve to do what has to be done to collect your money.

- Be sure to include the amount and number of days overdue.

Index by Title

Index by Subject

(**Boldface** numbers indicate chapter introductions. Numbers in parentheses are document numbers, found at the top of each letter. They are followed by page numbers.)

for quantity purchasing, (6-05, 6-07), 123, 125

and thank you letter, (4-12), 86

Inducements to buy

being first in the field, (5-06), 102

closing the sale, **95-96**

confirming points of agreement, (5-07), 103

customization, (5-02), 98

free home trial, (5-04), 100

offering introductory special, (5-03), 99

offering pre-approved car loan, (14-20), 336

price used as, (5-09, 5-10, 5-11), 105, 106, 107

product demonstration, (5-05), 101

relating success stories, (5-01), 97

Insurance

selling, **316**, (14-10, 14-11, 14-12, 14-13, 14-14), 326, 327, 328, 329, 330

Interviews, **199**, (*see also* Job offers; Job search; Resumes)

for career change, (8-01), 201

request, with executive search firm, (8-02), 202

thank you for, (8-03), 203

Introductions

of new market for existing product, (2-09), 41

of new products to old customer, (2-12), 44

of one's replacement, (2-11), 43

of oneself as consultant, (2-03), 35

of oneself as new to position, (2-02), 34

Introductory specials

as inducements to buy, (5-03), 99

Investments

selling, **316**, (14-01, 14-02, 14-03, 14-04, 14-05), 317, 318, 319, 320, 321

Invitations

to new product presentation, (1-11), 15

to store party, (12-03), 289

to tour plant, (2-08), 40

to visit trade show booth, (1-12), 16

Involvement devices, **241-242**, (*see also* Reply cards)

use of, (2-03), 35

J

Jargon, avoiding, **301-302**

Job offers, (*see also* Interviews; Job search; Resumes)

response to, (8-07), 207

Job performance

congratulations on job well done, (11-14), 274

congratulations on promotion, (7-01), 131

request for raise, (8-18), 220

request for transfer, (8-20), 222

Job search, **199-200**, (*see also* Interviews; Job offers; Resumes),

networking letter, (8-04), 204

request for letter of recommendation, (8-08), 208

response to ad, (8-05, 8-06), 205, 206

resume cover letter, (8-10, 8-12, 8-16), 210, 212, 217

seeking advice for, (8-09), 209

K

Key words

use of, **285-286**

L

Last resort letters, (4-07), 81

Lateness

apologizing for, (7-33), 163

Lead generators, **4**

Leave of absence

request for, (8-19), 221

Legal action

responding to threat of, (7-66), 196

Letter resumes, (8-15), 216

M

Magazines

as sources of leads, (1-03, 7-03), 7,

(7-63), 193

Speeches
   congratulations on, (7-06), 136

Stores
   announcement of new, (1-06), 10

Surveys, (see also Questionnaires)
   generating feedback from, (7-27),
      157
   used in direct mail, (10-10), 252

T

Target audience, (10-03, 10-08), 245,
   250

Termination
   request for advice after, (8-09), 209

Testimonials
   follow-up letter with, (4-09, 4-10),
      83, 84
   used to close the sale, **95-96**, (5-11),
      107

Thank you letters, **74, 130**, (see also
      Appreciation letters; Follow-up
      letters)
   for attending fund-raiser, (7-23), 153
   for business, (6-01, 7-15, 7-22, 7-26),
      119, 145, 152, 156
   for comments about employee,
      (7-11), 141
   for compliment, (7-08), 138
   and customer goodwill, **117-118**
   for enthusiasm, (7-24, 11-14), 154,
      274
   for evaluation, (7-25), 155
   even though it did not work out,
      (13-04), 306
   for favors given, (7-16), 146
   for giving time, (7-10), 140
   for interview, (8-03), 203
   for job, (7-14), 144
   for meeting, (7-17), 147
   for opportunity to quote, (3-12), 62
   for referrals, (13-06, 13-07), 308,
      309
   for response, (7-18), 148
   for setting up sales call, (7-09), 139
   for suggestions, (7-12, 7-13, 7-19,
      7-20, 7-21), 142, 143, 149,
      150, 151
   for visiting trade show booth, (4-12),

86

Title-only mailings, (2-07), 39

Toll-free numbers, (14-10), 326

Tone
   establishing, in letters, **129-130,
      301-302**

Trade journals
   enclosing reviews in solicitation,
      (13-03), 305
   used to respond to objection, (5-13),
      109

Trade shows, **4**
   invitation to visit, (1-12), 16
   missed you at, (1-13), 17
   thank you for visiting, (4-12), 86

Transfers
   request for, (8-20), 222

U

Unresponsive
   approach to someone who is, (2-05),
      37
   using fax to reach person who is,
      (9-07), 237

Urgency, (see also Faxes)
   creating a sense of, (5-08, 5-15), 104,
      111

W

Warranties
   customer misunderstanding of,
      (7-64), 194
   offered in follow-up letter, (4-19), 93

Welcome letters
   to new customer, (14-15), 331
   to new job, (1-02, 11-08), 6, 268
   to new resident, (1-01), 5

Workshops
   announcement of, (12-12), 298
   for computer professionals, (1-18),
      22
   confirmation of terms of, (3-07), 57

ATTENTION COMPUTER USERS!

All the Letters in this Book are Available on Computer Disks

All **308 letters** and other documents in *Encyclopedia of Money Making Sales Letters* are available on computer disks for IBM-compatible and Macintosh computers. They are in text (ASCII) file format, for use with any word processor. The disks are not copy protected.

Simply locate the letter you want in this book, call it up on the disk from within your word processor, and customize and print it out, quickly and easily. **You must have this book to use the disks.**

YES. Please rush me the disks for the computer indicated below, for **$42.90** ($39.95plus $2.95 shipping).

___ IBM 5 1/4" disk   ___ IBM 3 1/2" disk   ___ Macintosh (all models)

_____

___ I have enclosed a check or money order for **$42.90** ($39.95 plus $2.95 shipping). (Do not send cash)
Make checks payable to: Round Lake Publishing

Charge to my ___Visa ___MasterCard

Card number

Expiration Date ____/____ Signature _____

Name _____ Phone # (   )_____
    Please print

Company _____

Address _____

City _____ State _____ Zip _____

MAILING INSTRUCTIONS

1. **Fill out card**
2. **Detach from book**
3. **Fold, address-side out**
4. **Enclose payment inside card**
5. **Tape three edges of card and mail**

Tape all three sides

Fold Here

BUSINESS REPLY MAIL

FIRST CLASS MAIL   PERMIT NO. 105   RIDGEFIELD, CT

POSTAGE WILL BE PAID BY ADDRESSEE

Round Lake Publishing Co.
P.O. Box 1084
Ridgefield, CT 06877-9919